KNOWLEDGE IN AN UNC...

Knowledge in an Uncertain World is an exploration of the relation between knowledge, reasons, and justification. According to the primary argument of the book, you can rely on what you know in action and belief, because what you know can be a reason you have and you can rely on the reasons you have. If knowledge doesn't allow for a chance of error, then this result is unsurprising. But if knowledge does allow for a chance of error—as seems required if we know much of anything at all—this result entails the denial of a received position in epistemology. Because any chance of error, if the stakes are high enough, can make a difference to what can be relied on, two subjects with the same evidence and generally the same strength of epistemic position for a proposition can differ with respect to whether they are in a position to know.

In defending these points, Fantl and McGrath investigate the ramifications for debates about epistemological externalism and contextualism, the value and importance of knowledge, Wittgensteinian hinge propositions, Bayesianism, and the nature of belief. The book is essential reading for epistemologists, philosophers who work on reasons and rationality, philosophers of language and mind, and decision theorists.

Jeremy Fantl is Associate Professor in the Philosophy Department at the University of Calgary.

Matthew McGrath is Professor in the Philosophy Department at the University of Missouri.

Knowledge in an Uncertain World

JEREMY FANTL AND MATTHEW MCGRATH

OXFORD
UNIVERSITY PRESS

Great Clarendon Street, Oxford OX2 6DP

Oxford University Press is a department of the University of Oxford.
It furthers the University's objective of excellence in research, scholarship,
and education by publishing worldwide in

Oxford New York

Auckland Cape Town Dar es Salaam Hong Kong Karachi
Kuala Lumpur Madrid Melbourne Mexico City Nairobi
New Delhi Shanghai Taipei Toronto

With offices in

Argentina Austria Brazil Chile Czech Republic France Greece
Guatemala Hungary Italy Japan Poland Portugal Singapore
South Korea Switzerland Thailand Turkey Ukraine Vietnam

Oxford is a registered trade mark of Oxford University Press
in the UK and in certain other countries

Published in the United States
by Oxford University Press Inc., New York

First published 2009
First published in paperback 2011

British Library Cataloguing in Publication Data
Data available

Library of Congress Cataloging in Publication Data
Data available

Typeset by Laserwords Private Limited, Chennai, India
Printed in the United Kingdom by
Lightning Source UK Ltd., Milton Keynes

ISBN 978–0–19–955062–3 (Hbk)
ISBN 978–0–19–969467–9 (Pbk)

Contents

For Frances Dickey and Faye Halpern

Introduction

You're watching your favorite source for news—FoxNews—and, following a look at Sports, they turn to their lead story—'Lawsuit: Huge Atom Smasher Could Destroy World':

> Walter F. Wagner and his colleague Luis Sancho have filed a federal lawsuit seeking to stop work on the Large Hadron Collider, a gigantic atom smasher on the Franco-Swiss border that's set to start operations in May. Physicists hope its incredible energies will form briefly-lived new particles that could shed light on the origins of the universe, among other marvels. The plaintiffs' concerns? That the LHC could accidentally create strange new particles that would instantly transform any matter they touched, engulfing the Earth, or, even worse, make a rapidly expanding black hole that could consume the entire planet.
>
> '[T]he compression of the two atoms colliding together at nearly light speed will cause an irreversible implosion, forming a miniature version of a giant black hole,' reads the lawsuit, filed in U.S. District Court in Honolulu. '[A]ny matter coming into contact with it would fall into it and never be able to escape. Eventually, all of earth would fall into such growing micro-black-hole [*sic*], converting earth into a medium-sized black hole, around which would continue to orbit the moon, satellites, the ISS, etc.' (Wagenseil 2008)

You're concerned. You suspect that the lawsuit overstates the risk. The chances are going to be at best small: *physics*-small. But the fate of all humanity and the Earth itself is at stake. Here is a perfectly natural question for you to ask: do the scientists in charge of the machine *know* that the machine is safe?

The naturalness of this question suggests two things about the relationship between the scientists' knowledge and whether they should turn on the collider. First, if they do have knowledge, then they can go ahead and turn it on. Second, at least in this case, the potential costs are so great that unless they know, or at least unless their evidence is good enough to know, that the machine is safe, they shouldn't just go ahead and turn it on.[1]

Scientists certainly have excellent evidence that the LHC is safe. The official website of the LHC, addressing worries about its safety, tells us that,

> Despite the impressive power of the LHC in comparison with other accelerators, the energies produced in its collisions are greatly exceeded by those found in some cosmic rays. Since the much higher-energy collisions provided by Nature for billions of years have not harmed the Earth, there is no reason to think that any phenomenon produced by the LHC will do so.
>
> Cosmic rays also collide with the Moon, Jupiter, the Sun and other astronomical bodies. The total number of these collisions is huge compared to what is expected at the LHC. The fact that planets and stars remain intact strengthens our confidence that LHC collisions are safe. The LHC's energy, although powerful for an accelerator, is modest by Nature's standards. (CERN 2008)

Worries that LHC collisions aren't safe, according to spokesperson John Gillies, are 'complete nonsense ... The LHC will start up this year, and it will produce all sorts of exciting new physics and knowledge about the universe ... A year from now, the world will still be here' (Muir 2008). Of course Gillies was right: the world is still here.

But did Gillies know this? Did he and the other scientists know that the LHC would not create dangerous black holes, for instance? On the website of CERN, you can find what are in effect knowledge-claims. Here is one in terms of 'ruling out possibilities': 'the fact that the Earth and Sun are still here rules out the possibility that cosmic rays or the LHC could produce dangerous charged microscopic black holes' (http://public.web.cern.ch/public/en/LHC/Safety-en.html). An independent assessment of the safety of black-hole scenarios concludes with a claim to have *shown* that no logically possible black hole evolution path could lead to a disaster.[2] But how could the scientists know? Isn't there at least *some* chance that the operation of the LHC would lead to disaster? And if there is, doesn't it follow that they don't know?

[1] If you visit the website of the organization Citizens Against the Large Hadron Collider, you will see the banner 'Stop the LHC—until we know it's SAFE!' (http://www.LHCdefense.org).

[2] 'In this paper we reviewed the framework for the conjectured production of mini black holes at the LHC and we have motivated the necessity of analyzing the possible danger that could come with the production of mini black holes. After this we discussed the (logically) possible black hole evolution paths. Then we discussed every single outcome of those paths (D0–D3) and showed that none of them can lead to a black hole disaster at the LHC' (Koch et al. 2009: 13).

Let's start with the question of whether there is a chance of disaster. Isn't there at least *some tiny chance*? Perhaps, but if so, it is negligibly small or, in the words of the 'Report of the LHC Safety Study Group', not 'conceivable' (Blaizot et al. 2003: 13, e.g.). So says a selection of pro-LHC scientists:

> Dr William Unruh: 'Maybe physics really is so weird as to not have black holes evaporate,' he said. 'But it would really, really have to be weird.' (Overbye 2008)
>
> Professor Frank Close: 'The chance of this happening is like you winning the major prize on the lottery 3 weeks in succession; the problem is that people believe it is possible to win the lottery 3 weeks in succession.' (Edwards 2005)
>
> Dr Nima Arkani-Hamed: 'The Large Hadron Collider might make dragons that might eat us up.' (Overbye 2008)

These passages are torn between telling us that there is no chance of disaster at the LHC (Close's 'the problem is that people believe it is possible to win the lottery 3 weeks in succession') and telling us that there is a chance, but one that is insignificant or just silly to take seriously (Arkani-Hamed's 'might make dragons').

How can we accept both the claim that the scientists know the LHC is safe and the claim that there is some tiny possibility it is not safe? The scientists' own ridiculing of the possibility of its being unsafe gives us a hint: knowledge that it is safe is compatible with there being a chance that it isn't safe, but only if that chance is dismissible—dismissible not merely for theoretical purposes, but for the very practical purpose of starting up and continuing to operate the LHC.

In this book, we investigate questions about the relation between knowledge and chance of error, in isolation from the specifics of the LHC. A fundamental thesis of this book is that you can rely on what you know to be true; you can put it to work, not just as a basis for belief but as a basis for action.[3] In the coming pages we will try to make clear what precisely this thesis amounts to, and what reasons there are to think it is true. Throughout we have our eye on the fallibilist view that, even if the chance must be insignificant, knowing something is compatible with some chance that what we know is wrong. We hope to provide a way for a fallibilist, and not only an infallibilist, to accept our thesis that you can put what you know to work.

[3] Our slogan 'put knowledge to work' owes something to the title of John Hyman's (1999) paper, 'How Knowledge Works', and there are certain similarities between his view and ours. We discuss Hyman's view in Chapter 3.

We begin in Chapter 1 with an argument that fallibilists should find appealing the idea of a place for the pragmatic in knowledge. In particular, they should find appealing the 'idle doubts' thesis, according to which knowing a proposition *p* requires a probability which need not be 1 but is high enough to make the chance of not-*p* idle, both for belief and for action. This thesis provides neat solutions to a number of difficult problems for fallibilism. But acceptance of the idle doubts thesis is seen to lead fallibilists to 'pragmatic encroachment'—a problematic result according to which whether you know something can vary with what's at stake for you, even if your evidence and general intellectual position with respect to what you know remains constant. In Chapter 2, we turn our attention to epistemic contextualism and discuss whether it makes it possible for fallibilists to do the work the idle doubts thesis allows them to do without requiring the pragmatic to encroach on knowledge. Our conclusion is that whether the fallibilist should go contextualist or 'pragmatist' depends on whether there is a good principled case for something like the idle doubts thesis.

Chapter 3 presents the central argument in the book: a positive case, independent of the question of fallibilism, for a pragmatic condition on knowledge. The principle we defend is that what you know is warranted enough to justify you in both action and belief, or KJ. KJ is a fleshing out of the intuitive 'idle doubts' thesis, and like it, requires pragmatic encroachment, at least when combined with fallibilism. In Chapter 4, we broaden our argument to include, not only knowledge, but justification for believing as well: what you are justified in believing is warranted enough to serve as a justifier, both practical and theoretical. Our principles about justification in believing commit us to denying certain conceptions of outright belief and its relations to degrees of confidence or credences. We discuss and defend these commitments in Chapter 5. (One central theme in the book is how to reconcile binary notions relevant to epistemology (belief, knowledge, being justified simpliciter in believing) with graded ones (credence, strength of epistemic position, and degree of justification).) Chapter 6 considers how our conclusions allow us to view current debates on the value and importance of knowledge. Finally, in Chapter 7, we ask whether, if our principles require the fallibilist to accept pragmatic encroachment, we should accept pragmatic encroachment or reject fallibilism. We have also included at the end of the book a glossary of key terms and principles.

We began working on the ideas leading to the publication of this book during the summer of 2001. Since that time we have benefited from the support of a number of institutions. The Killam Trust of Canada provided Jeremy with a Killam Resident Fellowship in the winter of 2008 and the University of Missouri provided Matthew with research leave funded by the University of Missouri Research Council in the 2007–8 academic year. The Departments of Philosophy at the University of Missouri (Andrew Melnyk, Chair) and the University of Calgary (Ali Kazmi, Chair) have also been tremendously supportive.

Some of the arguments in Chapters 2 and 3 are anticipated in our critical study in *Noûs* of John Hawthorne's and Jason Stanley's books. Versions of Chapter 1 were presented at the University of Wisconsin and Northwestern University, after which it was published as 'Advice for Fallibilists: Put Knowledge to Work' in *Philosophical Studies* 142. The Springer Publishing Company has generously allowed us to reuse much of that material here. Various incarnations of Chapter 3 were presented at the Universities of Rochester, Iowa, Minnesota, and Manitoba, and the Arché Workshop on Epistemic Contextualism at the University of St. Andrews. Material from Chapter 5 was presented in a talk at Northern Illinois University. An early draft of a paper that turned into Chapter 6 was presented at the International Conference on the Value of Knowledge at Vrije Universiteit in Amsterdam. We are grateful to the audiences in all these venues for their many worrisome and insightful objections and suggestions.

Masashi Kasaki, Mike Steiner, and Jonathan Vertanen read complete versions of drafts of the book, and provided both stylistic and valuable content-oriented insights. Ram Neta and two anonymous referees for Oxford University Press also provided extensive and detailed critiques. Peter Momtchiloff, Catherine Berry, and Tessa Eaton at OUP were extremely helpful and gracious in dealing with last-minute requests and changes. In addition, we'd like to thank all of the following friends, colleagues, and commentators, whose thoughts were particularly valuable (again, or worrisome) in the developing of the arguments in the book: Kent Bach, Jessica Brown, Al Casullo, Juan Comesaña, Earl Conee, Keith DeRose, Frances Dickey, Trent Dougherty, Richard Feldman, Richard Fumerton, Sandy Goldberg, John Greco, Ish Haji, Faye Halpern, Peter Hanks, John Hawthorne, Geoffrey Hellman, David Henderson, Robert Howell, Jason Kawall, Jon Kvanvig, Jennifer Lackey, Adam Leite, Clayton Littlejohn, Jack Lyons, Andrew Melnyk, Mark Migotti, Adam Morton, Ted Poston, Baron Reed, Mark Schroeder, Ernest Sosa, Jason Stanley, Chris Tillman, and Thane Weedon.

1

Fallibilism

We all make mistakes, and not only when we purposely ignore our evidence or coax ourselves into believing what we would like to believe. Our primary sources of information about the world are fallible at least in the sense that they sometimes lead us to false beliefs. This is true of memory, testimony, inductive reasoning, perception, and even introspection. So much is uncontroversial, though perhaps not of obvious epistemological interest. But we can bring these general fallibility considerations closer to our epistemic home.

We sometimes make mistakes even when our evidence seems no worse than it is for many of our current beliefs which we now would call knowledge. You might think you know that your spouse went to work today. But there have been people with evidence apparently just as good as yours but whose spouses didn't go to work that day, for some reason (fill in the story as you like). Or consider our students' propensity to believe (and take themselves to know) what their professors tell them about matters of fact. When Matt teaches his students Chisholm, for example, he usually tells them, truthfully, that he took Chisholm's last seminar at Brown, and that the seminar was on the topic of intentionality. However, if he instead told them that the topic was epistemology, they'd believe it every bit as much. Just for kicks, Matt might tell his students this next year. His misinformed students would then seem to have equally good evidence as his correctly informed students.

We can go further, as any reader of Descartes' *Meditations* knows. It is at least initially plausible that a dreamer, in her bed dreaming she is reading a book, has just as good evidence that she is reading a book as you have that you are, even though, in her case, she is not. So, perhaps general considerations of fallibility touch on even paradigm cases of putative perceptual knowledge. To go to the full extreme, imagine a brain in a vat with the same experiential states and apparent memories as you have. It is at least somewhat plausible to think that this subject has just as good evidence as you have for many 'obvious' claims, such as *I have a body, I interact daily with a number of other people*, etc. But this subject is completely wrong.

What should we make, epistemically, of these 'bad cases'? One familiar sort of skeptic, of course, wants to appeal to the bad cases to show that, contrary to what we think, we *don't* have knowledge in the corresponding 'good cases'. Against this, the fallibilist holds her ground: the existence of these bad cases, and even our acknowledgement of them, does not undermine our knowledge in the good cases. The fallibilist allows that we can have *fallible* knowledge.[1]

1 CONCEPTIONS OF FALLIBILISM

1.1 The logical conception

In what respect is your evidence in the bad case supposed to be just as good as your evidence in the good case? The usual answer is that, if the bad case is chosen correctly, you have the *very same evidence* as you do in the good case. And if it's the same evidence for the same proposition then, since the proposition is false in the bad case, the belief in the good case is based on evidence that fails to entail the proposition believed. The upshot, then, is that for at least much of what we think we know there is a logical gap between our evidence and the proposition believed.[2]

This brings us to our first conception of fallible knowledge, the logical conception:

> To fallibly know that *p* is to know that *p* on the basis of evidence that fails to entail that *p*.

[1] The term 'fallibilism' originates from Charles Sanders Peirce (see, e.g. his (1897)), but the idea that knowledge can be in some sense fallible is not new with him. Lehrer (2000: 71), for example, finds it in Reid. We talk throughout this chapter of fallibilism about knowledge. But fallibilism can be true of other epistemic concepts as well—e.g. justified belief. Generally, fallibilism about epistemic concept E is the doctrine that you can fallibly exemplify E. Ours, then, is a weak conception of fallibilism in that it claims only that we *can* have fallible knowledge. Most fallibilists, of course, motivated by intuition that we *in fact* know many things, will stand by a stronger version as well: that we do have fallible knowledge. For most of our arguments, the difference won't make a difference, so we will speak as if, assuming fallibilism, someone fallibly knows something. If we sweated the details, the 'someone' would have to be a possible person. Again, all our arguments should work under this interpretation.

[2] The language of 'entailment' and 'logical gaps' throughout should be understood in terms of what is standardly called *broadly logical truth*, which is broader than narrow logical truth in that it also includes some 'conceptual' and *a priori* knowable truths.

Corresponding to this conception of fallible knowledge is the widely endorsed doctrine of *logical* fallibilism:

(LF) You can know something on the basis of non-entailing evidence.[3]

There are reasons to think the logical conception doesn't capture all the ways in which knowledge can be fallible. One familiar problem is that any proposition whatever entails a necessary truth. If *p* is a necessary truth, then whatever your evidence is for *p*, it entails *p*. Does this mean that all our knowledge of necessary truths is infallible? Presumably not: suppose you know some necessary truth on the basis of testimonial evidence. Such knowledge seems hardly infallible, though your testimonial evidence entails the necessary truth. This problem doesn't show that LF is false—LF isn't a biconditional—but it does show we need a broader conception of fallible knowledge.

A second problem for the logical conception arises from the fact that there is at least some case to be made that much contingent perceptual knowledge, memory knowledge, and testimonial knowledge, if it is based on evidence at all, is based on evidence that entails the truth of what is believed. The so-called disjunctivists Snowdon (1980/1: 195) and McDowell (1994), who claim that there is no highest common factor present in both veridical and non-veridical sensory experience, argue that in the good case you know that there is, say, a table before you on the basis of evidence such as *I see that there is a table before me*, whereas in the bad case your evidence is merely *I seem to see that there is a table before me.* Timothy Williamson (2000), though he does not endorse disjunctivism about sensory experience, agrees that there is no highest common evidential factor across good and bad cases. The victim of the evil demon has different evidence than you do.

This clears the way for claiming that while you often base your belief on entailing evidence, your twin in the bad case does not. If this is how it is for all of your knowledge, LF is false. And even if LF is retained because there is some knowledge based on non-entailing evidence, one might doubt whether the logical conception of fallibly knowing can do all the work we need done: do you *infallibly* know, say, that you taught a Tuesday/Thursday schedule in the fall of 2002 when you base your belief on the evidence *that you remember that you did* (and so on entailing evidence)?[4]

[3] Proponents are too many to list. They include Peirce, Moore, Chisholm, Feldman (1981), Conee and Feldman (2004*b*), Cohen (1988), and Stanley (2005*a*).

[4] Some epistemologists might feel uneasy about the claim that memorial beliefs are based on evidence (and similarly for perception). If so, they might prefer the following, still broadly logical,

What the two problems suggest is that our intuitions about fallible knowledge do not perfectly track the existence of a logical gap between evidence and the truth.[5] But perhaps the relevant gap isn't logical, but epistemic, i.e. between our actual justification and some stronger justification. Indeed, it seems to us that in *Meditation I* Descartes was arguing for precisely such an epistemic gap rather than a logical one. His appeal to actual and possible mistakes is used to show us that our justification falls short—falls short of making it impossible or unreasonable to doubt. Even if the good case and the bad case involve different evidence, with the good case involving objectively truth-connected evidence missing in the bad case, still the knowledge that there are actual and possible bad cases might give us reason to doubt. The justification we have falls short epistemically, even if it counts as 'infallible' with respect to objective truth-connections.

1.2 The weak epistemic conception

We want to distinguish two epistemic conceptions of fallibly knowing and corresponding fallibilist doctrines, a weak and a strong. Here is the weak:

> To fallibly know that *p* is to know that *p* despite *p*'s not being maximally justified for you.

The corresponding doctrine is:

> (Weak Epistemic Fallibilism (Weak EF)) You can know something even though it is not maximally justified for you.

As the name suggests, there is a good case to be made that fallibly knowing in the weak epistemic sense is *weaker* than fallibly knowing in the logical sense. We agree with Conee and Feldman (2004*b*: 285) that if you have fallible knowledge in the logical sense, then your evidence or justification is imperfect.

conception of fallibly knowing. To fallibly know that *p* is to know that *p* on the basis of a justification the having of which fails to entail that *p*. Both of the concerns about fallibly knowing in the first logical sense apply to this view as well.

[5] Baron Reed (2002) construes fallibly knowing as knowing on the basis of a Gettierizable justification, i.e. a justification which is such that believing on that basis fails to entail that your belief is non-accidentally true. Since the Gettier condition is associated with the truth-connection, this conception seems very much in the spirit of the original logical conception. As Reed notes, it fares better than the latter on fallible knowledge of necessary truths. It is less successful, though, at handling the worries derived from disjunctivism and Williamsonian epistemology.

It would be better if it *were* truth-entailing.[6] This is a reason to think that fallibly knowing on the logical conception implies fallibly knowing on the weak epistemic conception. But arguably, something infallibly known in the logical sense can still be fallibly known in the weak epistemic sense. If you know *Plato taught Aristotle* on the basis of entailing evidence—e.g. that you remember that it is so—this is still compatible with your justification being imperfect. Your justification might not be enough, for example, to make you reasonable in investing complete confidence in this proposition (or in the evidence on which it is based), or even as much as you would in other propositions, e.g. *Plato is believed to have taught Aristotle*, let alone *here is a hand*.[7]

Weak EF gives us a form of fallibilism that many epistemologists can accept, whatever they think about objective truth-connections. Defenders of LF ought to accept it, as should deniers. The defender of Weak EF can concede something to the skeptic that needs to be conceded—our justification is not perfect—while steadfastly maintaining that perfection is not required for knowledge.[8]

But is imperfection all that we must concede to the skeptic?

[6] In cases in which you know a proposition p on the basis of inference from another known proposition q, which doesn't entail the former proposition, your justification isn't necessarily improved by swapping any old entailing evidence r for evidence q. For it could be that r itself is less justified for you than q. But assuming that the entailing evidence r is at least as justified as the non-entailing evidence q, the swap improves your justification for the inferred proposition p.

[7] We are certainly not the first to specify an epistemic conception of fallible knowledge. One finds it in Feldman (2003: 122), at least suggested in Hetherington (2005), and in Reed (2002). We have found, though, that epistemologists often write as if fallibly knowing in this weak epistemic sense is obviously equivalent to fallibly knowing in the logical sense (or in Reed's case to his account in terms of Gettier-proof justifications).

[8] A referee asks how 'maximal' justification should be understood. Should it be understood as justification as good as we ordinary humans can achieve? As could possibly be achieved by any beings? Either way, the worry is that if the skeptic is right, it will follow that we are infallibly justified in the weak epistemic sense. If no possible being can have any significant degree of justification for its beliefs, then it won't be hard to have justification that high. So, doesn't the weak epistemic conception depend for its adequacy on the falsity of radical skepticism, and isn't this problematic?

We do not understand maximal justification in terms of the best justification any being could have, at least if 'could have' is understood in terms of metaphysical possibility. Think about it this way. If the skeptic is right, the skeptic is showing us that there is something we can't have: good justification. It doesn't follow that if the skeptic is right good justification is no justification at all. The same applies to a relation of *better justification than*. If the skeptic is right, then good justification—the justification we thought we had—is better justification than the justification we can have. It doesn't follow that the relation of *better justification than* never applies. But if we can make sense of good justification and *better justification than* independently of what justification can at least metaphysically be achieved, then why can't we understand maximal justification independently of what justification can metaphysically be achieved? Like this: maximal justification is justification which is good justification and such that no justification is better justification than it.

1.3 The strong epistemic conception

On the strong conception, to fallibly know is to know despite the fact that there is a non-zero epistemic chance, for you, that not-*p*. The corresponding doctrine is:

> (Strong Epistemic Fallibilism (Strong EF)) You can know that *p* even though there is a non-zero epistemic chance for you that not-*p*.

Before defending this approach, we need to answer some immediate worries concerning our use of 'epistemic chance'.

Consider the following dilemma. Either epistemic chance is a measure of the degree to which your evidence entails a proposition, i.e. a measure of partial entailment of a proposition by your evidence, or it is a measure of how justified the proposition is for you. If the former, then there is some non-zero epistemic chance that not-*p* iff your evidence doesn't entail that *p*: fallibly knowing on the strong epistemic conception boils down to fallibly knowing on the logical conception, and Strong EF is equivalent to LF. If epistemic chance is instead a measure of justification, then the strong epistemic conception boils down to the weak epistemic conception, because there being some non-zero epistemic chance that not-*p* amounts to there being some gap between the justification *p* has and maximal justification. Strong EF, then, is equivalent to Weak EF. So, whichever epistemic chance amounts to, the strong epistemic conception adds nothing new: Strong EF is equivalent to either LF or Weak EF.

This dilemma assumes we are forced, from the start, into choosing which of the two specified possibilities epistemic chance amounts to. But we are not. There is an independently comprehensible notion of epistemic chance, distinct from both the concepts of partial entailment by the evidence and strength of justification. This will become clearer after we consider the arguments below for the claim that much of what we think we know has an epistemic chance for us less than 1.

Here is a second worry. Philosophers versed in epistemic logic might be frustrated by our taking Strong EF seriously. Isn't epistemic chance, along with all epistemic modals—it's possible that *p*, it could be that *p*, it might be that *p*—simply *defined* in terms of knowledge in such a way that Strong EF must be false? On a standard definition, these are defined as true (relative to S) iff *p* is consistent with what S knows. If this is right, then clearly Strong

EF is stronger than Weak EF, since the latter is pretty clearly true and the former is contradictory!

We do not deny that for certain purposes, e.g. in doing epistemic logic or doing formal semantics, it is fine to stipulate certain meanings or truth-conditions for epistemic modals. But no stipulative definition can resolve the question of whether the notion of epistemic chance, as it figures in our thought about gambles and lotteries, is definable in terms of knowledge. Compare the following consideration. On standard assumptions in epistemic logic, 'K*p*' is true at a world iff '*p*' is true at every world compatible with the subject's knowledge. Plug in any logical truth for *p* and 'K*p*' comes out true at any world for every subject. But this hardly shows that all subjects know all logical truths.

We now turn to the arguments for the claim that much of what we take ourselves to know has an epistemic chance less than 1. As long as one keeps one's focus directly on paradigm instances of perceptual knowledge, one might be happy denying that knowledge is compatible with an epistemic chance of error. Is there really a chance for you that you are not reading right now? That you lack hands? But when we turn to other propositions we ordinarily take ourselves to know—facts one might find in history books (e.g. *Plato taught Aristotle, Napoleon was the emperor of France, Spain was once a world power*), as well as facts about our own lives (e.g. what your mother's maiden name was, where you went to college), facts about the physical world (e.g. in the Eastern United States it will snow more this January than this July), etc.—it seems harder to insist that there is no epistemic chance of error. For one thing, it just seems intuitively that there is a chance. But these intuitions can be backed with arguments. We consider two.

First, it can seem that conjunctions of propositions we take ourselves to know admit of accumulating risk.[9] Though we might be perfectly happy claiming to know individually each member of a set of historical propositions, for example, we are far less happy claiming that we know conjunctions of them, even relatively short conjunctions in some cases. The natural explanation of this reluctance is that there is too much of a chance that the conjunction is false. But how could any chance that the conjunction is false arise if for no conjunct is there a chance that it is false? One might think the relevant instance of conjunction-introduction is responsible for the added risk, not

[9] Similarly, it can seem that disjunctions of propositions we take ourselves to know admit of decreasing risk.

the conjoined propositions. There is something odd about this suggestion. It doesn't *feel* like the accumulation of risk is due to any riskiness in the instance of conjunction-introduction: assuming each is true, the conjunction is true, surely, so one thinks. A better explanation of accumulated risk is that for at least some conjuncts there is a very small chance that it is false. And if this is true of some of the things we know, it is presumably true for many of them. Such considerations give us reason to think that for many of the propositions we think we know, they have an epistemic chance for us which is less than 1.

Notice that the notion of epistemic chance employed here can't be equivalent to that of partial entailment by the evidence. Your belief might, as it happens, be in a necessary truth. There are surely some such beliefs (e.g. mathematical beliefs) such that, were we to conjoin sufficiently many, we would not be reasonable to believe the conjunction. A fair explanation of our reluctance, again, would be that there is too great a chance that the conjunction is false. But the conjuncts, because necessary, are (wholly) entailed by any evidence. Matters aren't as clear when we ask whether the notion of epistemic chance at work here is a measure of strength of justification, so that having probability 1 for *p* amounts to *p*'s being maximally justified. The issue is whether justification can improve even once it leaves no epistemic chance of error. We can make some progress on this question after considering a second argument for the claim that many of the things we take ourselves to know have an epistemic chance less than 1.

Would it be rational for you to stake your life on the proposition that Plato taught Aristotle? It seems to us it would not. Perhaps it would be different for Plato himself when he was meeting with Aristotle for a lesson. Perhaps during the lesson Plato would be rational to accept such gambles. But your justification is as not strong as this. Now, whether it is rational to accept a gamble on *p* depends, not on your subjective degree of belief, or on objective chances beyond your ken, but on how epistemically likely *p* is for you, i.e. on its epistemic chance for you. Thus, the fact that for a great many propositions *p* which we take ourselves to know there are possible gambles on *p* that we would not be rational to accept is a good reason for thinking that much of what we take ourselves to know has an epistemic chance for us less than 1.

One might object to this argument on the grounds that the rationality of degrees of belief is what is relevant to rational choice between gambles but that a subject can be rational in having a degree of belief less than 1 for a proposition even though the proposition has epistemic probability 1 for her.[10] We find this position hard to maintain. The subject, when asked why she turned down the high-stakes gamble on *p*, will be equally happy giving any of the answers: 'I just cannot be absolutely sure', 'there is just a tiny chance', 'there is a remote possibility'. They all amount to the same thing for her. Moreover, suppose the subject gives the first answer only. We ask her, 'why can't you be sure?' A very natural answer to this question is to give one of the two remaining answers, invoking talk of epistemic chance or possibility. What would be very peculiar indeed, and we think incoherent, would be to say, 'Of course it is impossible that *p* is false, and there is a zero chance that it is false, but I can't be sure it is false'. These remarks, moreover, seem just as bad when made in the third-person case: 'there's a zero-chance for her that it's false, but she can't be sure it is'.

Given the connection between epistemic chance and rational gambles, it becomes more plausible to think that what we've called Strong EF is stronger than Weak EF. Strong EF implies Weak EF (justification which leaves a chance of error is not maximal justification), but the converse is perhaps plausibly deniable. Perhaps there are or could be some beliefs which are so well justified for you that it would be rational to gamble on their truth no matter what the stakes even though they are still imperfectly justified. If you had a substantially better answer to a skeptic than Moore does, your justification even for *here is a hand* might be improved, even if there is no hypothetical gamble on the proposition—with a positive payoff if the proposition is true—that you would not be rational to take. (Were this not possible, however, Strong EF and Weak EF would be equivalent; this would not affect the substance of any subsequent argument.)

We have given two *arguments* that, for many of the things we take ourselves to know, there is a chance that these propositions are false. But supplementing these arguments is the strong intuition that we could just be wrong about such matters as whether our spouse will be home by 6 p.m. tonight, whether at least one baseball team will score at least seven runs in at least one game in the next full baseball season, whether Plato taught Aristotle, etc. The chance we're wrong is slight, but there is some chance. And in some cases arguably one could even calculate it (e.g. in the baseball case).

If much of what we take ourselves to know lacks probability 1 and if we do generally know what we take ourselves to know, then, Strong EF must be correct. The same *might* be true of LF. But the matter is less clear. So,

[10] Thanks to Ram Neta here.

the dialectical situation is as follows. If LF is false, skepticism is not clearly assured; perhaps Williamson is right that evidence simply varies between the good and the bad case in such a way that you infallibly know in the logical sense in the good case but not in the bad case. On the other hand, if Strong EF is false, the case for a fairly robust skepticism is almost irresistible.

Because of its proper place at the center of the philosophical discussions of fallibilism, we will hereafter refer to Strong EF simply as 'fallibilism'.[11]

2 THE MADNESS OF FALLIBILISM

Fallibilism is *mad.* Here is Lewis (1996):

> If you are a contented fallibilist, I implore you to be honest, be naïve, hear it afresh. 'He knows, yet he has not eliminated all possibilities of error.' Even if you've numbed your ears, doesn't this overt, explicit fallibilism *still* sound wrong? (550)[12]

Talk of 'eliminating' possibilities of error might seem too close to knowing them to be false, in which case this clashing conjunction is a denial of a principle of epistemic closure. But closure is not the real issue. If fallibilism is true, the following clashing conjunctions should be true in many cases:

I know that p but there is a chance that not-p.

I know that p but it is possible (it might/could be) that not-p.

Don't these just sound wrong, at least when one is careful to read both conjuncts as simultaneously endorsed, rather than reading the second conjunct as a correction to the first? The same goes for appropriate third-person versions:

She knows that p but there is a chance, for her, that not-p.

She knows that p but it's possible, from her perspective, that not-p.

If these sorts of statements are often true, as the fallibilist must admit, why the discomfort? If they're right, why do they feel so wrong?

[11] Those who seem, if in some cases hesitantly, to endorse Strong EF include Klein (1980*a*: 197), Dougherty and Rysiew (2009), Feldman (2003: 122), and Lehrer (2000: 219–20). Opponents are easier to find: Bach (forthcoming), DeRose (1991), Hawthorne (2004), Huemer (2007), Stanley (2005*a*), Williamson (2000), along with just about everyone working on epistemic modals in the philosophy of language.

[12] Or from Unger (1975: 195): 'He really *knew* that it was raining, but he *wasn't* absolutely *certain* it was.'

Consider, also, dialogues that seem to support the claim that 'S knows that *p*' entails 'there is no epistemic chance, for S, that not-*p*':

Dialogue 1:

Attorney for the Defense: Is there a chance that the man sitting here in the courtroom today is not the man you saw that night?

Witness: I know he's the guy. So, no, there is no chance.

Here the witness' knowledge claim answers the defense's question in the negative, which is just what we would expect if the entailment held. A second dialogue (cf. Hawthorne 2004) tests the contrapositive entailment from 'There is an epistemic chance, for S, that not-*p*' to 'S doesn't know that *p*'. If the entailment held, we would expect that if you conceded the former and were asked 'so you don't know, do you?' you would feel forced to answer, 'no', and this is what we find:

Dialogue 2:

Witness: OK, I admit, there's a chance that the man sitting there isn't the guy I saw that night.

Defense: Ah, so you don't know this is the man you saw, do you?

Witness: No, I don't.

There are of course many other dialogues in which we speak of epistemic chance. But it might be held that the naturalness of these dialogues gives us at least some reason to think that the clashing conjunctions above clash because they express genuinely contradictory propositions. For it seems that the knowledge claim in Dialogue 1 simply settles the matter of whether there is a chance negatively, and it seems that the concession 'I don't know' is forced in Dialogue 2. And why would this be, unless strong epistemic fallibilism were false?[13]

You usually take yourself to know that Plato taught Aristotle. It seems you do know this. But when you think about it, or consider arguments from accumulated risks and possible gambles, it also seems there's a chance you're wrong about this. But try putting these two thoughts together: you

[13] Other tests for entailment seem to support the claim, as well. The conditionals 'If I know that *p*, there's no chance that not-*p*' and 'If there a chance that not *p*, then I don't know that *p*' seem plausible, which is what is predicted by the entailment thesis.

know something but there's a chance you're wrong about it. That's awful! As appealing as it might be to hold off the skeptic, it is mad, isn't it?

Before we consider how the fallibilist might respond, let us get a second set of clashing conjunctions on the table, the 'Moorean' clashes:

> *p* but there is a chance that not-*p*.
>
> *p* but it is possible (it might/could be) that not-*p*.

As if these aren't bad enough, they have the following obvious entailments:

> *p* is a proposition which, though true, has a chance of being false.
>
> *p* is a proposition which, though true, might be false.

These certainly sound wrong. But if fallibilism is true, these statements should express propositions which we can and should believe to be true. Indeed we can *know* them to be true. But, as Michael Huemer (2007) has recently argued, the claim that we can know such things seems obviously false.

When we turn to dialogues to test the claim that '*p*' entails 'the epistemic chance, for S, that not-*p* is zero', we get a very different result than we got before. While the first dialogue is fine,

Dialogue 3:

Defense: Is there a chance, do you think, that the man you saw that night isn't the man sitting here?

Witness: No. He's the man.

the second one, which tests the contrapositive entailment, is unsuccessful:

Dialogue 4:

Witness: There's a chance that this is not the man I saw that night.

Defense: So, this isn't the man you saw last night.

Witness: Wait, I didn't say that!

If the entailment went through, the witness should be expected to concede the inference the defense draws, which the witness won't (and rightly so). This is reason to reject the claim of entailment. We should expect as much, given that the other Moorean clashes ('*p* but I don't believe that *p*', '*p* but I don't know that *p*', etc.) do not express contradictory propositions.

This should not console the fallibilist. For, just as you cannot properly assert, nor rationally believe, let alone know, the propositions you would express by uttering the standard Moorean paradoxical sentences, '*p* but I don't believe that *p*' or '*p* but I don't know that *p*', the same goes for '*p* but there is a chance that not-*p*'. If strong fallibilism is true, it is hard to see *why* this would be. You can know *p*, despite the fact that there is a non-zero chance that not-*p*. Why couldn't a self-conscious fallibilist, then, also *know* that there is a non-zero chance for her that not-*p*—say, after reflecting on facts about gambles and accumulating risk? If so, she should also be able to come to know the conjunction *p and there's a chance for me that not-p.*[14]

So the fallibilist has to do several things. She has to explain why the clashing conjunctions in the first group seem wrong, even though they can and presumably often are true on her view, and she must do this while also making sense of why the test dialogues seem to support the claim that there is a genuine entailment from 'S knows that *p*' to 'there is no chance, for S, that not-*p*'. In the case of the second group, the Moorean clashes, she must explain why these seem not only unassertable but even rationally unbelievable and unknowable (by the speaker or thinker), though if strong fallibilism is true they should be very easy to know.

Lewis is no doubt right that, between fallibilism and skepticism, fallibilism is the 'less intrusive madness' (1996: 550). But one would like, of course, to endorse fallibilism without being mad. The question is how to do this.

3 HOW TO BE A FALLIBILIST

We will discuss three proposals for handling the troubling data.

Proposal #1: Scope confusions

It is plausible that the conditional 'if you know then you can't be wrong' seems correct because we take 'can't' to have wide scope (see Feldman (2003: 124)), i.e. to be equivalent to 'it can't be that you know that *p* and are wrong'. Could scope confusion, together with the factivity of knowledge, help to explain the clashes above? We doubt it. It's much harder to get the epistemic

[14] Notice, no similar problem arises with the explanation of why you can't rationally believe or know the truth of *p but I don't know that p*. One standard line is that in rationally believing *I don't know that p* you have a defeater which prevents you from rationally believing *p*.

Is a similar line available to the fallibilist? Could the fallibilist say that knowledge is compatible with having a chance of error but that the recognition of this chance strips you of that knowledge? This suggestion is highly implausible. Knowledge becomes very elusive indeed: all you need to do is think about fallibilism as it applies to your beliefs and you lose knowledge left and right.

modal to assume wide scope over a conjunction than over the antecedent of a preceding conditional. It is a *misreading* of '*p* but it might be that not *p*' to read it as meaning that it might be: *p* but not-*p*. And in any case this would wrongly diagnose Moorean clashes as contradictory, which they are not.

Proposal #2: Contextualism

Of course, Stewart Cohen (1988) told us how to be fallibilists: accept contextualism. Perhaps as soon as we mention that there is a possibility of not-*p*—or as soon as that fact becomes salient—the standards for knowledge rise so high that only absolute certainty (probability 1) is enough to count as knowing. This explanation is more promising than the postulation of scope-confusion, but not particularly plausible.

It is somewhat plausible to claim that when *specific* error possibilities are mentioned or taken seriously, possibilities that are consistent with and at least putatively explanatory of your apparent evidence, the standards for knowing rise so that to count as knowing you must be able to 'eliminate' those possibilities (cf. Cohen 1999). So, if I mention the possibility that your car has been stolen and driven away, this might lead you to retract a knowledge-claim about the location of your car, and perhaps the retraction is correct, in that the knowledge-claim is now false. However, the salience of the fact that it might be that not-*p* doesn't conjure up any specific possibilities of error. The well-informed reader might recall that Lewis himself insists on reading the noun 'possibility' in a rather technical way which ensures it has a certain degree of specificity.[15] But in the ordinary English statement, 'I know that *p* but it's possible that not-*p*', this technical reading is not in force.

In any case, it is too strong to say that when the mere fact that there is a chance that a particular proposition *p* is false becomes salient the standards for knowledge rise so high that probability 1 is required for truly being said to know. We do find 'I know that *p* but it might be that not-*p*' odd, but the recognition of this oddness doesn't seem to turn us into skeptics. Might the standards, instead, rise just high enough so that one cannot truly attribute knowledge of the particular proposition? But how high is this, and what mechanism would explain the standards rising to precisely this height but no higher?

15 Lewis: 'A possibility will be specific enough if it cannot be split into subcases in such a way that anything we have said about possibilities, or anything we are going to say before we are done, applies to some subcases and not to others' (1996: 552).

More importantly, though, it seems there are ways of making the chance that not-*p* salient while maintaining, quite properly, that one knows that *p*. The next proposal suggests that very thing.

Proposal #3: Gricean infelicity

The most plausible explanation, in our view, is to appeal to infelicity of a broadly Gricean kind: the clashing conjunctions can be true, but are problematic to assert because they 'implicate' or in some way 'impart' something false. Why might this be? We can rule out from the start the claim that these statements aren't assertable because they are so obviously true. Far from it, they seem positively wrong not trivially right. And appealing to their obvious truth wouldn't help explain why there seems to be something wrong with believing them, in any case.

Trent Dougherty and Patrick Rysiew (2009) suggest a better Gricean explanation. The reason 'I know that *p* but it's possible that not-*p*' seems wrong is that uses of 'it's possible that not-*p*' in standard conversation impart that there is a significant possibility or chance that not-*p* and not merely the sort that accompanies all fallible knowledge. Why should this explain the oddity? We are told: 'a significant chance of error may well prevent one from knowing' (130). We will ignore the 'may well' hedge, because if it's read too weakly the resulting account can't explain what it aims to explain.

The account we are interested in, then, has two parts:

Part 1: Assertive utterances of 'it is possible that *p*' and the like conversationally impart but do not require for their truth that not-*p* is a significant possibility.

Part 2: If not-*p* is a significant possibility for a person then the person doesn't know *p*.

What's wrong with asserting, 'I know that *p* but it's possible that not-*p*', is that in one breath you are saying that you know and in the next you conversationally impart something that entails that you don't know. This is conversational or pragmatic self-defeat.

The dialogues we considered earlier are explicable because normally when you ask 'is there a chance that not-*p*?' you are getting your audience to focus on the question of whether there is a significant chance that not-*p*. The hearer can then answer this question by saying 'No, I know that *p*'. Similarly, in uttering, 'yes, there is a chance that not-*p*', the speaker is pragmatically imparting that there is a significant chance that not-*p*. No wonder, then, that the hearer can reply, 'so you don't know that *p*'.

Dougherty and Rysiew go on to say (130) that if one factors out this normal conversational implication the resulting statements don't sound so problematic. Statements like:

> The possibility that not-*p* is ridiculous and not worth considering. I know that *p*.

and

> Of course there is always some chance that I'm wrong, *anything is possible*, but I know that *p*.

do not seem clearly wrong. They do not seem clearly right either.[16] But here is where the hard work in epistemology comes in.

So far, so good. But what about the Moorean clashes? Here the Dougherty/Rysiew account needs supplementation. A natural thought is to claim that in asserting that *p* you are 'representing yourself' as knowing that *p*, or at least you are conversationally imparting that there is no significant chance that not-*p*. If either of these proposals is correct, we can see why there is a clash. Although you are not stating a contradictory proposition, you are conversationally imparting *both* that you know *and* that you don't, or perhaps alternatively *both* that there is no significant chance that not-*p and* that there is a significant chance that not-*p*.

Can the propositions expressed by the Moorean clashes be reasonably believed and even known? Yes. They seem not to be because, hearing or reading the sentence, you turn your mind to the wrong proposition: *p but there is a significant chance, for me, that not-p*. That proposition *can't* be reasonably believed, though it can be true. But the proposition expressed by Moorean clashes can be reasonably believed and known because you can reasonably believe that something is the case and also that there is an *in*significant chance that it isn't the case, and an insignificant chance is still a chance. Keeping separate the proposition expressed and the proposition that would normally be conversationally imparted, the problem seems to go away.

16 See also the physicists' comments in the Introduction on the possibility of disaster involving the Large Hadron Collider. Notice the pressure in at least some of the comments to collapse the minimal probability to zero.

Finally, the Gricean account nicely explains the successful dialogue we considered before in which the defense asks whether there is a chance that the man the witness saw isn't the defendant and the witness answers by saying 'No, he's the man'. Why does this dialogue succeed if there is no entailment? A plausible explanation is that the question the defense aims to get the witness to answer is whether there is a significant chance of this. The witness can answer *that* question by saying, 'He is the man', because asserting this conversationally imparts that any chance there is *isn't* significant.

All this sounds promising. There is just one remaining task: we need to give an account of, or at least say something about, what makes an epistemic chance that not-*p* significant for a person. One sort of account ties significance to the absolute probability of the proposition in question.[17] So, if a proposition is exceedingly improbable, then that is enough to make it insignificant, but if a proposition is, say, fairly probable, it is significant. No doubt one would have to say that the threshold involved is vague.

This account will not do. In some cases, where much is riding on how you act, depending on whether *p* is true or not, even a small chance of error must be taken seriously. In such situations, people will be prepared to say 'Although it is very unlikely, it might be that *p*'. This use of 'it might be that *p*' does not conversationally impart that there is a large chance of error, since it is well-known to all involved that there is only a very small chance. But, in such situations, they do imply that the chance of error is significant. And notice that the successful dialogues we considered can and do take place even when it is clear to all parties involved that there is at best a very small chance that the relevant proposition—that the defendant isn't the man the witness saw—is true. (The defendant is known to have been in the vicinity, etc.) And, of course, both sets of clashing conjunctions clash just as much when it is clear that the chance of error is very small. The clash can only be mitigated by making clear that the chance of error is not worth taking seriously.

This suggests a second, *pragmatist,* account of significance. The chance that not-*p* is significant just in case it is not *idle.* Perhaps the chance that not-*p* is significant just in case it is high enough to make it improper to *put p to work* as a basis not only for belief, but, as our reflection on high stakes cases motivates, for action as well. What exactly is involved in 'putting knowledge

[17] Dougherty and Rysiew suggested this response in correspondence.

to work' is something we spend much of this book investigating. What we want to stress here, at the outset, is that fallibilists have a reason to join us in investigating these matters.

We are not the first to notice an intuitive connection between knowledge and idleness of the chance of error. Here is Roderick Chisholm, writing in 1966:

> When a man takes precautions, he prepares for the worst, even though he may not expect it to happen. For example, he may not believe his house will burn, but he takes precautions by buying fire insurance. But if he *knows* that a given proposition is true, then, it would seem, there is no point in his taking precautions against the possibility that the proposition is false. If, somehow, he knew that his house would never burn, then, it would seem, there would be no point in his insuring the house against fire or otherwise taking precautions against the possibility that his house might burn. Suppose, then, we say that a man knows *h* to be true, provided that no matter what he may do, he has the right to rely upon *h*— that is to say, no matter what he may do, he does not have the duty to take precautions against the possibility that *h* is false. (Chisholm 1966: 13)

Chisholm goes on to reject this proposal because of the possibility of high-stakes cases in which we know but should nonetheless take precautions, but it is clear that the intuition is there. And he finds the same pragmatist thought in the scholastic claim that one who knows is 'safe from error'.

3.1 A neglected Gricean proposal: gradable knowledge?

The reader might worry that we have neglected another Gricean proposal, which doesn't call for an account of significant chances of error, and so might seem to avoid the turn to pragmatism. The proposal is based on the idea that knowledge is gradable. If fallibilism is correct, it might seem that knowledge can come in higher and lower grades, depending on how strong your justification or probability is. The bare 'know'—unmodified by adverbs clarifying the strength of our knowledge—followed by the concession 'it might be that not-*p*' might then seem wrong because if there really is some chance for you that not-*p*, then you should have explicitly modified 'know' accordingly, by saying 'I know pretty well that *p* but it might be that not-*p*', or something of the sort.

The claim that knowledge is gradable can be questioned. There is no reason, given fallibilism at least, to deny that you can know with more or less probability, but this doesn't imply that knowledge is gradable in anything like the way that, say, height is or affection is. Compare 'home run'. Home runs depend on, and vary with respect to, factors that come in degrees: how far the ball traveled, how hard it was hit, how skillfully, etc. There are, in some sense, better and worse home runs—home runs that are more or less majestic, more or less lucky, etc. But whether a hit is a home run is a binary matter. There is no reason the fallibilist shouldn't say the same thing about knowledge. (Also relevant here are the linguistic considerations against gradability adduced by Stanley (2005*b*).)

But suppose the claim about gradability is relaxed so that it is merely the claim that one can know with more or less probability. We still doubt this minimal sort of 'gradability' can be used to explain away the apparent wrongness of the clashing conjunctions. We say the bare 'I know' all the time, with respect to propositions we have only fallible justification for. In fact, on most forms of fallibilism at least, we rarely have infallible justification for anything we bother to claim to know. So, why should the use of the bare 'know' clash at all with a concession of a possibility of error? The fallibilist might retreat to the claim that the clash stems from our intuitive belief in infallibilism, but this is no longer a Gricean account; it is just an error theory; and similarly the fallibilist might retreat to some sort of content-shifting hypothesis, but this is to turn to contextualism again.

Finally, suppose knowledge is gradable, contrary to what we have said. Would it then follow that knowledge is consistent with a significant chance of error? Not at all. Either 'A knows that *p* better than B knows that *p*' entails 'A knows that *p*' or it doesn't. If it does then even knowing that *p* to some degree will be compatible with only an idle chance of error. If 'A knows that *p* better than B knows that *p*' doesn't entail 'A knows that *p*', then knowing that *p* to some degree would be compatible with a non-idle chance of error, but knowing that *p* would not be. That is, knowing well enough to know is consistent only with an idle chance of error. In short, if there are good reasons to think that knowledge is consistent only with an idle chance of error, then the possibility that knowledge comes in degrees is no bar to this.[18]

The appeal to idleness has a second benefit to fallibilists, to which we now turn.

[18] It is not a good response to say: 'I don't know what you mean by "knowing".' For one thing, the response is given using the bare 'know'. For another, 'I don't know what you mean by "happy"' would be a very poor response to someone who asked whether 'A is happier than B' entails that 'A is happy'.

4 HOW PROBABLE TO KNOW?

If fallibilism of our strong epistemic sort is true, then there can be knowledge without probability 1. But presumably there can't be knowledge with probability 0, probability 1/2, or even probability 2/3! (If you know you are one of four invitees to a dinner party, and you know nothing of the identity of the others other than that one is 20 years old, one is 30 years old, and one is 40 years old, do you know the first one you'll see isn't 30 years old? No, not even if you are convinced of it.) These considerations raise the question of just how probable a proposition must be for you in order for you to know it. A parallel problem affects the other forms of fallibilism we have discussed. If you can know based on non-entailing evidence, just how broad must the range of logical possibilities be in which your evidence matches the truth if you are to know? If you can know without having perfect justification, just how imperfect can that justification be, if you are to know? Once the pertinent absolute status—having entailing evidence, perfect justification, probability 1—is deemed overly demanding, we can ask just how high your relative status must be. Laurence BonJour makes the urgency of the problem vivid:

> One very obvious question to ask about the weak conception [of knowledge] is *how* likely the truth of the proposition must be to satisfy this weaker version of the reason or justification condition... There is no very obvious way of answering this question, and the even more striking fact is that almost none of the advocates of the weak conception of knowledge have ever seriously tried to do so. Even more important, it is simply unclear what sort of basis or rationale there might be for fixing this level of justification in a non-arbitrary way. However problematic the strong concept of justification may be in other ways, its intuitive significance and importance is clear. But nothing like this seems to be true for the weak conception. (2002: 43)

We hope it is clear how our pragmatist account can help here. How probable must *p* be for *p* to be known? It must be probable enough to be properly put to work as a basis for belief and action. Just to be clear: this doesn't mean that you must be able to act on *p* if you know *p*. We know plenty of facts which are irrelevant to our practical situation (e.g. *Jupiter has more moons than Earth*). It means that the improbability of not-*p* doesn't *stand in the way* of *p*'s being put to work as a basis for action and belief. In the case of practically irrelevant facts, what stands in the way of their being put to work isn't their improbability.

This gives us a lower bound on the probability for *p* needed to know. But it would be nice to say more. Of course, we can't expect to give a necessary and sufficient condition for knowledge in terms of probabilities short of 1. So we shouldn't ask for *that.* But it would be nice to be able to fill in the scheme below:

> Your probability for *p* is knowledge-level iff...

where having 'knowledge-level' probability is understood as having a probability for *p* which is high enough for knowledge.

Given our account, a plausible filling yields this:

> Your probability for *p* is knowledge-level iff the probability that not-*p* doesn't stand in the way of *p*'s being put to work as a basis for belief and action.

We explore these issues much more fully in subsequent chapters. For now, we simply note that our pragmatist approach promises to provide a plausible answer to the threshold problem for fallibilists.[19]

5 MORE MADNESS?

All this should sound welcome to the fallibilist, and we expect that it *would* be received as such, if it weren't for one small detail. It looks like the sort of pragmatist fallibilism we are recommending allows whether you know that *p* to vary with variations in practical stakes. After all, we say that your probability for *p* is knowledge level only if it can be put to work in belief and action. Fallibilism allows that this probability can be enough for knowledge even if it is below 1. So, suppose it is: you know that *p*, and can thus put *p* to work in belief and action. But we can suppose that what's at stake for you in whether *p* is fairly low: not much hinges for you in action on

[19] Conee and Feldman (2004*b*: 296) endorse a 'criminal' standard: knowledge requires justification beyond reasonable doubt for you. This is fine as far as it goes, but one would of course like to know, roughly, what it takes for a doubt to be reasonable. When it is very unlikely that *p*, can it still be reasonable to doubt that *p*, say, if the stakes are high? They don't tell us. Notice that the pragmatist account helps provide an answer.

whether it's true or false. If the stakes were sufficiently high, though, you would not be proper to put *p* to work in action. In that case, you won't know that *p*.

There is nothing particularly mad about the idea that stakes can affect knowledge by affecting belief. Nor is there anything particularly mad about the idea that as stakes rise, what it's proper to do and what it's proper to base action on can change. What is mad is the idea that whether you are in a position to know could be affected by stakes. But that is precisely what the pragmatist approach requires. Whether you can properly put *p* to work in action is independent of whether you in fact believe it: you might not be proper to put *p* to work as a basis of action even if, because you believe it, you *do* put it to work.

Why is the idea that stakes can affect *being positioned to know* so mad? One possibility is simply the intuition that stakes shouldn't be at all relevant to knowledge, unless relevant to belief—to whether you do believe. But a deeper obstacle is the conviction about what sorts of considerations are alone relevant. One standard position in epistemology has it that whether you are in a position to know that *p* is a matter of your standings on exclusively truth-relevant dimensions like how strong your evidence for/against *p* is, how reliable are the belief-forming processes available to you which would produce a belief that *p*, how strong your counterfactual relations to the truth-value of *p* (how sensitive, how safe your available basis is for believing that *p*), etc.[20] Call your profile of these factors with respect to *p* your *epistemic position with respect to p*. Epistemic positions can be stronger and weaker. Yours can be

20 As a first stab, a dimension is truth-relevant iff the stronger you are positioned along it with respect to a proposition *p* the more probable *p* is in some suitable sense. So, e.g., the more reliably formed your belief is the more likely that it is true (here the relevant probability is presumably some sort of objective probability). The better your belief that *p* fits the evidence the more likely *p* is *for you* (here the probability involved is presumably not objective but epistemic).

We are sympathetic to this probabilistic conception of epistemic position, but it is not the only one. For example, Peter Klein (1980*a*) argues that having 'intrinsically probabilistic evidence' for *p* never makes *p* completely justified. But a proposition 'may have a probability of less than one and still be completely justified' (197). Therefore, a proposition may have a higher probability—based on intrinsically probabilistic evidence—for you than a proposition that is completely justified, but the latter fail to be completely justified. It is plausible that whatever measure of justification is 'completed' for the former proposition but not the latter does not measure any probabilistic dimension. Therefore, followers of Klein may resist strictly probabilistic interpretations of 'strength of epistemic position' and 'strength of justification'. They are welcome to substitute their own conception of 'strength of epistemic position' here and throughout the book. The only point that is required for our purposes is that, whatever the preferred conception of epistemic position, it is not constituted essentially—even partially—by practical stakes.

stronger than it used to be, and stronger than someone else's.[21] Variations in being positioned to know, according to the traditional view, have to coincide with variations in strength of epistemic position. Call this view:

> (Purism about Knowledge) For any subjects S1 and S2, if S1 and S2 are just alike in their strength of epistemic position with respect to *p*, then S1 and S2 are just alike in whether they are in a position to know that *p*.

What makes the idea that stakes matter to being positioned to know mad is that your stakes don't seem to matter to your strength of epistemic position. That you have a lot at stake in what you do depending on whether *p* simply has no impact on your standing on any truth-relevant dimension with respect to *p*. If it has no such impact, then if it has an impact on being positioned to know, purism about knowledge is false. To deny purism about knowledge because of a pragmatic condition on knowledge is to commit to what Jonathan Kvanvig calls *pragmatic encroachment*.[22] Pragmatic encroachment seems mad because it entails the falsity of purism. Purism—many will say—seems clearly true.

But the fallibilist who recoils at the thought of denying purism or allowing pragmatic encroachment should bear in mind her tasks: to explain away the apparent madness of fallibilism and to give us some idea of what it takes for a probability to be 'knowledge-level'. To retain purism (and deny pragmatic encroachment) she must perform these tasks without appealing

[21] We will not have much to say about comparative strength of epistemic position, other than the following rather straightforward assumptions. First, the relation expressed by 'S1's epistemic position with respect to *p* is stronger than S2's is with respect to *q*' is to be asymmetric and transitive. Second, strength of epistemic position is assumed to be such that:

(1) Subjects who score equally well on each and every truth-relevant dimension with respect to *p* have equally strong epistemic positions with respect to *p*.

(2) If a subject S1 scores at least as well on each truth-relevant dimension with respect to *p* as S2 does with respect to *q*, and S1 scores better on one or more such dimensions with respect to *p* than S2 does with respect to *q*, then S1's epistemic position with respect to *p* is no worse than S2's is with respect to *q*.

Thanks to Baron Reed for discussion on (2).

[22] When Kvanvig (2004) initially coined the term, he seemed to use it for any view that imposes a pragmatic condition on knowledge. But, if infallibilism is true, such conditions allow that knowledge is fixed by strength of epistemic position alone, and that the pragmatic conditions are automatically satisfied when you have the fixed strength of epistemic position that is necessary and sufficient for knowledge for all subjects in all contexts. This is not so much pragmatic encroachment on knowledge, but rather mere pragmatic consequences of knowing. We reserve the term for views that deny purism.

to a conception of significant chances of error that allows stakes to play a role—that allows significance to vary without corresponding variance in your strength of epistemic position with respect to *p*. The fallibilist purist, then, has a tall order.

Our advice to fallibilists is this: if you don't want to budge on skepticism, at least *think* about budging on purism.

2

Contextualism

1 BACKGROUND

The recent surge of interest in the question of pragmatic elements in knowledge arose out of a debate over contextualism. Contextualism holds that the semantic content of knowledge attributions varies with the context of speech. In the 1980s, Stewart Cohen ((1986) and (1988)), building on earlier work by Gail Stine (1976), David Lewis (1979), and Peter Unger (1984), argued forcefully that contextualism provides a satisfactory resolution of skepticism. By forcing us to consider and take seriously possibilities of error that we normally neglect, Cohen argued, the skeptic is able to raise the epistemic standards a person must meet to be truly described as knowing. The skeptic can indeed raise these standards so high that virtually all knowledge attributions will count as false. So, in a sense, skepticism, the position that we know little or nothing, is right at least when the skeptic has succeeded in raising the standards. This is a concession to the skeptic. But, Cohen claims, the real reason we find skepticism worrisome is that we have taken it to imply that we were wrong all those times in ordinary life when we claimed to know. This worry is misplaced. In ordinary contexts in which the skeptic has not exploited the potential to raise standards, the standards are fairly low, low enough so that a very good many of our ordinary knowledge attributions are true.

All this will be familiar to anyone who has kept abreast of the contextualism debate over the last couple decades. But what is also familiar is the worry that the contextualist resolution of skepticism is too easy, that it is an instance of a general strategy that could be used to 'solve' a great many philosophical problems (Stanley 2005*b*: 155). If it seems we are pulled in two directions, we can always postulate that the relevant terms have different semantic contents depending on which pull we feel. It seems near consensus in the literature that if the contextualist solution to skepticism is to be plausible we need some independent evidence that the content of knowledge attributions can vary with speech context in ordinary non-philosophical contexts. And not only that. We need evidence that the variation can be rather dramatic. It would do little good for the contextualist to argue, for example, that 'knows' is vague and that all vague predicates are context-sensitive. This would show only that the epistemic standards associated with 'knows' can vary minimally.

Another contextualist, Keith DeRose (1992), and later Cohen (1999) as well, rose to the challenge by turning to *practical* cases:

Bank Case A. My wife and I are driving home on a Friday afternoon. We plan to stop at the bank on the way home to deposit our paychecks. But as we drive past the bank, we notice that the lines inside are very long, as they often are on Friday afternoons. Although we generally like to deposit our paychecks as soon as possible, it is not especially important in this case that they be deposited right away, so I suggest that we drive straight home and deposit our paychecks on Saturday morning. My wife says, 'Maybe the bank won't be open tomorrow. Lots of banks are closed on Saturdays.' I reply, 'No, I know it'll be open. I was just there two weeks ago on Saturday. It's open until noon.'

Bank Case B. My wife and I drive past the bank on a Friday afternoon, as in Case A, and notice the long lines. I again suggest that we deposit our paychecks on Saturday morning, explaining that I was at the bank on Saturday morning only two weeks ago and discovered that it was open until noon. But in this case, we have just written a very large and important check. If our paychecks are not deposited into our checking account before Monday morning, the important check we wrote will bounce, leaving us in a *very* bad situation. And, of course, the bank is not open on Sunday. My wife reminds me of these facts. She then says, 'Banks do change their hours. Do you know the bank will be open tomorrow?' Remaining as confident as I was before that the bank will be open then, still, I reply, 'Well, no. I'd better go in and make sure.' (DeRose 1992: 913)

The Airport Case

Mary and John are at the L.A. airport contemplating taking a certain flight to New York. They want to know whether the flight has a layover in Chicago. They overhear someone ask a passenger Smith if he knows whether the flight stops in Chicago. Smith looks at the flight itinerary he got from the travel agent and responds, 'Yes I know—it does stop in Chicago.' It turns out that Mary and John have a very important business contact they have to make at the Chicago airport. Mary says, 'How reliable is that itinerary? It could contain a misprint. They could have changed the schedule at the last minute.' Mary and John agree that Smith doesn't really *know* that the plane will stop in Chicago. They decide to check with the airline agent. (Cohen 1999: 58)[1]

We will examine in some detail how one might argue for contextualism based on these cases. But before we do that, we need to consider an objection—we think a decisive one—about the choices of cases.

Even if one could use the bank and airport cases to argue successfully for contextualism, there is some worry that it would only be a Pyrrhic victory. Yes, contextualism would be true. But the inference to a contextualist treatment of skepticism would appear jeopardized. As Jessica Brown (2006: 422) and Jonathan Schaffer (2006: 88) have pointed out, these cases involve *both* the raising of error possibilities to salience ('Banks do change their hours' in Bank Case B and 'They could have changed the schedule at the last minute' in the airport case) and the shifting of practical environment.[2] But salience and practical environment represent distinct potential mechanisms for raising the standards for knowing.[3] Even if the cases do support contextualism, therefore, we cannot draw the conclusion that salience of error by itself is sufficient to raise the standards for knowing. Perhaps practical environment is doing all the work. But practical environment seems irrelevant to the skeptical problem at least in its modern forms. The skeptic doesn't affect your practical environment in any important way, nor even does he attempt to get you to worry about practical concerns. His questions about whether you can rule out certain counterpossibilities are idle. Salience is doing all the work, if anything is. As Brown puts it, the bank and airport cases fail to control separately for salience and practical environment. This is fine if one's purpose is only to demonstrate the truth of contextualism, but problematic if one's ultimate purpose is to support the contextualist resolution of skepticism.

(It is, of course, no accident that salience of possible error should enter the cases given that practical environment does. When more rides for you in

[1] One might nitpick about these cases, and in particular about whether the relevant proposition, in both cases, is about a schedule or about a future occurrence. We will simply assume that in both cases it's the future occurrence which is under discussion.

[2] Alas, this is also true of the train cases in Fantl and McGrath (2002). The term 'practical environment' is due to Hawthorne (2004: ch. 3).

[3] DeRose singles out salience and practical environment as potentially independent mechanisms for raising the standards, and further distinguishes between 'mentioning' and 'considering' aspects of salience (1992: 914 ff.). Cohen notes only the role of practical environment in bringing the possibility of error to salience (1999: 61). For both, though, there is the assumption that salience does some work. Because this variable is not isolated in the various cases, the assumption is open to question.

your decision depending on whether *p*, it is to be expected that you would pay closer attention to possibilities of error you would normally ignore, and rightly so. Few would deny that practical environment with respect to *p* can affect how strong your epistemic position must be in order to act on *p*. This is a point long stressed by decision theorists.)

The bank and airport cases were thus poorly chosen if the goal was to lay the foundation for the treatment of skepticism. A better choice of cases would be ones in which practical environment was clearly irrelevant but one speaker has been considering (and taking seriously) various possibilities of error while the other speaker hasn't. If one makes the necessary changes to the original cases, however, we are inclined to agree with Brown (2006) that it is less clear that the knowledge-denials are true.[4] Practical environment, in other words, seems a more effective way of raising standards than salience. Brown imagines varying the airport case by stipulating that Smith, having overheard Mary and John worry about the possibility of a misprint, says to himself 'And how likely is *that*?', and notes that our intuitions seem to come down more clearly for Smith and against Mary and John.[5]

To be clear: we do not deny that there is some intuition that the High speakers—the speakers with a lot at stake—in these modified cases still speak the truth (here we agree with Schaffer (2006)); our point is only that these are the sorts of cases that contextualists should focus on if their goal is to support their solution to skepticism. In fact, we see the prospects for contextualism here to be fairly good, at least prima facie. The same sort of vacillation we feel about philosophical skepticism—BIV skepticism, say—we feel about more humdrum skeptical claims such as the claim that we don't know our car hasn't been stolen.

[4] So called 'experimental philosophers' have recently turned their attention to whether our intuitive responses to these practical cases are as predicted and, in particular, whether practical environment or salience represent the more forceful feature. We discuss the general relevance of the experimental work so far in n. 14.

[5] Unlike Brown, Schaffer seems to think that once we remove salience of possible error, there is no difficulty with the intuition that the subject knows in high-stakes cases. In his version of the high-stakes bank case, however, he fails to emphasize relevant features of the practical environment (see Schaffer (2006)). There is no mention of the option of going in and checking, as there is in DeRose's original case. Schaffer even seems to be suggesting that his subject Sam is fine to come back tomorrow. But we can all agree that practical environment can generate different demands on how strong one's epistemic position must be to take certain 'efficient' acts rather than their 'safe' alternatives. So, taking salience out, it should still be possible to generate the intuition that the subject really needs a strong epistemic position to just plan on coming back to the bank on Saturday, a stronger position than he in fact has. Once this intuition is in place, it would be surprising if intuitions about knowledge didn't track it.

But what is originally viewed as a mere means to an end can acquire interest of its own after it is seen not to lead to that end. And this is what has happened with the bank and airport cases. If these cases—with the elements of salience removed or at least ignored—are accommodated better by contextualism than its rivals, this might be evidence that contextualism can explain the relevance of practical environment to knowledge attribution, something which has interest independently of skepticism. In the remainder of this chapter, we will examine just how much mileage the contextualist can get out of the bank and airport cases, with the elements of salience ignored.

In the background throughout this chapter is the question whether what we have argued for in Chapter 1—that fallibilists should 'put knowledge to work'—should be understood as a thesis about the content of knowledge-attributions rather than as a thesis about knowledge. Perhaps knowledge itself can be kept free of any 'pragmatic encroachment' if we allow pragmatic factors a role in (and only in) the determination of the content of knowledge-attributions. We advised the fallibilist to at least think of budging on purism. Contextualism might seem to offer all that our pragmatist account does without requiring one to budge on purism—it might seem to offer the fallibilist all of the benefits of our pragmatism without the costs.[6]

2 A TAXONOMY OF POSITIONS

When an important new view, such as contextualism, appears on the philosophical scene, it is not long before a cottage industry arises devoted to the formulation and evaluation of views in its general neighborhood. Here we offer a brief taxonomy, which will be useful as we proceed.[7] We identify three core views, though the list isn't exhaustive and will be supplemented somewhat even later in this chapter.

[6] But didn't we argue in Chapter 1 that the contextualist account of the oddity of 'I know that *p* but it might be that not-*p*' is not convincing, because thinking generally about 'possibilities that not-*p*' isn't specific enough to raise any epistemic standards? Yes, but this needn't be the end of the story. For if the contextualist can show the fallibilist how to put 'knowledge' to work, she might be able to explain the oddity of such remarks (and their Moorean counterparts) by means of Gricean accounts that piggyback off the one we employed. The rough idea would be that in uttering 'it might be that not-*p*' one conveys that there is a significant chance of error and the thought of there being a significant chance of error has a tendency to raise epistemic standards. The contextualist needn't, of course, give a distinctively contextualist resolution of every puzzle.

[7] Ours is similar to MacFarlane (2005*a*), but we emphasize more than he does the various possibilities for combining the views discussed.

First, we have contextualism. For the contextualist, the *content* of knowledge-attributions shifts with context.

> (Contextualism) The semantic content of knowledge-attributing sentences varies with the context of use.[8]

A second sort of shiftiness is shiftiness in what, epistemically, it takes to *satisfy* the content of a given knowledge-attribution, or more precisely:

> (Impurism) How strong your epistemic position must be—which purely epistemic standards you must meet—in order for a knowledge-attributing sentence, with a fixed content in a fixed context of use, to be true of you varies with your circumstances.[9]

As we saw in Chapter 1, two likely candidates for standards-shifting circumstances are practical environment and salience of possible error. If one combines impurism with the rejection of contextualism one arrives at the *subject sensitive invariantism* (SSI) of Hawthorne (2004) and Stanley (2005*b*).[10] SSI might have much to be said for it, but one shouldn't think that one is committed to rejecting contextualism if one rejects purism. Impurist contextualism is a perfectly consistent view.[11] It is, in fact, suggested

8 We should add, following Stanley (2005*b*), 'in a distinctively epistemological way'.

9 As this definition of impurism is written, the following view gets (incorrectly) classified as impurist: how strong your epistemic position must be in order for you to know that *p* depends solely on how strong your epistemic position with respect to *p* is; e.g. the more evidence you have, the more you need to have. This view is implausible in the extreme. We imagine that even traditional purists would prefer that epistemic standards vary with practical context than with epistemic position. However, on this view, knowledge that *p* can't vary holding fixed strength of epistemic position with respect to *p*. Therefore, this view is compatible with the purism as defined in Chapter 1. Obviously, we don't want impurism, as defined here, to be consistent with purism, as defined in Chapter 1. Therefore, we stipulate that under the label of 'circumstances' should be included only *features of your situation that are not truth-relevant with respect to p.*

The official definition of impurism is simply the material mode version of what we are here calling impurism. The formal mode is used here only to highlight the relationships between impurism contextualism and relativism.

10 Hawthorne calls his view 'sensitive moderate invariantism' and Stanley calls his 'interest-relative invariantism'. The label 'subject sensitive invariantism' is due to DeRose (2004).

11 A view like this is perhaps suggested by John Greco (2009). According to Greco, the label 'subject-sensitive invariantism' is inappropriate 'because it tends to obscure from view a possible version of attributor contextualism, i.e. one that allows the attributor context to be sensitive to the interests and purposes of the subject' (424). We say 'perhaps' suggested because it is not clear that the view Greco explicitly recommends makes the interests and purposes of the subject necessarily relevant to the truth of knowledge-attributions. As Greco says, on this view, 'some attributor contexts would be partly defined by subject interests' (425). But if there are good arguments for subject-sensitivity, this might tell in favor of making the truth of knowledge-attributions sensitive to the subject's interests and purposes in all contexts.

(perhaps unwittingly) by Lewis (1996), who proposes, in addition to his attributor-based 'Rule of Attention', a 'Rule of High Stakes', according to which 'when error would be especially disastrous, few possibilities are properly ignored' (556, n. 12). Unlike the Rule of Attention, which specifies that whether some possibility is properly ignored is fixed by what the attributor is attending to, the Rule of High Stakes leaves open whether the cost of error would be especially disastrous in the attributor's or the subject's context. If it is the subject's context that matters (as it is in Lewis' chosen example—the example of a jury whose false verdict could have disastrous consequences), then Lewis' contextualist Rule of Attention is conjoined with an impurist Rule of High Stakes. One of the main selling points of contextualism, though, has been its compatibility with purism.

A third sort of shiftiness is shiftiness in a parameter relative to which knowledge-attributions are true or false. To get the sorts of shifts needed, one can take this parameter to be a context of *assessment*, a context which a speaker is making or evaluating a knowledge-attribution.[12]

> (Assessment relativism) How strong your epistemic position must be—which epistemic standards you must meet—in order for a knowledge-attributing sentence, with a fixed content in a fixed context of use, to be true of you can vary with the context of assessment.

To illustrate, suppose Jill claims, 'Sally knows that *p*'. This knowledge-attribution can be assessed in any number of contexts. Suppose Bob has much at stake. Relative to his context, Jill's knowledge-attribution is false, let's assume. Relative to a more humdrum context, say Jill's own context, Jill's claim might be true. Assuming that the content of a knowledge-attributing sentence in a context of use is a knowledge-ascribing *proposition*, what assessment relativism tells us is that the truth or falsity of a knowledge-ascribing proposition varies with the context of assessment. Even though the leading relativist, MacFarlane, accepts a purist non-contextualist form of relativism, relativism is not incompatible with contextualism or with impurism or with their combination.

The fact that all these views are compatible points up the need to distinguish the *epistemological* question of whether impurism is true from both the *semantic* question of whether knowledge-ascribing sentences vary

[12] Here we assume, with MacFarlane (2005*a*), that every context in which 'S knows that *p*' is used is one in which it is assessed but that it's not true that every context in which 'S knows that *p*' is assessed is one in which it is used (as opposed to mentioned).

in content across contexts of use and the *metaphysical* question of whether knowledge-ascribing propositions can only be true relative to an index (e.g. a context of assessment). The traditional line on these questions is *no, no*, and *no*—a denial of all three of contextualism, impurism, and relativism. This is the received tradition in analytic epistemology. The maximally accurate if unwieldy name for such a view is *insensitive non-relativistic invariantism*. This view comes in two basic varieties, a skeptical and non-skeptical one. Following Hawthorne (2004), we'll refer to these as *skeptical* and *moderate invariantism*, respectively. Anyone who has even passing knowledge of analytic epistemology in the last fifty or so years knows that moderate invariantism is the orthodoxy. It is the view to beat.

With this rough taxonomy under our belts, we turn to the cases.[13]

3 THE PRACTICAL CASES

So far we've lumped the bank and airport cases together. But they differ in one significant respect. In Bank Case B, Keith—the High speaker, for whom much is at stake—denies *himself* knowledge, whereas in the airport case, the High speakers, Mary and John, deny *someone else*, Smith, knowledge. This difference is relevant to the construction and evaluation of arguments from the cases.

3.1 The bank cases

Here is our best rendering of the argument from the bank cases to contextualism:

(1) What Keith says in uttering 'I know it'll be open tomorrow' in Bank Case A is true.

(2) What Keith says in uttering 'No, I don't [know it'll be open tomorrow]' in Bank Case B is true.

(3) Keith's epistemic position with respect to the proposition *the bank will be open tomorrow* is exactly as strong in Case A as it is in Case B.

13 Some other sorts of shiftiness we will not consider include the following. Content relativism: what content a knowledge-attribution has in fixed context of use varies with the context of assessment. Non-indexical contextualism (MacFarlane 2009): what truth-value a knowledge-ascribing sentence with a fixed content has can vary across contexts of use.

(4) The best explanation of how all of (1)–(3) are true is that the content that the sentence 'Keith knows that the bank will be open tomorrow' has in the speech context Keith occupies in Case A is different from the content it has in the speech context Keith occupies in Case B.

So,

(5) The bank cases support contextualism over its rivals.

We will mostly ignore worries about (3) and about the move from (4) to (5). In the next few sections, we want to discuss how one might question the premises (1), (2), and (4).

3.1.1 Denying premise (1)

To deny premise (1) is to deny that what Keith says in Bank Case A is true. Keith has a strong epistemic position with respect to the proposition in question. The fact that two weeks ago the bank was open on Saturday is good evidence that this is its policy, so good evidence it will be open the following day, which is Saturday. Granted, the evidence isn't good enough to justify perfect certainty, an epistemic probability of 1. But, as we noted in Chapter 1, we have prima facie reason to think that the only way to hold off a robust form of skepticism is to allow for fallible knowledge. Translated into the language of knowledge-attributions, the acceptance of fallibilism amounts to the claim that at least in ordinary speech contexts a knowledge-attribution 'S knows that *p*' can be true even if S has an epistemic probability less than 1 for *p*. And if such a fallibilism is true, there will be cases like Bank Case A in which the subject does speak the truth.

Skepticism might be a price worth paying, but for now (until Chapter 7) we put it aside, as do most contextualists and their rivals.

3.1.2 Denying premise (2)

We said earlier that moderate invariantism is the view to beat. Premise (2) is where the moderate invariantist must stand her ground. She must insist that, because Keith's epistemic position in Bank Case B is quite good, as good (in the moderate invariantist's view) as it is in Bank Case A, Keith does know, contrary to what he says.

Against anyone who denies that Keith speaks the truth in Case B (or in Case A for that matter), DeRose (2005) argues *that is what ordinary competent speakers of the language say.*[14] This is a sort of argument from charity. Of course, if, in Case B, Keith was relying on some straightforward mistake of fact (though not a fact about knowledge!), it might be charitable to take him to be speaking falsely. But there seems to be no such mistake. If Keith was speaking non-literally, say by exaggerating, again he might charitably be taken to speak falsely. But the signs of exaggeration seem to be lacking. If Keith's wife pressed him, 'Well, but let's not exaggerate; you know it will be open', Keith could properly insist that he wasn't exaggerating in the least, that he meant exactly what he said when he said he didn't know.[15]

It is of course possible for the moderate invariantist to claim that Keith is making a mistake about whether he knows. To claim this would be to embrace an error theory. To be plausible, the postulated error would have to be explained in some way. The worry, though, is that the error can be explained only by appealing to ordinary folks' ignorance of the fact that, even when a lot is riding on one's action depending on whether a proposition is true or false, knowing the proposition is true requires only a fairly strong

[14] Doesn't recent work in experimental philosophy ('x-phi') cast doubt on this? There have been a number of x-phi studies of 'folk intuitions' concerning the bank cases (see May et al. (2009), Buckwalter (manuscript), and Feltz and Zarpentine (manuscript)), as well as concerning other practical cases (Neta and Phelan (manuscript)), and many of the authors claim to have called into question whether ordinary folk agree with the claim the high-stakes subjects don't know.

Of course, it could be that DeRose is right that people who are actually in relevantly similar cases do say what Keith says in the bank cases even if it isn't true that people react to the hypothetical bank cases by saying that what Keith says is true in Case A but not in Case B. That is: our intuitions about possible cases might not match up with how we would speak were we in those cases. As long as x-phi restricts itself to evaluating subjects' responses to cases, it lacks the force it would have were it to provide results about what people actually say when they are in the relevant cases themselves.

But should we take the recent results seriously even when it comes to intuitive responses to the cases? Even if DeRose doesn't explicitly say so, these are not arbitrary cases. Behind them, and motivating them, are two very plausible theoretical assumptions: first, that some sort of fallibilism is true, whether it be exactly ours or not, and second that if your epistemic position is fallible in the relevant sense, the gap between your position and a stronger one can make a difference to what you should do depending on your practical environment. An epistemologist can be expected to see that these assumptions motivate the bank cases, an ordinary non-philosopher, maybe not. So, there is a danger that a non-philosopher might react to Case B, or whatever variant of it is given in the vignette, by saying, 'Keith knows', but might also think Keith is just fine to plan on coming back the next day. This non-philosopher would not understand the point of the example. (And even philosophers might find themselves with the intuition that Keith is perfectly rational to wait until the next day and so lean toward the intuition that Keith is wrong when he denies himself knowledge.) We are not saying that these sorts of factors cannot be controlled for (though they are not in the work of May et al., Buckwalter, or Feltz and Zarpentine), but only that they need to be if these studies are to have any probative value.

In previously published work, our chief arguments for principles connecting knowledge and actionability do not rest on claims about what intuitions folk have about the bank cases or other stakes-shifting cases. We provide further such arguments in the next chapter.

[15] See Hawthorne (2004: 115–18) for further relevant discussion.

epistemic position, not an *extremely* strong one. The postulation of such errors would be detrimental to the view.

But there is an alternative, developed in some detail by Patrick Rysiew ((2001) and (2007)) and Jessica Brown (2006). What Keith is doing in Case B is *implicating* or *pragmatically imparting* a truth by stating a falsehood. Keith knows the bank will be open tomorrow. He says otherwise in order to impart an important truth. What is this imparted truth?

Rysiew favors a salience-based proposal. When Keith denies that he knows he is conveying the fact he can't rule out whatever possibilities of error are 'in the air', or at least the fact he can't rule out all such salient possibilities that are worth taking seriously. We are of course ignoring any role salience of possibilities of error plays in these cases. So, Rysiew's proposal needs to be reworked so that it is about practical environment rather than salience. Making the required change (see Brown (2006: 422–4)), we arrive at the view that in saying he doesn't know in Bank Case B, Keith is conveying, roughly, that he cannot properly rely on the proposition that the bank will be open tomorrow, because his epistemic position isn't strong enough.

This response to the contextualist has come to be known as a *warranted assertability maneuver*, or WAM. As Brown (2005) characterizes the maneuver:

> At the core of a WAM is the idea that the intuitions about contextualist cases can be explained by appeal to the truth-value of the propositions pragmatically conveyed by the knowledge attributions, rather than the literal truth-value of those attributions. (85)

In this case, the needed WAM is not merely that claiming 'I know' imparts that one can act on the proposition in question, though of course the WAMer will accept that WAM. Indeed, once Keith goes into the bank and checks with the teller, he can then say to his wife, 'Okay, so now we know. The bank is open tomorrow.' Saying this will impart that they are proper to rely on the bank's being open tomorrow. But a WAM on 'I know' will not explain why we are willing to go as far as to assert the negation, 'I don't know', which according to the WAMer, is false. To explain *that*, the WAMer posits a WAM on 'I don't know'. The WAMer is therefore putting forth a double WAMmy, if you will, under which 'I know that *p*' imparts that you can act on *p*, and 'I don't know that *p*' imparts that you cannot act on *p*. Keith doesn't say 'I don't know' for no reason; he says it to impart the information that he can't act on *p*.

Double WAMmies might seem suspicious. It is generally not the case that by asserting the negation of something P which imparts Q you thereby impart

~Q. To use Grice's example, if I wrote in a letter of recommendation that *Mr. X doesn't have excellent handwriting*, that wouldn't imply that he is a good philosopher, even though writing that he does have excellent handwriting implies that he isn't a good philosopher. But double WAMmies are not unheard of. If you say 'There's a gas station around the corner', then at least if your situation is normal (e.g. you're not working for the Yellow Pages), you imply that you can get gas there. If you say 'There is no gas station around the corner', then you imply that you cannot get gas there. Neither of these implications is semantic. So there are particular situations in which by asserting P you impart Q and by asserting ~P you impart ~Q.

But not even a mere double-WAMmy sufficiently explains the data. Keith does not merely fail to assert 'I know.' He asserts 'I don't know' and yet he *does* know. Suppose a man goes to lunch with his relatively youthful mother, who has arrived in town for a surprise visit. His wife is told by a friend that he was seen lunching with a lovely woman and displaying much affection toward her. Later the wife asks him directly, 'I heard you were at lunch with a beautiful woman, is that true?' The man will not say 'Yes, I went to lunch with a beautiful woman.' That would imply—if left bare—something false. Nor will he say, 'No, I didn't go to lunch with a beautiful woman.' He won't say this, even though what it implies—that he didn't lunch with some possible romantic interest—is true. So, although the WAM on the negation would impart *information*, he doesn't say it. Why? Because it is false, and he knows it is false. He would be lying to say that. We needn't assume the man has only the purist of motives. Perhaps the lie would get him into further trouble (if the mother and the wife talk), but it will get him into trouble because it is a *lie*.

Similarly, the mere existence of a double-WAMmy concerning knowledge won't explain why Keith says, 'I don't know'. In fact, assuming Keith *does know*, we would expect that he would refrain from saying 'I don't know', precisely because saying that would be saying something false. At least we would expect this unless Keith was mistaken about whether he knows. What would we expect Keith to say if he knew that the bank was open but couldn't act on it? Perhaps, 'Yes, I know it's open, but we'd better go in now just in case.' Or perhaps just, 'Let's not risk it.' Why convey the information by lying when the information could be conveyed just as well with the truth?

Of course, there are lies and there are lies. Sometimes, by avoiding a falsehood, you risk complications that your interlocutor would just be annoyed by. In such cases, the falsehood will count as a white lie. Perhaps it is only a white lie, in the above example, to say, 'No, I didn't have lunch with a beautiful woman.' Or suppose you know that there is a gas station around the corner but you also know it's been out of gas for a few weeks. You're asked by a motorist, 'Is there a gas station around here?' You might say, 'Well, yes, but you shouldn't go there. It's been out of gas and closed for weeks.' Better, perhaps, to just say 'No'. And in some cases, the true story will be even more complicated and the motorist just won't want to hear it. Sometimes the white lie is best (although the motorist will be annoyed if he sees the gas station, doubts your veracity, and then stops to see if he can get gas. He might mutter to himself, after checking the place out, 'I wish the guy would have told me the straight truth!').

Perhaps we should expect Keith in Case B to tell a white lie. But it's not clear how issues of politeness or a potentially annoyed interlocutor are relevant in Keith's situation. And the situation is more peculiar when we consider Keith's own first-person perspective. Keith will in fact be willing to say this to himself all alone: 'Gosh, if we wait till Saturday and the bank is closed, we will be in deep trouble. Do I know the bank will be open tomorrow? No, I guess I don't. I should go check inside.' In saying this to himself, he doesn't seem to be telling himself a white lie. Compare this to the gas station case. We don't lie to ourselves to avoid an annoyed interlocutor: 'There's no gas station around here!'

If the WAMer embraced an error theory, she would be able to give the needed explanation here. It's simple: we are prone to mistake what we pragmatically impart for what is entailed by the semantic content of the sentences we use, and this is what we do in the case in point (Rysiew 2001: 502–3)). Presumably, we do make some such mistakes (e.g. it can seem that if a person believes something she doesn't know it, or that if you like someone, you don't love them). However, if this sort of error theory is not to be a serious cost, we need to be given some story about why we make these particular mistakes; it is not adequate merely to remark that we do sometimes confuse or run together the semantic content and the propositions pragmatically implied. Why do we do it *here* rather than *there*?

So, the moderate invariantist can plausibly WAM premise (2) only if she combines her double WAMmy with an error theory. We have laid down a challenge for the WAMer to explain this error beyond the mere observation that we sometimes confuse semantics and pragmatics. In the absence of such an explanation, we deem the postulation of error a cost to the moderate invariantist's WAM, and so to moderate invariantism.

3.1.3 *Denying premise (4)*

Perhaps the moderate invariantist can resist the argument for contextualism without WAMing premise (2), by concentrating on premise (4). Premise (4) states, in effect, that a variation in semantic content is what best explains how Keith could have the same strength of epistemic position in both cases but could speak truly in saying 'I know' in Case A and in saying 'I don't know' in Case B, while maintaining the same strength of epistemic position. How might the moderate invariantist deny this claim?

Perhaps, when Keith says 'I know' in Case A he satisfies all the traditional invariant conditions on knowledge, while in Case B he fails to satisfy some traditional invariant condition on knowledge. If this explanation worked, it would seem superior to the contextualist explanation. Of course, the condition would have to be one which didn't affect strength of epistemic position. The natural thought is: *belief.* Maybe the High Stakes subject lacks knowledge merely because he lacks belief.

Jennifer Nagel (2008) puts the idea as follows:

> Whether one thinks of High-Stakes Hannah[16] as having a lower-confidence belief or a state of cognition that precedes arrival at settled belief, it's psychologically realistic to read her as needing more evidence either to make up her mind at all or to attain the same level of subjective confidence in High Stakes as she would have in Low. As a high-stakes/high effort subject, she should be expected to collect more information prior to settling on a fixed belief. (286)

However, you will recall that DeRose explicitly stipulates that his confidence level in the two bank cases is the same: his confidence doesn't go down. But is this legitimate—to just stipulate belief? According to Kent Bach (2005), it is not:

> I would not accept DeRose's stipulation regarding his high-standards version of his Bank case, according to which the attributor denies knowledge while 'remaining as confident as [he] was before that the bank will be open tomorrow' and yet concedes that he'd 'better go in and make sure' (1992, 913). It seems to me that unless he's trying to placate his wife, his belief would have to be shaken at least somewhat.

Why does Bach think that it is impossible to retain an unshaken belief in a proposition while failing to act on it? Now, Keith could retain a very strong

16 Nagel uses Stanley's reimaginings—in which the subject is Hannah—of the bank cases and related stakes-shifting cases, rather than DeRose's originals. The name obviously makes no difference.

degree of confidence for the proposition that the bank is open tomorrow, while nonetheless claiming that he'd better go in and make sure. Keith could explain himself well enough: 'Although I am extremely confident, I am not sure, and I need to be sure, and that is why I'm going to go inquire further.' But Bach probably has in mind not what Bayesians call 'credence', which is a graded matter, but rather outright belief, which is binary. And a plausible thesis about the relation between credence and outright belief is that you have an outright belief that *p* only if your credence in *p* is high enough so that it wouldn't stand in the way of your being moved to act on the basis of *p*. We discuss this pragmatic conception of belief and its role in our project more fully in Chapter 5. Here we just note that, if the pragmatic conception is correct, then Keith in Case B does not outright believe that the bank will be open the next day, because his confidence is apparently not high enough in the situation for him to act. We can interpret Bach as claiming that, to block the argument for contextualism from the bank cases, the moderate invariantist need not WAM premise (2). She can simply adopt the pragmatic conception of belief. If this conception provides at least as good an explanation as contextualism of Keith's speaking truth in both cases—that Keith believes and has knowledge in Case A, but fails to believe and so lacks knowledge in Case B—premise (4) is false.

But suppose we alter Case B by stipulating that Keith's confidence is sufficient to (irrationally) move him to act, so that, in Case B as well as Case A, he will act on *the bank will be open tomorrow*. So, in the modified Case B, Keith counts as having an outright belief. We would have to imagine Keith in Case B saying something like, 'Aw come on, I know it will be open. We'll just come back tomorrow.' Intuitively, Keith's knowledge-claim, 'I know' is false. But not because he lacks outright belief; we have stipulated that he does believe. Moreover, the mere fact that in Case B Keith has confidence sufficient to move him to act does not falsify the claim that Keith has the same strength of epistemic position with respect to *the bank will be open tomorrow*, because having enough confidence to move one to act is not a truth-relevant factor. So, modifying Case B in this way bypasses Bach's complaint and the basis of the objection to premise (4).

Nagel does not rely on a pragmatic conception of belief; she allows DeRose's stipulation that he believes in Case B, but does not think this provides solace for the contextualist:

> Given the differences in confidence ordinarily produced by differences in stakes, it's odd that High-Stakes Hannah is so confident, and one has to wonder how

> this peculiar confidence is understood by the reader of the case. One natural hypothesis that could explain the reader's tendency to ascribe a failure of knowledge to Confident High-Stakes Hannah is that the reader will naturally perceive her as having unfounded confidence ... [I]t's only psychologically plausible that High-Stakes Hannah could have high confidence of the sort stipulated on her slim evidence if she is compromised in her accuracy, for example by thinking hastily or in a way biased by wishful thinking ...
>
> Ordinarily, high- and low-stakes subjects think differently about problems complex enough to generate contrasting epistemic intuitions: we can make high-stakes subjects think like low-stakes subjects on such problems, but only by putting them under conditions where they think less accurately than their low-stakes counterparts. (291–2)

By adopting Nagel's proposal, the moderate invariantist can grant that Keith speaks truly in Case A and falsely in our modified Case B (in which Keith says 'I know'), and that Keith believes that the bank will be open tomorrow in both cases. But Keith's epistemic position is different in the two cases because the sorts of belief-forming processes Keith would have to use in a High-Stakes context in order to form a belief that p are not generally reliable processes. Premise (3) is false.

It's not clear why Keith would need to use different methods in Case B than he does in Case A. With equanimity—no more hastily and with no more bias than he does in Case A, and using exactly the same methods—he forms the belief that the bank is open tomorrow. He acts on that belief by waiting until the following day, to his wife's amazement and frustration. Of course, he's irrational in so waiting, for the risk is too great and the cost of going today is so small. But he nonetheless, without a second thought, does it. We still have the intuition that he speaks falsely when he says 'I know'. It is hard to see, given that his methods are equally reliable, he is equally cautious or incautious, etc., how his epistemic position is so much poorer in Case B than in Case A. Yet his 'I know' is true only in Case A. So we still are left without an explanation of this fact.

There are two ways Nagel might respond. First, she might say that his methods *can't* be the same because there is a difference between *memory-in-Low-Stakes-contexts* and *memory-in-High-Stakes-contexts*. But even if these mark out two relevantly distinct methods, and even if there is some way to determine that in Case B Keith is using *memory-in-High-Stakes-contexts* rather than, simply, *memory*, it's not at all clear which method puts Keith in the better epistemic position. Nagel points to psychological studies that show that unless a subject is rushed, on most markers of reliability, including those pertaining to memory, High-Stakes subjects tend to perform better than Low-Stakes subjects. So a mere difference between methods used, assuming Keith isn't being hasty and isn't rushed in Case B, won't be enough to secure an epistemic cost for Keith in Case B.

Second, perhaps the fact that Keith is the sort of person who does not change his methods when the stakes get high makes him epistemically vicious, so that even if he uses the same methods in Case A and Case B, he can't get knowledge in Case B. Of course, if it's the general disposition to fail to change methods when the stakes get high that makes Keith epistemically vicious—well, that's a disposition that Keith has in Case A as well and, therefore, Keith doesn't know even in Case A. So the worry must be that it's the manifestation of that disposition, of that vice, that stands in the way of knowledge in Case B and only Case B. Still, it's hard to see how the worry is justified. The methods used in Case A are good enough for knowledge in Low-Stakes contexts. They are no less reliable when used in Case B than they are when used in Case A, and nor do they perform worse on any other purely truth-relevant dimension across the two cases. And so, if moderate invariantism is true, it is hard to see why, even if the failure to change methods is somehow epistemically vicious, it is vicious in a way that poses an obstacle to knowing.

We don't see much hope in claiming that Keith fails to satisfy some traditional invariant conditions on knowledge (like belief or some traditional epistemic condition). What options remain for the moderate invariantist with respect to premise (4)? According to moderate invariantism, if Keith believes and has the same strength of epistemic position as he does in Case A, then the semantic content of Keith's utterance of 'I don't know' in the original Case B is false if the semantic content of his utterance in Case A is true. This looks simply inconsistent with the conjunction of premises (1) and (2). And so the moderate invariantist can't explain the truth of premises (1) and (2): according to the moderate invariantist, they can't both *be* true. But it appears they are.

But perhaps this is too quick. It assumes, for one thing, that if the semantic content of one of Keith's utterances is false, then what he says in uttering it is false: it assumes an equation between semantic content and the content of the speech acts, in particular the content of what is said or asserted.[17]

[17] What is said might be distinguished from what is asserted, but we will not explore this possibility. We will treat the two as equivalent.

But suppose that semantic content can come apart from speech act content. Then, if there is a nice story of how that happens, this story might be used to explain how what Keith says is true—thus preserving premises (1) and (2) unaltered—even though the semantic content of one of Keith's utterances is false—thus allowing for moderate invariantism.

Such a view is what Robert Stainton calls *speech act contextualism*. Speech act contextualism is invariantism about the semantic *content* of knowledge-ascribing sentences combined with contextualism about *what is asserted* in their use on particular occasions.[18] Both contextualism and speech act contextualism explain perfectly well how (1)–(3) could all be true. But which of these two putative explanations is most plausible?

The speech act contextualist will tout the fact that she needn't worry about many of the powerful linguistic arguments Jason Stanley (2005*b*) makes against mainstream contextualism. Stanley might be right in arguing that 'knows' does not exhibit the sort of behavior we find with expressions which clearly shift in their semantic content across contexts of attribution. But this leaves open the possibility that what ordinary people assert when they use 'S knows that *p*' varies from context to context. Consider an example loosely derived from Stainton (forthcoming). You can use 'There is a tiger in the next room' in a zoo to assert that, indeed, a tiger, a large striped cat, is in the next room. In another context—a gallery of paintings of animals—you could assert something quite different by using this sentence, viz. that there is a painting of such a tiger. If the gallery-owner said 'There are no tigers in the next room' to a potential patron who just asked 'I like the lions here, but do you have any tigers?', the gallery-owner would be *lying*—asserting something false—and not merely misleading the customer if there were no tigers in the next room but there were paintings of tigers. Perhaps, suggests the speech act contextualist, this is how it works for knowledge-attributions. In some contexts we use knowledge-sentences to assert that we possess knowledge while in others we assert something else, perhaps that we have an epistemic position high enough to act on the proposition at issue.

However, there are some notable difficulties incurred in moving from mainstream contextualism to speech act contextualism. For one thing, some

18 This view is endorsed by both Stainton (forthcoming) and Gilbert Harman (2007). For more on the distinction between speech act content and semantic content, see Herman Cappelen and Ernest LePore (2005).

of Stanley's (2005*b*) linguistic evidence seems to indict both views.[19] Another problem is that speakers don't seem to be able to distinguish clearly between what they are asserting and the semantic content of the knowledge-sentences they use, in anything like the way they can for the 'tiger' example. A third and deeper problem is that the moderate invariantist can use speech act contextualism to explain the truth of premises (1) and (2) only by relying on a sort of chauvinism that contextualists have wanted, naturally, to avoid.

The chauvinism comes in two sorts. First, if the sentence 'I know that the bank is open on Saturdays' has the same content in both cases, and if we continue to accept purism, we will have to say that in one of the two cases the semantic content of the sentence uttered is *false*, so that the sentence uttered is literally false. This is truth-value chauvinism. Second, because what is asserted is true in both contexts, in one of the contexts, but not the other, Keith asserts the semantic content of his utterance. This is chauvinism concerning who asserts semantic content. With regard to both sorts of chauvinism, it seems fair to ask, 'Which one? Which context gets the moderate invariantist's blessing?' The answer, of course, is Case A. But this begs the question against skepticism in a way that mainstream contextualism doesn't. The mainstream contextualist avoids these problems because she avoids all such chauvinism.

The speech act contextualist might reply that in neither context is the subject asserting/denying knowledge. But this option, though not chauvinistic in the second sense, seems highly implausible: if not in either such contexts, do people ever assert the semantic contents of epistemic sentences? And if they never do, how does 'know' get to have the content it has?[20] And how can we tell what content it has?

There is another way of denying (4), without committing to any chauvinism, but not one that is available to the moderate invariantist.[21] Consider the following account of how (1)–(3) could all be true:

[19] We have in mind especially the arguments from indirect speech reports and propositional anaphora on pp. 52–4.

[20] See Hawthorne (2004: 121–3) for related discussion.

[21] Another option is relativism, but we don't dwell on that option here because, strictly speaking, the relativist will not agree that all of premises (1)–(3) are true. For this could only mean that each is true in all contexts of assessment, which is not the case for (1) and (2). So, relativism is really not a threat to (4), at least assuming (1)–(3) are in place.

Really, the relativist rejects (1) and (2) as ill-formed or incomplete. They can be reformulated to be true, as follows:

(1R) What Keith says in Case A in uttering 'I know' is true in his context of assessment in Case A.

(2R) What Keith says in Case B in uttering 'I don't know' is true in his context of assessment in Case B.

> How can Keith's knowledge-attribution be true in Case A and his knowledge-denial be true in Case B, even though Keith's strength of epistemic position is the same across the cases? Because knowing something requires being proper to act on it (at least when what is known is pertinent to one's practical situation), and although Keith in Case A knows and has the same strength of epistemic position as Keith does in Case B, in Case B, because of his heightened stakes, Keith isn't proper to act on the relevant proposition, and so doesn't know.

This account appeals to the principle that if you know that *p* you are proper to act on *p* when the question of whether *p* is relevant to the question of what to do. Call this principle *Action.*[22] Call the above account the *pragmatist* account of how (1)–(3) could all be true. The pragmatist account has the hitch we noticed in Chapter 1: it is a form of impurism. It allows whether you know (or are in a position to know) to vary without a variation in your strength of epistemic position.

Impurism is counterintuitive. And it also seems to have troubling implications. For one thing, it threatens to allow for the possibility of knowledge coming and going 'with ease' (Hawthorne 2004: 176). It would seem to follow that you could lose knowledge not by forgetting information or obtaining new evidence, but in some cases by writing a sufficiently large check. If knowledge can come and go like this, we would expect odd-sounding temporal and modal embeddings to come out true: 'I know but wouldn't have known if more had been at stake for me', 'I know now, but earlier, when more was at stake for me, I didn't know even though I had the same evidence for what I believed'. These certainly sound problematic.

These implications concern a single subject. A second sort of implication concerns interaction between subjects, and in particular the transferability of knowledge (see MacFarlane 2005*b*)). If pragmatic factors encroach on

Of course, the contextualist will agree with (1R) and (2R). But the relativist will add that what Keith says in Case A in saying 'I know' is the negation of what Keith says in Case B in saying 'I don't know.' The contextualist will not agree with that.

We will not assess the argument for relativism based on (1R)–(5R), other than to say that (1R) and (2R) are not as intuitively compelling as (1) and (2).

22 To eliminate the qualification about relevance to the question of what to do, in Fantl and McGrath (2002) and (2007) we introduced a special notion of 'being rational to act as if *p*'. To be rational to act as if *p* is to be such that what one is rational to do is the same as what one is rational to do given *p*. The basic idea is straightforward: you are rational to act as if *p* iff the chance, if any, that not-*p* doesn't affect what you are rational to do. In Chapter 3, we will explore the idea of one's epistemic position being 'good enough' for action and belief in detail. Here we stick with the intuitive idea of its being proper to act on what one knows.

knowledge, then it seems that a knower's testimony need not, even if trusted, impart knowledge to the recipient, and not because the recipient has misleading counterevidence which the testifier lacks, but only because the recipient's practical environment is sufficiently different.

Given the implausibilities associated with the pragmatist explanation of how premises (1)–(3) in the pro-contextualist argument could all be true, one might simply rule such an explanation out, and so refuse to see it as posing any danger to premise (4), which asserts that contextualism provides the best explanation of (1)–(3).

But, of course, the contextualist has similar difficulties *bumped up a level.* That is, if the defender of *Action* must accept impurism, the contextualist must accept the use-to-mention conversion of impurism. The contextualist must claim that two subjects could be just alike in strength of epistemic position but one could truly self-ascribe knowledge while the other couldn't. Someone can come to falsely self-ascribe knowledge by writing a sufficiently large check. Contextualism would seem to predict the truth of odd-sounding temporal and modal embeddings such as, 'It is true for me to say, "I know", but had more been at stake for me, it would not have been true for me to say "I know"' and 'It is true for me now to say, "I know", but it wasn't true for me to say this earlier, even though I had the same evidence then'. And even if knowledge is transferable through testimony for the contextualist, the status of being able to truly call yourself a knower isn't. All this seems to be because the contextualist is committed to something very much like the use-to-mention version of *Action*: if you satisfy 'knows that *p*' in your speech context, then if *p* is relevant to your practical situation, you are proper to act on *p*. Moving the impurist consequences to the meta-level hardly constitutes a big improvement.[23]

Still, isn't it *some* improvement? Enough to carry the day? DeRose writes:

> In general, then, when it looks as if the contextualist has to say something strongly counter-intuitive, what he must say turns out to be, on the contrary, something fairly theoretical concerning the truth conditions of certain sentences. Do we really have strong intuitions about such things? (1992: 927)

One problem, here, is that we do have intuitions about whether *what a person said* on a particular occasion is true, and it seems the contextualist does have troubles with such intuitions. But there is a more serious difficulty. If you are

[23] Stanley (2005*b*: 116) makes similar points.

asked, not whether Keith's statement in Case B is true, but whether Keith knows in Case B, then if you are like us, you will find the *Action*-based reasoning very plausible.

Notice how attractive and easy the reasoning is: 'If Keith knows in Case B, he should be able to act accordingly, but given all that is at stake, he can't; his evidence isn't good enough, and so he doesn't know'. This reasoning is every bit as available to Keith in Case B. Keith thinks that since the stakes are high he needs knowledge to act, but he also thinks that knowledge is good enough—nothing more is needed. The difficulty for contextualism, here, is that *Action*-based reasoning seems extremely plausible in both our low-stakes context and in Keith's high-stakes context, and this is evidence that its plausibility doesn't depend on the particular epistemic standards in force in the speech context, but rather stems from the invariant conditions on knowledge: if you know something which is relevant to your choice situation then you are proper to act on it. In this way, it is no different than reasoning from the fact that not-*p* to the fact that so-and-so doesn't know it, or from the fact that a subject is Gettiered to the fact that he doesn't know (see Cohen 1999)). If *Action* identifies an invariant condition on knowledge, then at least assuming fallibilism is true in all but the most skeptical contexts—as we have been assuming all along in granting that premise (1) is true—impurism, too, will be true in all but the most skeptical contexts. And one of the main rationales for contextualism, at least in the work of its leading proponents, Cohen and DeRose, is to avoid impurism, to keep the pragmatic away from knowledge by allowing it to infect only 'knowledge'.

In response, the contextualist might grant that this *Action*-based reasoning is attractive and easy, but she might think it has been misrepresented. The reasoning is really bumped up a level; it is about 'knowledge' rather than knowledge. We are really reasoning thus: if Keith satisfies 'knows' in his context in Case B, then he should be able to act on what he believes, but given all that is at stake, he can't act on it; and so he doesn't satisfy 'knows' in his context. One obvious problem is that it seems plainly incorrect: the reader might react differently, but our reaction to this proposal is *it doesn't seem like we're reasoning about 'knowledge' here but about knowledge*! But another problem is that it is implausible to claim that this is how Keith reasons in Case B. Keith is surely *using* 'know' in his thinking, rather than mentioning it.

The pragmatist explanation of how all (1)–(3) could be true is hard to accept. It's hard to accept because it is impurist. What we take away from the bank cases, then, is not that they are anything like decisive evidence for contextualism, but rather that they make us vividly aware of a tension in our thinking about knowledge: we are pulled to purism on the one hand, and on the other to the claim that you can act on what you know, and these two come into conflict as soon as we allow fallible knowledge. If the best resolution of this tension is to uphold fallibilist purism at the cost of denying *Action*, then we suspect the bank cases will provide support for contextualism. But whether this is the best resolution is simply not clear until we see what can be said on behalf of *Action* and other pragmatist principles.

3.2 The airport case

Are matters different when we turn to the airport case? Our discussion here can be brief. In the airport case, the speakers are talking only about Smith. And so we have a single subject in a single circumstance, and so no need for an assumption, like (3), about sameness of epistemic position.

(1*) What Smith says in uttering 'I know the plane stops in Chicago' is true.

(2*) What Mary and John say in uttering 'Smith doesn't know it stops in Chicago' is true.

(3*) The best explanation of (1*) and (2*) is that the content of 'Smith knows that the plane stops in Chicago' varies across Smith and Mary and John's speech contexts.

So,

(4*) The airport case supports contextualism.

The very same objections that were raised against (1) and (2) can be raised against (1*) and (2*), and with equal (im)plausibility. And the same points about speech act contextualism apply to (3*).

Bach (2005) extends to the airport case his worry that we can explain Keith's self-denial of knowledge in Case B because in Case B he loses belief. Unlike DeRose's first-person bank cases, Bach endorses an error theory concerning the third-person airport case. You can correctly deny knowledge to yourself if you no longer count as outright believing because your threshold for outright belief has risen. But in the airport case you are denying knowledge to someone who does believe. Bach thinks that his is not a particularly troubling error theory, though, because, though 'it has people sometimes denying knowledge of people who have it, it does not have them generally confused about knowledge or "knowledge"' (78).

Even if the error theory is 'minimal', this treatment of Mary and John's knowledge-denial cannot be used to explain why Mary and John speak truly in denying knowledge to Smith: according to Bach they *don't* speak truly. So this move cannot be used to target (3*). It would have to take the form of an objection to (2*)—it would count as an explanation of why Mary and John deny knowledge to Smith, despite the falsehood of such a denial. It's because Mary and John think Smith's confidence isn't high enough for outright belief, and because outright belief is required for knowledge, that they think that Smith doesn't know. Of course, Smith's confidence is high enough for belief, even if theirs isn't. This is the mistake they make. Their error is fundamentally about psychology. They 'overproject' their own 'doxastic' situation, treating Smith's like their own.

This seems to us an implausible account of Mary and John. When asked why they deny Smith knowledge, it surely wouldn't raise any eyebrows if they said, 'He just doesn't have enough evidence.' If pressed by a philosopher, they might well add, 'Even though he believes it, he doesn't have the evidence he needs to know—he needs better evidence.' On Bach's account, they would be in error: Smith's evidence is good enough to know. So, it turns out that Bach's account does require postulating an error about knowledge and not merely about psychology. Nor is the mistake merely about whether a particular person knows. It is about how strong one's evidence needs to be to know. Ordinary folk—and philosophers—tend to overestimate how much evidence is needed.

Assuming that premises (1*) and (2*) are secure, is there an objection to (3*) along the lines of the impurist objection to (4) in the argument concerning the bank cases? Not obviously. What is different in the two arguments is that there is no plausible *Action*-based reasoning which can explain (2*). It is not plausible to reason: Mary and John have a lot at stake, and can't act on *the plane stops in Chicago*, and so don't know it does, and because they can't act on it, Smith doesn't know. So, one of the main barriers to (4) in the argument concerning the bank cases—the fact that there is a simple *Action*-based explanation of (1)–(3)—is not a barrier to (3*). At least as long as (2*) is secure, it seems there is no reason why the same pragmatist who gave the *Action*-based explanation in the bank cases can't accept a contextualist explanation of the truth of (1*) and (2*) here. A pragmatist can help herself to (3*). And to (4*), at least as long as contextualism isn't being equated with purist contextualism, which as we argued in section 2, it shouldn't be.

The purist contextualist might claim that her explanation, which explains the shift in content by appealing to a shift from 'knows' expressing one purist relation to its expressing another weaker or stronger purist relation, is more plausible than the impurist contextualist explanation, which will not take 'knows' to express a purist relation in any context (save a skeptical one). But this takes us back once again to the tension between purism, fallibilism, and *Action.* The purist contextualist explanation is initially more plausible, but only because purism is more plausible than impurism. But, then again, the *pragmatist* explanation of why Keith speaks the truth in Bank Case B is more plausible than any contextualist explanation.

So, the argument for contextualism from the airport case is more compelling than the argument for contextualism from the bank cases, and that is because there is no available pragmatist explanation of how (1*) and (2*) could both be true. But once the contextualist replaces (4*) with the conclusion that *purist* contextualism is true, all bets are off.

The contextualist might claim that a unified treatment of first-person and third-person knowledge-attributions is preferable to one that divides the cases. Because we can account for the truth of Keith's self-denial of knowledge in Case B without recourse to *Action*, and because this account squares with Mary and John's denial of knowledge to Smith, perhaps we should just go with that and leave *Action* (and impurism) behind.

The difficulty, though, is that *Action* is independently plausible. No sensible contextualist would claim that when the speaker is different from the subject, only features of the speaker's context are relevant to the truth-value of the speaker's knowledge-attribution. That the subject believes the proposition, at a minimum, is also required, and that is not a speaker factor. The plausibility of *Action* gives us prima facie reason to think that there are pragmatic conditions on knowledge, too. And if there are pragmatic subject factors, then first- and third-person cases *ought* to be treated differently, because speakers and subjects will often differ in pragmatic factors, just as speakers and subjects often differ in whether they believe a proposition.

DeRose (2004) claims that third-person cases like the airport case comprise *the problem with subject-sensitive invariantism.* We can now see that this claim is potentially misleading in two ways. First, the third-person cases, in which speakers, like Mary and John, are talking about a subject who isn't part of their context, pose problems for any sort of non-skeptical invariantism, whether SSI or moderate invariantism. The WAMs that the moderate invariantist offers, warts and all, should be available to the defender of SSI. Second, and more importantly, DeRose does not distinguish SSI in his paper from impurism. One can accept impurism without accepting SSI. Although we have taken no stand on the matter, perhaps DeRose is right that third-person cases show that one shouldn't be an invariantist—and so shouldn't accept SSI or moderate invariantism. But that wouldn't refute impurism. The impurist, too, can reach into the contextualist's playbook to cope with these cases.[24]

4 GATEKEEPING

When a practical situation is salient in which a certain high strength of epistemic position is clearly needed in order for a proposition to be epistemically fit to be the basis for action, speakers tend to deny knowledge to both the subjects in the high-stakes situation as well as subjects who clearly have a lesser strength of epistemic position with respect to *p* or some appropriately related larger class of propositions. (The salient stakes-situation needn't be that of the speaker, though this is certainly a common case.) This appears to be a fact.

Both the moderate invariantist and the contextualist have explanations of this fact, and both can be employed by the impurist. According to the moderate invariantist, there is a certain brute WAM that is in play when the relevant practical situation is salient. We say 'brute' because there is nothing about what knowledge is that can explain this WAM, nor can it be explained by general Gricean principles. To know, for the moderate invariantist, requires only having a fairly strong epistemic position with respect to *p*, and it can be crystal clear that a salient subject in a high-stakes situation does have a very strong epistemic position with respect to *p*, but just not strong enough for *p* to be the basis for action. Why would it be, then, that by saying 'He doesn't know' we convey that his epistemic position isn't good enough to serve as a basis of action, then? The only answer is that this is just how it is.

Similarly, the contextualist appeals to a brute content-shifting mechanism, very much in addition to the mechanism of salience of possible error,

[24] DeRose (2002) claims one can demonstrate the truth of contextualism from two premises: (1) warranted assertibility varies with the context of speech, and (2) the condition under which a proposition is warrantedly assertible is precisely the condition which constitutes a truth-condition for first-person attributions of knowledge. But as Blackson (2004) and Brown (2005) point out, even if (1) and (2) are true, it does not show contextualism is true. For, (1) and (2) are perfectly consistent with SSI, and more importantly for us, they are consistent with impurism.

to explain the phenomena. When the high-stakes situation is salient the standards anyone must meet to be truly described as knowing simply shift. Why? Again, the only answer is that this is how it is.

By contrast, the impurist has a more principled answer: the high-stakes subject *doesn't know*, and that is because knowledge is related to action in the way *Action* suggests. So far, this only explains why we deny knowledge to the high-stakes subject whose epistemic position isn't good enough to serve as a basis for action. It doesn't yet explain why we go on to deny knowledge to other subjects with no better epistemic positions. But there is a plausible story to be told here, though we are uncommitted on which form precisely it should take—whether a contextualist form or a WAM. And it is this: when a high-stakes situation is salient in which it takes a certain high strength of epistemic position to know, it is understandable that in order to truly or at least appropriately call someone else a knower that person must meet the standards relevant to the high-stakes situation. This is understandable, because arguably part of the point of knowledge-attribution is 'epistemic gate-keeping', to use David Henderson's (2009) term. In attributing knowledge to a person we are certifying that her epistemic position is good enough to be a basis for action and belief in *all* the stakes-situations under consideration. Which stakes-situations are under consideration is typically determined by which people or communities might have need of the relevant information.

For the invariantist impurist, this would constitute an error theory of our folk attributions, of the sort that we recommend that the moderate invariantist employ when explaining our folk habit of denying knowledge to high-stakes subjects. But for the impurist, this error theory is motivated by the independent plausibility of principles like *Action*, while for the moderate invariantist, there is no metaphysical connection between knowledge and action—no fact about what knowledge is—that explains the error. Consider 'epistemic egocentrism', a mechanism proposed by Royzman et al. (2003) for explaining why 'sophisticated' subjects—subjects with greater knowledge of a situation than more 'naïve' subjects—will tend to predict the naïve subjects' reactions as if those subjects shared the sophisticated subjects' knowledge and concerns. Though epistemic egocentrism has been used primarily as an explanation of why epistemically more sophisticated subjects go wrong in attributing non-epistemic psychological states to naïve subjects (see also Birch and Bloom 2004)), Jennifer Nagel (2010) argues that similar mechanisms might explain how sophisticated subjects could wrongly deny knowledge to more naïve subjects—that, for example, if possibilities of error are salient to a sophisticated subject but not to a naïve subject, the sophisticated subject might 'mistakenly [project] to the subject of evaluation ... [the] ascribers' own concern with error, and this projection is explained in terms of the central bias in human mental state ascription' (304).

Likewise, we might think, if *Action* tells us that our practical concerns—relevant as they are to whether we can act on *p*—are relevant to whether we know that *p*, we might well mistakenly project those same practical concerns onto lower stakes, 'naïve' subjects. If our knowledge-attributions are properly governed by *Action*, we can see how they might well be improperly guided by the egocentric version of *Action*: if you know that *p*, then I can act on *p*. And even if our concern with high-stakes is motivated not by our own high-stakes, but simply with the high-stakes of some salient subject, we might improperly project onto low-stakes subjects that very concern.

If *Action* is false, however, we have a less persuasive explanation of the mechanisms by which both moderate invariantism and contextualism explain our linguistic habits. Why would we deny knowledge to both high-stakes subjects and low-stakes subjects (wrongly, in both cases, as the moderate invariantist would have it), if the moderate invariantist is right and *Action* is false? Which concerns *relevant to whether the subject knows* do we wrongly project onto the subject? Likewise for contextualism: why would the standards for 'knowledge'-attributions be raised when the salient stakes go up unless it were also the case that the standards for *knowledge* get raised when the *stakes* go up?

Obviously, this is not a knock-down objection either to moderate invariantism or contextualism. But what it does do, we feel, is clear of the charge of *ad hocery* any impurist who uses contextualist standards-shifts or moderate invariantist WAMs or error theories in order to explain reactions to third-person cases. What seems equally (or more) ad hoc is to use those standards-shifts, WAMs, or error theories without the grounding provided by *Action*.

5 CONCLUSION

Where does all of this leave the fallibilist? In this chapter, we have considered the possibility that, instead of putting knowledge itself to work, the fallibilist could, so to speak, put 'knowledge' to work. The bank and airport cases were meant to provide the basis for an argument for putting 'knowledge' to work—for taking pragmatic elements to help determine the content of knowledge-attributions rather than to help determine whether any such content was satisfied. The airport cases do arguably provide some basis for contextualism. But the lesson of the bank cases isn't about knowledge-*attributions* at all; it is about knowledge, and it is this: purism, fallibilism, and the intuitive relations between knowledge and action together comprise a genuine philosophical puzzle; each is highly plausible, and they appear to be jointly inconsistent. To make progress here, we need to see what really can be said on behalf of principles asserting a strong knowledge–action connection, such as *Action* and the 'idle doubts thesis' presented in Chapter 1. If there is sufficient independent support for such pragmatist principles, then the fallibilist can make use of these principles themselves, rather than use-to-mention rewritings of them, in fending off the objections considered in Chapter 1. The goal of the next chapter is to provide this independent support.

3

Knowledge and Reasons

1 KNOWLEDGE AND THE PRAGMATIC

It is not particularly controversial that what you know bears on the proper conduct of your doxastic life. If you know something to be the case, you are proper to rely on it in forming and revising beliefs and in distributing and redistributing your degrees of confidence.

But what you know seems to have broader relevance. If you know something to be the case, it seems you are proper to rely on it in 'pragmatic' aspects of life: in your preferences, your intentions and plans, as well as in actions and decisions about what to do, including whether to continue or abandon a certain line of inquiry. Consider the following principles, which connect knowledge to the pragmatic:

> (Action) If you know that p, then if the question of whether p is relevant to the question of what to do, it is proper for you to act on p.[1]
>
> (Best Results) If you know that A will have the best results of your available options, then you are rational to do A.[2]

[1] For defenses of *Action* or something similar, see Fantl and McGrath (2002) and (2007), as well as Stanley (2005*b*) and Hawthorne and Stanley (2008).

[2] We argue for *Best Results* in Fantl and McGrath (2007). For a particularly ringing endorsement of this principle, see Sellars (1970). '[D]rawing heavily on the powers of that little word "know" ', he endorses the principle: 'To know that course A is, *all things considered*, better than course B, is to have *conclusive* reason for following A rather than B' (7; emphasis in original). We see this as an endorsement of *Best Results* because Sellars is explicit that the heavy work is done by the little word 'know'. It is not enough to have conclusive reason for following A rather than B, in Sellars' view, merely that A is all things considered better that B. But knowledge is enough. If by 'all things considered better' he meant something like 'has a higher expected utility', then the merely being all things considered better would be enough, and the little word 'know' would only contribute the truth-condition.

Some philosophers, worried that *Best Results* presupposes consequentialism, might prefer a principle we may call *Most Reason*: if you know that there is more reason to do A than to do any of its competitors, you are rational to do A. *Most Reason* doesn't prejudge the issue of consequentialism. We discuss the difference between reasons there are, reasons one has, and motivating reasons at some length in Chapter 4.

(Preference) If you know that *p*, then you are rational to prefer as if *p*.[3]

(Inquiry) If you know that *p*, then you are proper not to inquire further into whether *p*.[4]

These principles gain support from the fact that we cite knowledge to criticize or defend action, preference, and inquiry:

(Criticisms)

(1) The coach shouldn't have sent his tight ends out on fourth down. He knew the other team was going to blitz.

(2) You know it will have the best results if you just plead guilty. Why are you opting for a trial?

(3) You prefer white wine? But you know we're having steak!

(4) If you know the butler did it, why are you still bringing in suspects?

(Defenses)

(5) The coach knew the other team was going to blitz. That's why it made so much sense for him to hold his tight ends back to block.

(6) She's pleading guilty because she knows it will have the best results.

(7) Why do I prefer red wine? I know we're having steak.

(8) We now know the butler did it. That's why we stopped bringing in suspects.

These criticisms and defenses, and many others like them, provide evidence for the corresponding principles. Such criticisms and defenses are perfectly in order, and exactly what we would expect to find, if the principles *Action, Best Results, Preference,* and *Inquiry* are true.

Despite this evidence, these principles, and others like them, have been targets of proposed counterexamples. We'll consider just two, the first from Baron Reed, the second from Jessica Brown:

You are participating in a psychology study that is intended to measure the effect of stress on memory. The researcher asks you questions about Roman history—a

[3] Defended in Fantl and McGrath (2002).

[4] *Inquiry* may remind some of Peirce's contention that inquiry properly ends when we have removed the irritation of doubt (see, e.g. his *Collected Papers*). See also Schaffer (2006) and Levi (1980).

subject with which you are well acquainted. For every correct answer you give, the researcher will reward you with a jelly bean; for every incorrect answer, you are punished by an extremely painful electric shock. There is neither reward nor punishment for failing to give an answer. The first question is: when was Julius Caesar born? You are confident, though not absolutely certain, that the answer is 100 B.C. You also know that, given that Caesar was born in 100 B.C., the best thing to do in light of all your goals is to provide this answer ... Nevertheless, when you weight the meager reward against the prospect, however unlikely, of excruciating pain, it does not seem rational to attempt an answer. Does this show that you don't *know* when Caesar was born? ... It would be perfectly natural for you to say to the researcher, 'I *do* know this one, though it's certainly not worth risking a shock'. (Reed forthcoming)

A student is spending the day shadowing a surgeon. In the morning he observes her in clinic examining patient A who has a diseased left kidney. The decision is taken to remove it that afternoon. Later, the student observes the surgeon in theatre where patient A is lying anaesthetised on the operating table. The operation hasn't started as the surgeon is consulting the patient's notes. The student is puzzled and asks one of the nurses what's going on:

Student: *I don't understand. Why is she looking at the patient's records? She was in clinic with the patient this morning. Doesn't she even know which kidney it is?*

Nurse: *Of course, she knows which kidney it is. But, imagine what it would be like if she removed the wrong kidney. She shouldn't operate before checking the patient's records.* (Brown 2008: 176)

Reed takes his example to be one in which you know that giving the answer is best but you shouldn't give the answer. Brown takes hers to be one in which the surgeon knows that the left kidney is the diseased one, but is not proper to act on that information, i.e. by going straight to surgery without checking the chart. She must check further.[5] In general, for any such example

[5] The examples seem to work better against some principles than others. In Reed's example, it perhaps makes some sense for you to think to yourself, 'I know that Caesar was born in 100 BC, but I'd better not say it, just in case.' It makes, to our ears, much less sense to think, 'I know that it will have the best results if I give the answer—that it will have worse results if I fail to give it—but I'd better not give it, just in case.' *Best Results* is on better footing with respect to Reed's example than, for instance, *Action*. Brown's example is not even purportedly a counterexample to *Best Results*, but just to emphasize the point, compare what the nurse says in Brown's example to this: 'Of course she knows it will have worse results to check the chart than just to operate. Just operating will have the best results. But she shouldn't operate before checking the chart.' This sounds absurd. *Best Results*, we think, is not seriously threatened by either example.

to be successful, a subject must know the target proposition while failing to be proper in doing some relevant action or adopting some relevant attitude. Are these conditions satisfied?

One might argue that any fallibilist is committed to there being cases in which these conditions are satisfied. Fallibilism, as we understand it throughout the book, holds that you can know something even though there's a chance for you that it is false. But, the thought goes, if there's any chance at all that you are wrong, that chance can be exploited by raising the stakes so high that you aren't proper to rely on the proposition in your decisions and actions, despite the fact that you know. The examples merely exploit situations that are possible given fallibilism. So, the truth of fallibilism guarantees the existence of counterexamples to principles like *Action, Best Results,* etc. If examples like those from Reed and Brown don't seem decisive, it's only because we have some inclinations to infallibilism.

But there are different ways to be a fallibilist. A fallibilist need not say that any chance of error less than a fixed amount is good enough for knowledge. One possibility, which we developed on behalf of fallibilists in Chapter 1, is to say that knowledge is compatible with a chance of error but only an idle one. Of course, in the examples we have been discussing, the chance of error is not idle. And generally, relevance to the rationality of an action will make a chance of error non-idle. Therefore, it does not follow merely from fallibilism that there will be cases like Reed's or Brown's in which a subject knows something but isn't proper to act on that knowledge.

Can the counterexamples stand on their own? We are skeptical. Without changing the subjects' strengths of epistemic position, we can modify seemingly irrelevant features of the examples to pump intuitions for the opposite conclusions. For example, though Reed may be right that it doesn't raise eyebrows for you to say, perhaps with the right tone of voice, 'I *do* know this one, though it's certainly not worth risking a shock', it also wouldn't raise eyebrows for you to say, 'Do I really know that Caesar was born in 100 BC or am I just pretty confident of it? Well, I thought I knew this before, but after thinking about the risk, I guess I don't really know it after all. I'd better not answer.' Nor would it raise eyebrows, in Brown's example, after the student asks, 'Why is she checking the chart; didn't she examine the patient this morning?', for the nurse to reply, 'She did examine the patient this morning, but every good surgeon checks the patient's chart so that she *knows* which kidney to take out.'

The effect of these revised examples is to render the proposed counterexamples toothless. They (at best) reveal that the principles which they are meant to refute are not clearly true, prior to theorizing, and that the evidence from our habits of criticisms and defenses, which we cited above, is not decisive. But we already knew this.[6] We already knew that a principled argument for a link between knowledge and the pragmatic would be preferable to mere appeals to the intuitiveness of these principles and the linguistic data about criticisms and defenses. The purpose of this chapter is to supply such an argument, one that elucidates and provides a solid theoretical basis for the claim that you can put what you know to work.

2 WHAT YOU KNOW IS WARRANTED ENOUGH TO JUSTIFY

An examination of the principles we have been discussing, which link knowledge to the pragmatic, reveals that the activity or attitude cited in each case is one about which it makes sense to ask whether you are *justified* in doing or having it. This suggests that what these principles are getting at is a more general connection between knowledge and justification. We want to articulate this connection.

We regularly speak of facts as justifying us in certain actions, intentions, and beliefs. Someone running for the school board might assert 'I am qualified to serve on the board.' Asked what justifies him in thinking so, he replies by citing considerations such as his endorsements, his experience, etc. If these considerations are true, he is citing *facts* as justifying him in thinking what he does. If the facts he cites do justify him in thinking this, then he is justified in thinking what he thinks. You might wonder whether it is really the fact, rather than some mental state, which is the justifier. We postpone consideration of this worry, since the idea of appealing to facts as justifiers is quite familiar.

6 A contextualist can happily accept that the speakers speak the truth in all these cases. However, as we pointed out in Chapter 2, the contextualist herself has trouble explaining why there is an attractive piece of *reasoning* that favors denying knowledge in these cases: if the surgeon knows it's the left kidney, she should be able to act accordingly. She shouldn't need to bother checking; but she does need to check.

Start with the case of beliefs. What you know can justify you in having certain beliefs. If you have no idea that your car's battery is dead, then even if it is dead, the fact that it is dead doesn't justify you in believing further propositions, such as *the headlights won't turn on*. Facts of which you have no inkling cannot justify you in believing anything. Nor is it enough for a fact to justify you in believing something for you to believe the fact obtains, for your belief in the fact could itself fail to be justified. A mere true belief that your car's battery is dead is not enough for that fact to justify you in believing that the headlights won't turn on. But suppose you know that your car's battery is dead. Then its being dead can and does justify you in believing the lights won't turn on, as well as any number of other propositions suitably related to it.

When you know a proposition p, no weaknesses in your epistemic position with respect to p—no weaknesses, that is, in your standing on any truth-relevant dimension with respect to p—stand in the way of p justifying you in having further beliefs. We will recruit the term 'warrant' to express this idea. Knowing that p, as we shall say, makes *p warranted enough* to justify you in believing any q.[7]

Any q? No matter how utterly irrelevant p is to q? Does it even make sense to say that your car's battery being dead is warranted enough to justify you in completely unrelated propositions, such as *there is water under the surface of Jupiter's moon Europa*? It is plausible to say it does make sense. Suppose you were to argue for this conclusion about Europa on the grounds that your car's battery is dead. Obviously, the conclusion would not be justified by the premise: the complete absence of a relevant connection stands in the way. But does any weakness in your epistemic position for the battery proposition stand in the way? Are such epistemic weaknesses at all to blame, even partially, for the failure to justify the conclusion? We find it plausible to answer: no. If you know your battery is dead, one way your reasoning

[7] By speaking of 'p justifying you in ϕ-ing' here and throughout the book, we mean that p itself and not merely some larger proposition of which p is a component justifies you in ϕ-ing. Even if p itself justifies you, p might be able to do so only because certain enabling conditions are met: you must be able to believe the proposition, say, even if your ability to believe the proposition isn't part of what justifies you in believing it. To use an example from Robert Audi (2002), 'if a child has no concept of an insurance adjuster, then seeing one examining a damaged car and talk to its owner about deductibles will not function as a source of justification for the proposition that this is an insurance adjuster' (89). When the enabling condition is satisfied, it allows you to be justified, but it plays no part in justifying you: that you have a concept of an insurance adjuster does not form part of the evidence or reasons that justifies for you that this is an insurance adjuster. It allows the evidence you already have, itself, to justify you.

from this premise to the conclusion about Europa *can't* be criticized is by challenging the entitlement to the premise. Contrast this with the case in which you argue from the proposition that there are an even number of stars to the conclusion that there is water underneath the surface of Europa. Here we can challenge your reasoning in two ways: the premise offers no support for the conclusion and *even putting that consideration aside*, it isn't warranted enough to justify believing the conclusion. Thus, we leave '*q*' unrestricted: if you know *p*, *p* is warranted enough to justify you in believing *q*, for all *q*.[8]

When we turn to action, there seem to be cases in which what you know justifies you in doing certain things. Suppose, walking along the sidewalk with your son, you suddenly see a car careering onto the sidewalk, and thereby come to know that your child will be hit by the car unless you immediately seize hold of him and pull him back. It certainly seems that you are justified in taking this action. What justifies you? If, after the fact, your child asks why you did this, you can say: 'You would have been hit by the car if I hadn't seized you and pulled you back.' Here, you are citing as your justification a fact you know—a fact about the relation between your son and the car. Notice, as before, that if you had no inkling of the car's approach, the fact that your son would be killed would not justify you in grabbing your son, though it may entail that it is best to do so. Just as in the case of justifiers for belief, had you had no inkling of the existence of this fact, e.g. if the driver of the car is plotting to run you and your son down and wishes to appear to be driving normally, you would be perfectly justified in continuing your walk. We don't think those who spontaneously seize their children and yank them around, without any inkling that this is a good thing to do, are models of rationality. Nor would the fact justify you if you merely believed—without justification—that fact, despite your belief being true. But if you know the fact, then it does justify you in seizing your son.

Are known propositions always warranted enough to justify action? Some might answer 'no': knowledge is not always sufficient warrant in cases in which a lot is riding on your action depending on whether what you know is true. As David Owens (2008) puts the point, 'since I know my car is correctly parked, I know it would be wasting my time going to check it,' but

[8] It would not materially affect the main conclusion of this chapter, that fallibilist purism is false, to hold back from claiming that what you know is warranted enough to justify believing *any q*, and restrict *q* to 'appropriately related' *q*.

nevertheless I still judge that I ought to check it, and 'I make this judgement in light of what I know about the (remote) chance of it being parked illegally and the trouble involved in checking'; thus, he says, 'I screen-off the knowledge that it is in fact correctly parked in judging that I ought to check' (14).

In *screening off* bits of knowledge when deciding what to do, you retain the knowledge, but you can rightly exclude it when deciding what to do. What makes such exclusion proper is the '(remote) chance' that the car is illegally parked, i.e. a weakness in your epistemic position for *my car is legally parked.* If Owens is right, then even if known propositions are warranted enough to be theoretical justifiers (i.e. justifiers for belief), they are not always warranted enough to be practical justifiers.

We argue in Section 3 that this is a mistake. What you know is warranted enough to justify you in believing, doing, feeling, wanting, liking, hating, or intending anything at all.[9] More carefully, what we defend is the principle that what you know can justify:

(KJ) If you know that p, then p is warranted enough to justify you in ϕ-ing, for any ϕ.

We sometimes let ϕ go implicit, and so speak of p's being warranted enough to justify you or to be a justifier for you.

KJ is formulated in terms of sufficient warrant. Since this notion will be key in this chapter (and similar notions of justificational and credal sufficiency will be key for later chapters), we pause to say more about it. As we noted earlier, in saying that p is warranted enough to justify you, we are saying that no weaknesses in your epistemic position with respect to p—in your position along any of the truth-relevant dimensions—stand in the way of p justifying you. This explanation of being warranted enough to justify raises a number of questions. For one thing, one might ask which truth-relevant dimensions count for a proposition's justifying you. Any and all? Can falsity matter to whether p can justify you? Can the reliability of relevant processes? In this chapter, we stay neutral on what sort of weaknesses—weaknesses in your standing along *which* truth-relevant dimensions—can stand in the way of a proposition's justifying you.[10] For all we have said, one person

[9] Here, as we remarked in n. 8, one might want to carry through the restriction to appropriately related states and activities.

[10] In the next chapter we argue that the only dimensions that are relevant to a proposition's being sufficiently warranted to justify are those that matter to how justified p is for you. In this

might score much higher on many truth-relevant dimensions with respect to a proposition than another person, and just a little lower on those that count for whether the proposition is epistemically fit to justify you. The proposition might then be overall 'more warranted' for the first person than for the second, even though it is 'warranted enough' in our sense to justify the second person but not warranted enough to justify the first. But if we remember the technical definition, this is not surprising: although there are greater overall weaknesses in the second person's epistemic position for the proposition, the first person's epistemic position with respect to it is weaker on the dimensions that count.

One might also ask for more explanation of what it means to 'stand in the way' in the relevant sense. There is of course a causal notion of standing in the way: your physical weakness can stand in the way of your being a Sumo wrestler, your shyness can stand in the way of your dazzling your dinner guests. But there is also a notion of standing in the way which is not causal and concerns meeting a standard. Thus, your age or your country of birth can stand in the way of your being eligible to hold the office of President of the United States and your gender can stand in the way of your being a bachelor. What we are claiming, in endorsing KJ, is that when you know p no weaknesses in your epistemic position preclude p's meeting the standards for its justifying you.

We offer no analysis of the intuitive notion of 'standing in the way'. But we do think that, when Y does not obtain, the following counterfactual condition is *sufficient* for a subject's position on some dimension d to be something that stands in the way of Y obtaining: whether Y obtains can vary with variations in the subject's position on d, holding fixed all other factors relevant to whether Y obtains. Since we can vary whether a 30-year-old is eligible to hold the office of President of the United States by varying her age, holding fixed all other relevant factors, her age stands in the way of her being so eligible. If, in a certain situation, we can vary whether p justifies you in ϕ-ing by raising your strength of epistemic position, holding fixed all other factors relevant to whether p justifies you in ϕ-ing (such as your stakes, the connection between the question of whether p and the question of whether to ϕ, and what other countervailing reasons you have), then weaknesses in your epistemic position for p stand in the way of p's justifying you in ϕ-ing.

chapter, we stay neutral on this question. We do not assume, then, that p is sufficiently warranted to justify iff p is sufficiently justified to justify.

In slogan form: if merely strengthening your epistemic position can make a difference as to whether p justifies you in ϕ-ing, then weaknesses in your epistemic position stand in the way of its so justifying you.

We offer this counterfactual condition as a sufficient condition for standing in the way. It is not a necessary condition. None of us has strong warrant for *the number of stars is even.* This proposition doesn't justify you in believing, doing, feeling anything. But consider this (obviously peculiar) question: is your epistemic position for *the number of stars is even* strong enough for it to justify you in believing that Oswald shot Kennedy? Obviously, it doesn't justify you in this, but is it warranted enough? Again, consider the reasoning 'The number of stars is even, so Oswald shot Kennedy'. The reasoning is awful, because of the lack of relevant connection between the premise and the conclusion. But isn't it also bad because you aren't entitled to the premise? Because your warrant for it isn't strong enough? We are inclined to answer yes.[11] But the counterfactual condition *is* satisfied: merely strengthening your epistemic position doesn't make a difference to whether *the number of stars is even* justifies you in believing that Oswald shot Kennedy. The problem, of course, is that more than one thing stands in the way: weaknesses in your epistemic position as well as the lack of connection between the proposition and the contemplated action. Something similar holds of any married woman: two factors stand in the way of her being a bachelor, and so varying one, while holding fixed the other, won't make a difference to whether she is a bachelor.

One final remark before turning to the defense of KJ: KJ does not collapse theoretical and practical justification. It leaves entirely open, for instance, whether justification for action, unlike justification for belief, has an essentially instrumentalist or teleological structure. KJ does not assimilate practical to theoretical justification or vice versa; rather it posits that a single epistemic relation to a fact suffices for that fact to be epistemically sufficient to justify: knowledge is enough.

3 THE CASE FOR KJ

Our case for KJ depends on two principles about reasons. The first is akin to principles proposed by Unger (1974), Hyman (1999), and Hawthorne and

[11] We are inclined to answer yes in this case, but KJ does not commit us to doing so in every case in which some proposition isn't appropriately connected to the relevant ϕ. There may, in fact,

Stanley (forthcoming),[12] though only in the *sufficiency* direction.[13] We call it the *Knowledge-Reasons* Principle:

(KR) If you know that p, then p is warranted enough to be a reason you have to ϕ, for any ϕ.

3.1 The Theoretical Knowledge-Reasons Principle

The theoretical restriction of KR (restricting ϕ-ing to believings) should be relatively uncontroversial: if you know that p, then p is warranted enough to be a reason you have to believe that q, for any q. Certainly the cases suggested by Brown and Reed earlier in this chapter do not tell against this principle. For those cases are explicitly and exclusively about action and do not bear on any of the relevant beliefs. To accept the theoretical restriction of KR, all Brown and Reed would have to grant is that, if the subjects in their examples have knowledge, then what they know are reasons the subjects have to believe other propositions.

be good reasons for allowing propositions unconnected to some ϕ to be warranted enough to justify ϕ-ing even if no more warranted than some propositions connected to ϕ that aren't warranted enough to justify ϕ-ing. See Chapter 7 for discussion of this possibility.

12 Unger explicitly endorses the necessity direction: 'If S's reason (for something X) *is that p*, then S *knows* that p; and if S's reasons (for X) *are that p and that q* and so on, then S *knows* that p and S *knows* that q and so on' (1975: 200).

Hyman is concerned with *motivating* reasons—the reasons for which one acts and for which in general one ϕs—rather than *normative reasons*, those that go some distance toward justifying. He endorses a biconditional connection between knowledge and motivating reasons: 'A knows that p if and only if the fact that p can be A's reason for doing, refraining from doing, believing, wanting or doubting something' (1999: 442). Hyman's 'can be' is the 'can' of ability. We see more promise in interpreting Hyman's 'can' in terms of sufficient warrant than in terms of ability. You might well know something but lack the ability to use it as a reason for action (think of practically idle propositions). For Hyman's left-to-right conditional to stand a chance of being true, when 'can' is understood in terms of ability, the right-hand side must be understood disjunctively. But if it is, this misses something important, because what you know 'can' indeed be your reason for doing something, just not in the ability sense.

Hawthorne and Stanley (forthcoming) propose a 'Reason-Knowledge Principle': Where one's choice is p-dependent, it is appropriate to treat the proposition that p as a reason for acting iff you know that p. A natural question to ask about this proposal is how to understand the relation between the appropriateness of treating something as a reason and its being a reason. In a footnote, Hawthorne and Stanley claim that it is appropriate to treat a proposition as a reason only if it is a reason. We discuss Hawthorne and Stanley's proposal in more detail in Chapter 4.

13 One might wonder whether we shouldn't go further, in the spirit of Hyman, Unger, and Hawthorne and Stanley, and claim that knowing is necessary for being sufficiently warranted to have something as a reason. Such a stand is not necessary to achieve the aim of this chapter—the grounding of KJ. But is the necessary condition nonetheless true? We postpone consideration of this question until Chapter 4.

Some philosophers will be unhappy even with the theoretical restriction, on the grounds that facts can never be reasons you have, even when you know them, because something can be a reason you have only if it can be the basis on which you believe or act, and no fact can be such a basis. Only mental states meet this condition. It isn't the fact that the battery is dead that justifies you in believing that the lights won't go on—it's your *belief* that the battery is dead, and this belief is a mental state of yours. If so, then KR and KJ, even in their theoretical versions, are at best vacuously true, because facts or propositions are the wrong sort of thing to be reasons you have or to justify you. (Here we take up the worry we deferred at the beginning of Section 2.)

It is not clear that, even if facts cannot be bases for belief, they cannot still fail to be warranted enough to be bases for belief. Perhaps two things stand in the way of the fact that your battery is dead, when you are in ignorance of that fact, being a reason you have for believing that the lights won't go on: the fact that it is a *fact*, not a mental state, as well as your epistemic weakness with respect to that fact. But putting this issue aside, notice that something very much like our principles could be reinstated in a way which would satisfy the mental state theorist. We could say that when you know that *p*, *your belief that p* is warranted enough to justify you or be a reason you have. Our subsequent discussion could then proceed much as it does, with references to facts or propositions as justifiers and reasons replaced by references to the corresponding beliefs.

However, we think there is no compelling reason to modify all our principles in this way. We agree that if X is a reason you have to ϕ, then X must be the sort of thing that can in principle be the reason for which you ϕ, i.e. can be your motivating reason for ϕ-ing. But this is not the only desideratum to secure in an account of reasons-had. Here is another: if X is a reason you have to ϕ, then X must be the sort of thing that can be cited in support of your ϕ-ing. That is, it must be the sort of thing that can figure as a premise in a positive case for ϕ-ing. The 'motivational' desideratum might appear to favor the view that only mental states can be reasons-had, while the 'justificational' desideratum appears to favor the opposing view that only facts or propositions can be reasons-had. However, we think the fact/proposition view can accommodate the motivational desideratum perfectly well: in order for a fact or proposition to be the reason for which you ϕ, you must believe it and your believing it must appropriately explain your ϕ-ing. To say that facts or propositions are motivating reasons only if they are believed doesn't commit one to saying that it is really beliefs—belief states—which are motivating reasons.

We also want to recommend a more irenic alternative to the mental state theorist. If you are a mental state theorist, you should also acknowledge that facts can be motivating reasons in a derivative sense. Most fundamentally, perhaps, it isn't the fact that the battery is dead which serves as the basis for your further belief that your lights won't go on; it is your belief about the battery. But a fact that *p* can be said to be a basis for belief insofar as that fact is the content of a belief of yours which is such a basis. We suggest to the mental state theorist that there is no point in denying that facts can be 'bases', can 'motivate' or 'move' us in this derivative sense. We certainly do seem to cite facts as our bases for beliefs, actions, feelings, etc. Presumably, these theorists themselves will want to say that belief states can figure as a premise in an argument only in a derivative sense: a belief state can be said to be a premise in a good argument only insofar as its content is.

3.2 The Unity Thesis

Theoretical KR is very plausible. But there is reason to think that a stronger knowledge-reasons principle is true, one linking knowledge to practical as well as theoretical reasons. Suppose that, to use Owens' example, you do know that your car is correctly parked, and that therefore it is a reason you have to believe that you would waste your time by getting out of your armchair to check on it. Now, in your situation, here is something else you know: if indeed the car is correctly parked, the fact that it is correctly parked is then a reason there is to remain comfortably in your armchair. If you know both of these things, then at least assuming that your knowledge of the latter, of the conditional, is extremely probable (which is a reasonable assumption), you will know the conjunction. That is, you will know not only (9) and (10) but their conjunction:

(9) The car is correctly parked.

(10) If the car is correctly parked, then the fact that it is correctly parked is a reason there is to remain comfortably in my armchair.

But notice what follows from (9) and (10)

(11) The fact that the car is correctly parked is a reason there is to remain comfortably in my armchair.

So, if you can know the conjunction of (9) and (10), then presumably you can know (11). (We are not saying it follows that if you know the conjunction of (9) and (10) you know (11), only that there can be a case in which someone knows (9), (10), their conjunction, and on that basis knows (11).) But if you know (11), you *have* a reason to remain comfortably in your armchair, namely that the car is correctly parked. And this is obviously a practical reason.

The principle we are invoking here can be formulated thus:

> (*Reasons Link*) If you know that the fact that p is a reason there is for you to ϕ, then you have a reason to ϕ, namely p.

Reasons Link links knowledge of something's being a reason there is for you to ϕ to your having that something as a reason to ϕ. It links reasons there are—facts which favor ϕ-ing—to reasons you have to ϕ—considerations which go some distance toward justifying you in ϕ-ing. It doesn't link them in the standard 'factoring' way (cf. Schroeder 2007). *Reasons Link* doesn't claim that p is a reason you have iff p is a reason and you have p. Nor does it say that knowledge of a consideration that is a reason entails having that reason. It says that if you know that the consideration is a reason for the relevant action then you have a reason for that action—that very consideration.

Reasons Link suggests that theoretical KR doesn't exhaust the relation between knowledge and reasons. Knowledge bears important relations to practical reasons. In particular, knowledge of the existence of reasons-there-are suffices for having a practical reason.[14] It is not clear, though, that *Reasons Link* can get us all the way to the full unrestricted KR. But the fully general

[14] A similar sort of argument might be used to argue that Theoretical KJ can be strengthened. Suppose you know that the car being correctly parked outweighs all other considerations bearing on whether you should remain comfortably in your armchair, so that you know that it is a *conclusive reason there is for you to remain comfortably in your armchair.* If you know this is a conclusive reason there is for you to remain comfortably in your armchair, it seems you have a conclusive reason to remain comfortably in your armchair, namely that the car is correctly parked. The principle guiding this reasoning is:

> (*Conclusive Reasons Link*) If you know that p is a conclusive reason there is for you to ϕ, then you have a conclusive reason to ϕ.

This principle suggests that Theoretical KJ doesn't exhaust the relation between knowledge and justifiers. But it does not yet show us that the full KJ is true. Nonetheless, even the restricted version of KJ implied by *Conclusive Reasons Link* is enough to falsify fallibilist purism, because many of the relevant cases are precisely cases in which the subject knows, for example, that there is conclusive reason for doing the relevant action.

version of KR follows from KR's theoretical restriction together with a 'unity thesis' about practical and theoretical reasons:

> (The Unity Thesis) If p is warranted enough to be a reason you have to believe that q, for any q, then p is warranted enough to be a reason you have to ϕ, for any ϕ.[15]

According to the Unity Thesis, any proposition that is warranted enough to be a reason you have for belief is also warranted enough be a reason you have for action or anything else. We can see the plausibility of the Unity Thesis by reflecting on our habits of deliberation.

When trying to determine what is true—that is, in forming beliefs—we draw conclusions from the reasons we have. The same goes for trying to decide what to do. Here, too, we draw conclusions about what to do—we form intentions—from the reasons we have. We bring reasons into our reasoning knowing that we might draw all sorts of conclusions from them along the way, some practical and some theoretical.[16] Suppose your sister calls you on the phone to tell you about plans for her upcoming visit to see you. She tells you, and you thereby come to know, that she'll be ready to be picked up at the airport at 8:00 a.m. and will need a ride to your place. You might well include this proposition in your reasoning and at some point draw a practical conclusion from it, e.g. 'I'll be there at 8:00 sharp with my car', but you might also draw along the way any number of theoretical conclusions as well, e.g. that she'll be tired when she arrives, that you'll not be able to drop the kids off at preschool, and so on. You don't segregate reasons by whether they are available for drawing practical or theoretical conclusions. But if the Unity Thesis were false, we should expect to find segregation, if not always, at least when something significant is at stake, and when the stakes are high we should expect consistent segregation.

This is not what we find. Even when the stakes are high we do not find segregation; rather, when the stakes are high, we are more careful about using a consideration as a reason to believe—as careful as we are about using it as a reason to act. On your hike, you come to a frozen pond. Do you walk across or walk around the frozen pond? Walking around will take a while, but you

15 What we are calling the Unity Thesis is to be distinguished sharply from Levi's (1980) 'unity of reason thesis', according to which practical and theoretical reasoning are structurally alike.

16 Here it is not crucial precisely what a practical conclusion is. Whether it is an action, an intention, or plan, or even an 'ought' judgment, still, we draw practical conclusions from the same premises from which we draw theoretical conclusions.

don't want to fall through the ice.[17] How do you decide? The crucial issue is whether the ice is thick enough to hold you. Suppose you do some checking (you call the park authorities) and come to know that the ice is thick enough. So *the ice is thick enough* becomes a reason you have to believe other things (e.g. that it is perfectly safe to cross it). It would then be very odd not to allow this knowledge into your practical reasoning. We can, of course, imagine you reflecting, and coming to think, 'But it would be horrible to fall in ... ' and perhaps 'Maybe I shouldn't risk it.' But these reflections bear on the use of *it's thick enough* as a reason for belief, too: 'Is it really thick enough? Would I really be fine?' What we don't find is the following thought: 'Yes, it's thick enough, so as far as whether I'll be fine to cross, I will, but I can't bring that fact into my deliberations about what to do.' We are not saying it is impossible for someone to do this, that it is impossible to segregate theoretical and practical reasons. We are saying such segregation is not the familiar aspect of our reasoning which we would expect it to be if the Unity Thesis were false.

Our claims here are bolstered by empirical research that has, ironically, been used in an attempt to undermine intuitions concerning DeRose's bank cases that support views like ours. As we noted in Chapter 2, Jennifer Nagel has pointed to psychological research supporting the claim that, as the stakes go up, we tend to be more reluctant to form beliefs on matters relevant to questions about what to do: we hold off believing until more evidence comes in. But why would this be if we are so happy to segregate theoretical and practical reasons? If this habit were commonplace, we'd expect to find that, even in high-stakes situations, we'd form beliefs as easily as we do in low-stakes situations.

We want to go further than merely the observation that we don't find the segregation we'd expect to find. We find segregation positively peculiar, even irrational. When *p* becomes available as a basis for theoretical conclusions, it is 'barmy' (to use an expression suggested by one of our informants) to ignore *p* in one's decision-making and planning. The kind of segregation that would be perfectly reasonable if the Unity Thesis were false is not reasonable at all.

Strictly speaking, we have argued only for the claim that warrant sufficient to justify belief is warrant sufficient to justify action. However, similar considerations can also be given concerning other states for which we can have reasons, such as emotions, feelings, intentions, etc. (here the emphasis on reasoning would have to be toned down with regard to some of these

[17] Thanks to Mark Migotti for suggesting this example.

states, though there clearly is such a thing as responding to reasons in these cases). We conclude, in general, that if *p* is warranted enough to be a reason you have for belief, it's warranted enough to be a reason you have for not only for action but for anything. This is the Unity Thesis.

3.3 A worry about the Unity Thesis[18]

Perhaps there are cases in which we engage in theoretical reasoning for its own sake, and not for the purpose of figuring out what to do. Because the stakes are presumably lower in such cases, perhaps they present counterexamples to the Unity Thesis, even if we are right that cases—like the ice case we have considered—do not. Perhaps, *p* can be warranted enough to be a reason you have to believe anything in the course of dedicated theoretical reasoning, but isn't warranted enough to be a reason you have for doing something once *p* is employed in practical deliberation. The infallibilist who thinks that only what has probability 1 can be a reason you have has an easy way with this objection, but what can the fallibilist say?

First, suppose the Unity Thesis is too strong and all that is true is that when we are in the course of practical reasoning, *p* is warranted enough to be a reason for belief only if it is warranted enough to be a reason for action. This would not jeopardize our argument against fallibilist purism. If all we could ground is the truth of KJ restricted to situations in which one is doing practical reasoning, that principle would still undermine fallibilist purism.[19]

Second, we think the worry raised does not undermine the Unity Thesis. There are two sorts of cases to consider, one in which there is no possibility of acting upon the reason for belief, and one in which there is such a possibility. To illustrate the former case, suppose that you are far from the ice and have no desire to cross it, anyway. But you are thinking about the ice and speculating about who it might hold, how thick it might be, and other ice-related matters of no particular consequence. In that case, you might well be able to allow the proposition that the ice is thick enough to hold you into your dedicated theoretical deliberations even if you would not be able to allow that proposition into your practical deliberations were you right in front of the ice, desiring to reach the other side of the pond, and faced with the decision. But as things stand, you do not have an option of crossing the

[18] Thanks to a referee for raising the concern discussed here.
[19] See also n. 8.

ice. What's preventing the proposition that the ice is thick enough to hold you from being a reason you have for crossing the ice is not any epistemic weakness with respect to the proposition, but rather the fact that you have no desire to cross the ice and couldn't do it anyway, even if you tried.

But perhaps you can engage in dedicated theoretical deliberation even while faced with the decision about whether to cross the ice. You try to put out of your mind the proximity of the ice and just start speculating, out of curiosity, about the ice. Suppose you know and have as a reason for belief that the ice is thick enough to hold you. But, of course, when you now turn your mind to whether to cross the ice or not, it might seem you cannot just employ that knowledge. Is this a counterexample to the Unity Thesis? We think not. If you know the ice is thick enough to hold you, then in this situation you know that the fact that it is thick enough is a reason for you to cross it. You can reason to this knowledge in your purely theoretical deliberation. Now, do you *have* a reason to cross it? Yes: that it's thick enough to hold you. Here we appeal to the principle *Reasons Link* discussed above. You have this reason even if you aren't engaged in practical deliberation. Suppose a third party says: 'He knows the fact that the ice is thick enough to hold him is a reason for him to cross it; but he doesn't have any reason to cross it, because he's not trying to decide whether to cross it.' Again, the word 'barmy' comes to mind.[20]

KR follows straightforwardly from the Unity Thesis and KR restricted to belief.[21]

[20] These worries can be pushed a step further. Suppose you're not faced with any ice-crossing decision. And suppose *the ice is thick enough* is warranted enough to be a reason for belief. Is it also warranted enough to be a reason to hold conditional preferences such as *preferring to cross the ice rather than go around on the condition that one is faced with the decision*? The short answer is *yes, but your knowledge is 'junk knowledge' and this fact about it stands in the way of its being a reason you have for the conditional preference.* See Appendix II for the long answer.

[21] In Fantl and McGrath (2002), we were relying on the broadly Humean framework presupposed in standard 'Bayesian' decision theory. Thus, we assumed that what you are rational to do is a matter of evidence together with fundamental preferences. This assumption now seems to us unnecessary (one certainly needn't be a Humean about rational action to be sympathetic to knowledge/action links such as *Action* and *Preference*). The apparatus of reasons allows us to stay neutral on debates about the role of preferences and desires in rational action. Humeans will insist that a fact cannot be a reason a person has unless it connects appropriately with some desire or pro-attitude; anti-Humeans will disagree. We don't need to take any stand on the matter. Humeans and their opponents can agree on what it takes for a fact to be warranted enough to be among your reasons (knowledge is good enough) even if they disagree on what it takes to be good enough in other ways, e.g. whether there must be an appropriate connecting pro-attitude.

The switch from preferences to reasons has another side benefit. As we emphasized in Fantl and McGrath (2002) and (2007), stakes can matter to rational action. But notice that with the appeal to reasons, we needn't assume that only your own stakes—or, more precisely, only your practical

3.4 Safe Reasons

KR alone does not entail KJ, but it does when conjoined with

> (*Safe Reasons*) If p is a reason you have to ϕ, then p is warranted enough to justify you in ϕ-ing, for any ϕ.

Suppose your bank offers two options for checking accounts, and you're trying to decide which option to choose. High Yield pays interest on your money, but has a two-dollar monthly fee. Economy Plus offers no interest, but is free. It seems that you have a reason for choosing High Yield—that it will pay interest on your money—and that you have a reason for choosing Economy Plus—that it won't cost you a monthly fee. You might well weigh these reasons: 'I'll get interest on my money if I choose High Yield, but I'll avoid a monthly fee if I choose Economy Plus. What's more important—getting interest on my money, or avoiding a monthly fee?' Nowhere in this reasoning is there a place for consideration of the relative probabilities involved—the chance that the bank won't pay you interest if you choose High Yield and the chance that Economy Plus will cost you a monthly fee. When we weigh reasons we *have*, we do so without taking into account the relative probabilities (or more generally the weaknesses in the warrant[22]) of respective reasons.

According to *Safe Reasons*, this is just what we would expect. If both are reasons you have, then the chance that they are false can't stand in the way of either reason justifying you in doing anything. Suppose, in this case, it's more important to you that you will get interest on your money than that the account won't cost you a monthly fee (perhaps because you'll have enough money in the account for the interest to offset the monthly fee). Thus, suppose that the fact that High Yield will pay you interest on your money justifies you in choosing the High Yield account. In that case, clearly, the chance that High Yield won't offer interest on your money doesn't stand in the way of it justifying you in choosing High Yield. But nor does the

interests—matter to what you should do. Suppose you know that someone else is in grave danger and that, with only a small inconvenience, you could save the person's life. On certain (plausible) theories of reasons, you then have a reason to help this person, whether or not it serves your interests. So others' interests, if known, can make a difference to your practical reasons even if they don't make a difference to your own interests.

22 We ignore features of warrant other than probability in what follows, but everything we say can be generalized to warrant.

chance that Economy Plus will charge you a monthly fee stand in the way of it justifying you in choosing Economy Plus (or, for that matter, choosing High Yield). As predicted, both reasons you have are warranted enough to justify you in choosing either option. What determines which option you are justified in choosing is simply how the reasons weigh up, without regard to their probabilities.

Of course, we can come to take account of the relative probabilities if the chance of falsehood gets high enough. If you get evidence that the bank is thinking about eliminating interest payments on its checking accounts (though there is a good chance it won't) but that it is contractually obligated to keep its Economy Plus plan free, it looks like you would do well not to ignore the possibility when making your decision. In fact, the probabilities might be such that once you get this new information, you should choose Economy Plus rather than High Yield. That is, that Economy Plus is free might now justify you in choosing Economy Plus even though it didn't before when there was a greater probability that High Yield would pay you interest on your money.

Notice, though, that after you get this new information, you stop weighing the reasons in the same way. You do not still reason this way: 'High Yield will pay me interest on my money, but Economy Plus won't charge me a monthly fee. Which is more important?' You don't reason this way but allow the probabilities of each proposition to play a role in your decision. If you *did*, this would be evidence that *Safe Reasons* is false. Why? Because if you did, it would be evidence that both would be reasons you have. But, even so, it would only be the chance that one of the reasons (High Yield) is false that stands in the way of it justifying you in choosing the respective option. Therefore, one of the reasons you have wouldn't be warranted enough to justify you in choosing one of the options.

However, *Safe Reasons* is indeed safe. We do not reason this way, even in cases like this one. We do not weigh reasons we have while covertly taking their probabilities into account. Rather, in this case, you plausibly would reason like this: 'It's not really sure that High Yield will pay me interest on my money, but for sure Economy Plus won't charge me a monthly fee. I'll go with Economy Plus.' And this reasoning is again what is predicted by *Safe Reasons*. For, again here, you are not taking into account the probabilities of the reasons you have. In particular, you aren't taking into account the chance that *it's not really sure* that High Yield will pay you interest on your money, nor the chance that *for sure* Economy Plus won't charge you a monthly fee.

But might you take into account probabilities when the stakes get really high? Consider again the ice example and how we might weigh reasons when standing before the frozen pond. Suppose you know that the ice is thick enough to hold you (you're a Canadian experienced in these matters and, what's more, you've read in the local paper it is over 6 inches thick, more than enough to hold an average adult). And suppose that this knowledge provides you with a reason to walk across the pond, viz. that it's thick enough to hold you. There are various ways in which this reason might be defeated and so fail to justify you in walking across the pond. You might know, for instance, that you are prone to disastrous falls when you walk on ice, whether the ice is thick or not. Weighing your reasons for walking across and your reasons for walking around, then, you might find that your reasons for walking around are weightier: 'I want to get around the pond as soon as possible. I don't want to fall through the ice, but the ice is thick enough to hold me, so that's not going to happen. But I am prone to disastrous falls on ice, and I really don't want to do that. The risk of a fall is not worth the extra time it would take to walk around the pond. I'll walk around.'

Here you weigh one reason—that the ice is thick enough to hold you—against another—that you are prone to disastrous falls on ice. The stakes are high. The cost of falling through the ice is tremendous. But you nonetheless do not take probabilities into account. One reason is defeated by another, and the defeat has nothing to do with how probable either reason is. Even improving your epistemic position so that it is *epistemically certain* for you that the ice is thick enough, this reason would still be defeated by your known propensity to bad falls on ice.

The picture of having reasons suggested by *Safe Reasons*, then, is a 'ledger-keeping' one; as the Tortoise said to Achilles, 'Whatever Logic is good enough to tell me is worth *writing down*' (Carroll (1895: 280)). When a proposition is a reason[23] you have to ϕ—when, say, it is a conclusion of justifying theoretical deliberation—it gets put in the ledger with countervailing reasons and *weighed* against them. But the probabilities of these reasons don't get recorded alongside.

None of this is to deny that we can have reasons that are explicitly about probabilities, or that we can weigh such reasons against reasons that aren't explicitly about probabilities. For example, we might weigh the proposition that there is a 90% chance of rain against the proposition

[23] Importantly, these are complete reasons you have to ϕ. See n. 7.

that the umbrella is cumbersome. Again, when we do this, we don't take into account the probability, for example, of the proposition that there is 90% chance of rain. But, we might think, the mere fact that we do weigh reasons about probabilities against reasons that aren't about probabilities suggests another way that *Safe Reasons* might be false. Consider the following counterproposal:

> That the ice is thick enough to hold you is a reason you have to walk across the pond. But there's a chance you're wrong about this. And the stakes are so high—you'll freeze to death if you fall in, and walking around the pond isn't so bad—that the chance of error is too great. You should walk around the pond. Your reason to walk across—that the ice is thick enough—is defeated by a further reason—that the chance the ice isn't thick enough makes the risk of walking across the pond too great. In short, although you do have a good reason to walk across the pond, this reason doesn't justify you in walking across.
>
> Of course, were it absolutely certain for you—were there no chance that it isn't thick enough—then that the ice is thick enough would justify you in walking across the pond. Therefore, in this case, the weakness in your epistemic position is standing in the way. That the ice is thick enough is a reason you have to walk across the pond, but that it's thick enough isn't warranted enough to justify you in walking across the pond. *Safe Reasons* is false.

While we do sometimes weigh reasons about probabilities—probabilistic reasons—against reasons that aren't about probabilities, most of us do not find ourselves weighing the sorts of reasons suggested by this rejoinder to *Safe Reasons*. We do not find ourselves weighing p—a reason to ϕ—against *there is a serious risk that not-p*—a reason not to ϕ. Again, consider what the weighing of competing reasons feels like in uncontroversial cases:

> There is a 90% chance of rain, so that's a reason I have to take my umbrella, but the umbrella is also really cumbersome. What's more important, the chance it will rain, or the fact it's really cumbersome?
>
> The High Yield account will pretty surely pay me interest on my money, but the Economy Plus account won't charge me a monthly fee. What's more important, that the High Yield account will pretty surely pay me interest, or that the Economy Plus account won't charge me?

Contrast these examples with:

> There's a serious risk the pond isn't thick enough to hold me, so that's a reason I have to walk around it. But the pond is also thick enough to hold me, so that's a reason I have to walk across it. Which is more important, the serious risk that it isn't thick enough or the fact that it is thick enough?

People don't normally weigh these kinds of reasons in the way we'd expect them to if people normally could have both of them at once. We'd expect to find people explicitly weighing up reasons concerning actual results against conflicting reasons concerning expected results. We find no such thing. People do vacillate: 'This ice is very thick. Surely it will hold me. But ... there's a real possibility it won't. I better not risk it.' Perhaps even with the right halting tone of voice someone might say, 'The ice will hold me (won't it? *surely* it will, right?). Forget it. I'll play it safe and walk around.' What you don't find is the likes of, 'Hmm, the ice might not hold me. That's one consideration. Another is that it will hold me.'

The opponent of *Safe Reasons* should not reply, 'We don't weigh them because it is so clear that *there is a serious risk the ice isn't thick enough to hold me* beats *the ice is thick enough to hold me*.' To the contrary, if we could and did have both reasons, it seems very plausible that *the ice is thick enough to hold me* should beat *there is a serious risk the ice isn't thick enough to hold me*, because A) the former entails that the serious risk alluded to in the latter doesn't obtain and B) it seems that *walking across will have the best results*—entailed by the former—should beat *walking around has the best expected results*—entailed by the latter.[24] After all, we care more about getting the best results than getting the best expected results.[25]

Think, finally, about the ways we challenge the practical reasoning leading to a decision. You and a friend are deciding whether to walk across the ice. The friend reasons: 'The ice is thick enough to hold us; it's a long way around, let's walk across.' You might want to resist the conclusion—because you think it isn't justified. How do you question the argument? You could

[24] This would be an embarrassing consequence for those who think you can have both reasons in high-stakes cases. For one would end up having to say that in high-stakes cases you really are fine to perform the risky act—board the train in our high-stakes train case, wait till Saturday to deposit the check in Keith DeRose's bank case B. But the cases are set up so that it is very plausible that you shouldn't perform the risky act.

[25] For a discussion of the relation between our principles and Bayesian decision theory, see Appendix I.

question the connection between the premise (that the ice is thick enough to hold the two of you) and the conclusion, or you could question the premise that the ice is thick enough. What you won't do—and it seems you can't properly do—is concede the premise but then raise worries about whether it might be false: 'Yes, I agree, the ice is thick enough to hold us; but while that is true, it might not be true, and if it isn't (which it is) and we walk across, we'll be in real trouble (which we won't).' Raising concerns about whether there is a real risk about walking over the ice amounts to challenging the entitlement to the premise, to challenging its status as a reason you *have*.[26] But if *Safe Reasons* were false—if p could be a reason you have for ϕ-ing, even though p isn't warranted enough to justify you in ϕ-ing—it should be perfectly legitimate to concede the premise and then proceed to raise concerns about whether it is overridden by the risks associated with its falsehood.

If something is a reason you have, it should be epistemically safe to put to work in the way we have described. Of course, if fallibilism is true, then small chances of error accumulate as you add more and more fallibly known premises, and so when reasoning from a very large set of such premises you can't jointly take each premise for granted, whether the reasoning is theoretical or practical. Thus, no fallibilist can say that when you have a reason, you get to put it to work in *any* reasoning in which it figures. But accepting fallibilism doesn't mean sucking all the marrow out of reasons. When p is a reason you have to ϕ, that doesn't give you free reign in all reasoning involving p and a large number of other premises; but it ought to have some implications for whether to ϕ. You ought to be able to weigh p—the reason to ϕ—against reasons you have to do some alternative to ϕ-ing, without worrying about the chance that p is false. This is what *Safe Reasons* assures us.

3.5 Deriving KJ

Does adding *Safe Reasons* to KR really get us KJ? To get to KJ from KR don't we need, not merely *Safe Reasons*, but rather the following connecting claim?

> If p is warranted enough to be a reason you have for ϕ-ing, then p is warranted enough to justify you in ϕ-ing, for any ϕ.

[26] Of course, by raising these concerns, we do not challenge the claim that it is available as a motivating reason.

The only difference between this claim and *Safe Reasons* is the replacement of 'is a reason you have' with 'is warranted enough to be a reason you have' in the antecedent. But, still, doesn't this need to be argued for instead of, or in addition to, *Safe Reasons*?

No. The connecting claim is guaranteed by *Safe Reasons*. Suppose *Safe Reasons* is true and the connecting claim is false. Then, for some ϕ, p is warranted enough to be a reason you have for ϕ-ing, even though p is not warranted enough to justify you in ϕ-ing. Because p is not warranted enough to justify you in ϕ-ing, the consequent of *Safe Reasons* is false. What stands in the way of it being true? Your epistemic weakness with respect to p. But if your epistemic weakness stands in the way of your satisfying a necessary condition on p's being a reason you have for ϕ-ing, then your epistemic weakness stands in the way of p's being a reason you have for ϕ-ing. This is to say that p isn't warranted enough to be a reason you have for ϕ-ing, which violates the assumption that the connecting claim is false. Therefore, the connecting claim is true if *Safe Reasons* is and is not needed as an independent premise.

KJ follows from KR and *Safe Reasons*.[27] This completes our case for KJ.[28]

[27] Here is the explicit deduction of KJ from KR and the connecting claim, with all the quantifier scopes explicitly articulated:

(1) For all S, p, if S knows that p, then, for all ϕ, p is warranted enough to be a reason S has for ϕ-ing.

(2) For all S, p, ϕ, if p is warranted enough to be a reason S has for ϕ-ing, then p is warranted enough to justify S in ϕ-ing.

Therefore:

(3) For all S, p, if S knows that p, then, for all ϕ, p is warranted enough to justify S in ϕ-ing.

(1) is KR, (2) is the connecting claim, guaranteed by *Safe Reasons*, and (3) is KJ.

[28] We remarked in n. 7 that we are using 'justify' to mean 'is a full justifier'. Similar remarks hold for 'reason'. You might worry about how we build full reasons and justifiers, if fallibilism is true. Our principles do not address this question. Consider the full reason you have to cross the pond in the ice example. It is not simply that the ice is thick enough to hold you (which strictly speaking might not be a reason in favor of walking across at all) but rather a conjunction of other propositions: e.g. that it's good to get to the other side as quickly as possible and that walking across is quicker than walking around. Now, given fallibilism, if the probabilities of enough of the conjuncts are close to a threshold at which we wouldn't be able to know them—if we 'just barely know them'—then we will not be in a position to know the conjunction, and so might not have the full reason to walk across.

Worries about building knowledge of conjunctions from knowledge of conjuncts are familiar for fallibilism. This is the well-known problem of saving something like 'multi-premise closure'. In Chapter 7, we discuss whether the retention of the full MPC is a reason to accept infallibilism.

4 KJ AND FALLIBILIST PURISM

KJ is of interest in its own right, since it articulates broader connections between the concepts of knowledge and justification than those typically recognized. But it is also of interest because of what it implies. We argue in this section that if KJ is true, then either fallibilism or what we have called 'purism' about knowledge is false. Fallibilism, again, is the thesis that you can know something to be the case even though there is, for you, a non-zero epistemic chance that it is not the case. Purism about knowledge is the doctrine that two subjects just alike in their strength of epistemic position with respect to a proposition *p* are alike with respect to whether they are in a position to know that *p*.

It will help if we work with a more precise definition of being 'positioned to know'. Being positioned to know can be defined in terms of sufficient warrant, as follows: you are in a position to know that *p* iff *p* is warranted enough, for you, to be known by you. That is: you are in a position to know that *p* iff no epistemic weaknesses with respect to *p* stand in the way of your knowing that *p*. It is of course crucial here that belief is not reckoned among the truth-relevant factors that determine strength of epistemic position. (Were belief among those truth-relevant factors, then on this definition of 'positioned to know' it would follow that you are positioned to know iff you know.)

If KJ is true, then fallibilist purism is false. Suppose Matt fallibly knows that the train about ready to leave the station is a local train. The local goes to Foxboro and on to Providence, the express directly to Providence. Matt is a casual sightseer. His preferred destination at the moment is Foxboro, although he wants to see Providence, too. He can either board the train or inquire further as to its destination. But Matt knows it is the local, and so by KJ the fact that it's a local is warranted enough to justify him in boarding it. And since nothing else stands in the way, that's what Matt should do: board. Of course, since Matt *fallibly* knows, the small chance of error could have made a difference to what he should do if the stakes had been sufficiently high. And it could have made such a difference compatibly with all of Matt's truth-relevant factors with respect to *it is a local* remaining as they are. Let Jeremy be such a subject. Jeremy should not board; he should check further. But if he shouldn't board, then *the train is a local* doesn't justify him boarding. The chance of error is too great. Jeremy's probability, therefore, is not high enough, and so constitutes a weakness in his epistemic position which stands in the way of *the train is a local* justifying him in boarding. (Notice that our counterfactual sufficient condition is satisfied: holding fixed all factors relevant to whether *the train is a local* justifies him in boarding, other than his epistemic probability for *the train is a local*, we can vary whether this consideration justifies him by raising the probability sufficiently.) So, *the train is a local* isn't warranted enough to justify Jeremy in boarding it. Since Matt and Jeremy have the same strength of epistemic position with respect to this proposition, but only Matt knows (or is in a position to know), it follows that purism is false.

The general argument, in brief, is this:

(i) If KJ and fallibilism are true, then there are pairs of subjects, like Matt and Jeremy above, which falsify purism.

(ii) So, if KJ is true fallibilist purism is false.

All the work is in defending (i). The illustration we just ran through, alone, should get us most of the way there. But we here develop the defense in detail.

Suppose KJ and fallibilism are true. If fallibilism is true, then someone fallibly knows something. And if someone fallibly knows something, then there is a possible subject, call him *Low*, who is in a position like Matt's above in these respects:

(a) he is faced with a choice between doing an 'efficient' act A or a 'safe' act B;

(b) the proposition p is about the world (and not at all about his stakes), and p is connected to the question of whether to do A in such a way that p is fitted in all non-epistemic respects to justify his doing A, as opposed to B; and

(c) he fallibly knows that p.

(In the case of Matt, p is *the train is a local*, A is *boarding*, and B is *inquiring further*.) Given KJ, p is warranted enough to justify Low's doing A, and is appropriately connected to the question of whether to do A, and so p justifies Low in doing A. (We now have our Matt. Next we construct Jeremy.)

Because Low *fallibly* knows that p, there is some non-zero epistemic chance for him that p is false. Because this chance is non-zero, and because p itself is about the world, the small chance of p would make a difference concerning whether to do A or B had the stakes been higher. Let High (think: Jeremy) be such a high-stakes subject, who has the same epistemic chance for *p* as Low does and who generally has the epistemic position Low does with respect to *p*, and who satisfies (a) and (b). High *isn't* justified in doing A, though; he should do B instead. So, *p* doesn't justify High in doing A. Yet, holding fixed all other factors relevant to whether *p* justifies High in doing A, we can vary whether *p* so justifies High by strengthening High's epistemic position along the probability dimension. Therefore, *p* is not warranted enough for High to justify him in doing A. By KJ, High doesn't know that *p*, even if he happens to believe that *p*. High's epistemic weaknesses with respect to *p* stand in the way of his knowing that *p*, and so High isn't in a position to know that *p*. But Low is, even though Low and High have the same strength of epistemic position with respect to *p*. It follows that the pair of Low and High falsify purism.

This argument makes use of ancillary assumptions. In particular, these:

(A1) If fallible knowledge is possible, then it is possible for there to be a subject, Low, who is in a position like Matt's, i.e. who satisfies (a)–(c) above.

(A2) If there is such a possible subject, Low, in a position like Matt's, then there is a possible subject, High, in a position like Jeremy's, i.e. who is such that (a) and (b) hold of him, and who has the epistemic position with respect to *p* that Low has.

(A3) If a subject is in a position like Jeremy's, then *p* isn't warranted enough to justify him in doing the 'efficient' act, A.

Given KJ and these assumptions, fallibilist purism is false.

One might object to (A1) on the following grounds. Only propositions about probabilities and utilities—or about expected utility—can justify action, and so only such propositions can be relevant in all non-epistemic respects to justify an action.[29] Therefore, (A1) is false because there are no propositions which make (b) true—there are no propositions about the world (and not about stakes) which are suited to justify action. This is implausible for two reasons. First, given the plausible claim, which could be supported in the way our Unity Thesis is, that what is warranted enough to justify action (and the pragmatic) is warranted enough to justify belief, the claim

[29] Something like this objection may be at work in Feldman (2007).

that only propositions about expected utility can justify action would lead to the absurd conclusion that there are no propositions about the world (and not about stakes) which can justify belief. Second, this objection requires a rather radical revision in an everyday picture of how reasons play a role in our decisions. Why is Sam going to the store? Because he's out of milk. Why is the manager bringing in a lefty? Because the batter has a much better average against righties. Why are you giving the paper an F? Because it was submitted two months late. Sam isn't going to the store because he's *probably* out of milk, nor is the manager bringing in a lefty because the batter *almost certainly* has a much better average against righties, nor are you giving the paper an F because it was *definitely* handed in two months late. The motivating reason behind the action in all these cases is a proposition about the world. But for the token actions to be justified, what motivates them—what they're based in—must be the very same reason that justifies taking those actions. And, of course, if you ask Sam what his reason is for going to the store, he will say *I am out of milk.* He presents this as a justifying reason and not merely a motivating one.

One might object to (A2) on the grounds that stakes have a direct bearing on epistemic position. Now, there are obviously some cases in which by raising stakes on whether *p* your epistemic position with respect to *p* changes, as when you have some special evidence of a correlation between the high stakes and whether *p*. But it is implausible in the extreme that changing stakes will always make the relevant difference to your strength of epistemic position. Consider probability: if you are offered a suitable gamble on whether the die will come up 6, this does not plausibly change the probability for you that the die will come up 6, nor does it change the probability for you that it will come up 1–5. The matter seems no different if the chance that not-*p* is low enough for you to fallibly know that *p*.

One possible objection to (A3) is this: Jeremy's high stakes stand in the way of *the train is a local* being warranted enough to justify him in doing the efficient act, boarding; so, the problem isn't that he isn't warranted enough.[30] The problem, rather, is that the standard his warrant has to meet in order for *the train is a local* to justify him is too high. We accept the premise and deny the conclusion. Yes, the high stakes do stand in the way, but so do

[30] In personal communication, Juan Comesaña and Brian Weatherson each raised an objection like this.

weaknesses in his epistemic position. Why think his high stakes stand in the way? The difference-making condition is satisfied: with suitable variations in stakes while holding all other relevant factors fixed, you can vary whether *the train is a local* justifies Jeremy. But this same condition is satisfied for warrant as well. Both of these factors stand in the way. To say that only the standard Jeremy's warrant must meet stands in the way, but not Jeremy's strength of epistemic position itself, is like a racer saying, 'I didn't lose because of my speed. I lost only because of the other guy's speed.'[31]

All three ancillary assumptions look good, then. Therefore, if KJ is true, fallibilist purism is not. This result might be surprising to a reader who skipped Chapter 1. In that chapter we advised fallibilists wanting to answer David Lewis' charge of 'madness' and Bonjour's worry about arbitrariness to take seriously the following two-part account of *significant chance of error*:

(Part I) Knowledge that p is incompatible with there being a *significant* chance that not-p.

(Part II) If there is a non-zero chance that not-p, the significance of this chance that not-p is not simply a matter of not-p's probability, i.e. it can vary holding fixed not-p's probability.

This account, as we saw, can be used to give a broadly Gricean explanation of why conjunctions such as 'I know that p but there is a chance that not-p' and 'p but there is a chance that not-p', which would seem to be perfectly true and knowable if fallibilism were true, sound deeply wrong and even mad. The price the fallibilist pays for taking our advice, as we noted, is the denial of purism. And this is because the barebones account of significant chance of error just sketched rules out fallibilist purism. KJ neither introduces nor removes the conflict with fallibilist purism; it was there already in the barebones account. KJ is just a way of putting flesh on these bones, a way of explaining more clearly what significance of the chance of error is: the small chance that not-p is significant iff it stands in the way of p's being a *justifier*. And the argument for KJ provides independent support for a claim that the fallibilist should find helpful to take on in any case.

[31] We could, of course, reformulate KJ and the rest of the principles in terms of difference-making rather than sufficient warrant; if we did we would avoid this objection. One advantage of appealing to sufficient warrant is that we can apply it to cases in which there is no appropriate connection between p and ϕ, as we did earlier in considering whether *the number of stars is even* is warranted enough to justify you in getting a flu shot tomorrow. In Chapter 7, however, we consider a challenging argument that this isn't an advantage.

5 A WEAKER VERSION OF KJ

The term 'justification' is ambiguous. In common parlance, when we say that you are justified in doing something, we often mean that you are permitted to do it—that it isn't something you shouldn't do. But epistemologists often use 'justification' as an *obliging* notion: you are justified in believing something only when you should believe it rather than withhold or disbelieve it. In KJ, which conception did we have in mind?

We think it does not matter. Whether justification is construed in the obliging way—in terms of what you *should* believe or do—or the permitting way, the arguments retain their force. When justification is taken in the obliging way, of course, the resulting principles are stronger. So, we take ourselves to have made a compelling case for the claim that what you know is warranted enough not only to permit you to ϕ but to oblige you to ϕ, for any ϕ.

Some readers will worry that, despite our arguments, this obliging version of KJ (which we will hereafter simply call KJ) is too strong. All we should accept, instead, they might suggest, is the permitting version, which we will call

(KP) If you know that p, then p is warranted enough to permit you to ϕ, for any ϕ.

The proponent of KP might say that, in the frozen pond case we considered earlier, if you know that the ice is thick enough to hold you, then you may walk across the ice. It is rationally permissible for you to do so—even though it's not true that you *should* walk across. When you know in a case like this, multiple incompatible courses of action are permissible for you. So far, this is consistent with KJ.[32] However, the proponent of KP might go on to say, if we bumped up your epistemic position with respect to *the ice is thick enough to hold me* sufficiently, there would be only one permitted action, walking over the ice. Therefore, p is not warranted enough to oblige you to ϕ. This is inconsistent with KJ.

[32] In addition to worries about falling on the ice and other such defeaters, there is also a question of whether, even if it were certain that it would hold you, you really would be obliged to walk across. In the literature on practical reasons, some philosophers have argued that although you are always *permitted* to choose what you know and are even certain will have the best outcome you aren't always *obliged* to do so, if the goods involved are merely 'attractive' or 'enticing' (cf. Dancy 2003).

One might hope that in replacing KJ with KP one is spared from having to reject fallibilist purism. Not so. Notice that our argument in Section 4 for the claim that the truth of KJ ensures the falsity of fallibilist purism is unaffected by our choice of how to construe 'justify', whether in terms of permission or obligation, and when 'justify' is given the permitting reading, KJ becomes KP. So that argument shows that KP rules out fallibilist purism.

KP undermines fallibilist purism just as well as KJ does, seems to spring from the same considerations that suggested KJ, and some would find it more palatable. Nonetheless, we think that KJ, and not just KP, is true. Consider what the proponent of KP would need to say in order to reject KJ. Presumably, she should not reject the first premise in the argument for KJ: the theoretical version of KR—that if you know something, then it is warranted enough to be a reason you have to believe things. KR, restricted to belief, has nothing to do with permission or obligation. Nor does the unrestricted version, which adds only the Unity Thesis—a second principle that does not involve notions of permission or obligation. Her target, we think, would have to be *Safe Reasons.* She would have to contend that p can be a reason you have for ϕ-ing, even though p isn't warranted enough to justify you in ϕ-ing.

In challenging *Safe Reasons*, a proponent of KP might insist that, especially when it comes to actions, a reason you have to ϕ is warranted enough only to permit you to ϕ, not to oblige. Weakening the principle in this way, though, raises all the same questions about the weighing of reasons concerning expected results with those concerning actual results: 'On the one hand, the ice might not be thick enough. On the other hand, it is thick enough. Which is more important?' If one accepts the permitting but not the obliging version of *Safe Reasons*, one will think it is permissible to answer this latter question in either of two ways. But, first, one will still be committed to the claim that we do weigh such reasons against one another, which, as argued above, we don't. And, second, unless one is to reject the very plausible principle *Conclusive Reasons Link*, which states that

> if you have a reason which you know to be a conclusive reason there is for you to ϕ, then you have a conclusive reason to ϕ,

understanding *Safe Reasons* as 'merely permissive' amounts to allowing that it can be permissible not to ϕ even when you have a conclusive reason to ϕ. We avoid these problems with the full and unmodified *Safe Reasons.*

We suspect that the driving concern behind the move from KJ to KP is over close calls in high-stakes situations. Suppose you just barely know that the ice is thick enough to hold you. It's a close call. If so, *the ice is thick enough* is a reason you have to walk across, but you won't know that it is. But if you don't know that it is a reason you have, then surely you can't be criticized for failing to be appropriately responsive to it by walking across the pond. And if you can't be criticized for walking around the pond, then it's hard to see how it can be the case that you *should* walk across the pond. Of course, if it wasn't a close call whether you knew and had *the ice is thick enough* as a reason—if your epistemic position for it were sufficiently stronger—then you *could* be criticized for walking around. Therefore, in close calls, it seems that your epistemic weakness with respect to what reasons you have can stand in the way of those reasons obliging you: *Safe Reasons* is false, and so the case for KJ fails.[33]

In short, the argument is as follows. There can be close calls when it comes to what you know and what reasons you have and, when there are such close calls, you can't be criticized for not responding appropriately; and if you cannot be so criticized, then what you know isn't warranted enough to make it the case that you *should* respond in the appropriate ways.

There are two main difficulties with this argument. First, it is not clear that, in such close calls, you can't be criticized for ϕ-ing. It is true that you can't be criticized as much, or in all the same ways, as you can in cases in which the call isn't close. But that doesn't mean that you aren't subject to

[33] One way to respond to this worry is by insisting that there is no such thing as a close call when it comes to what reasons you have and what you know. If you know, on this view, you must know that you know. If p is a reason you have to ϕ, then you must know that p is a reason you have to ϕ. Does this response require an infinite number of iterations of knowledge? And if so, doesn't it lead to skepticism, because we never know 'all the way up'?

The issues are complicated here. One worry is about requiring infinite numbers of beliefs. But the relevant iterations should really be iterations of *being in a position to know* rather than knowledge. So that is not a serious problem. But there is still some worry about whether we are in a position to know things like the thousandth iteration of *I'm in a position to know* on the proposition *Bush is president.* Perhaps the worry is about iterations exceeding our grasp. Another suggestion, which takes account of our decreasing grasp of the higher and higher iterations, would run something like this: if you are in a position to know that p, then if you determinately understand *I am in a position to know that p*, then you are in a position to know that you are in a position to know that p. It isn't crazy to think that we are in a position to know all the relevant iterations on *Bush is president* until our determinate understanding 'runs out'. This doesn't even seem to conflict with fallibilism about being in a position to know.

A more serious worry against the 'no close calls' strategy is found in Williamson's (2000: ch. 2) anti-luminosity argument, which we will not address here.

legitimate criticism at all for failing to respond appropriately to what even the objection grants are reasons you have and you know.

Second, if there can be close calls when it comes to knowledge and the having of reasons, then there can presumably be close calls when it comes to what you should do. This is apparent in any case on standard views of what one should do. For example, in certain utilitarian views in ethics, there can certainly be close calls concerning what you morally should do: although you cannot know it, A will produce just barely higher overall happiness than B; despite the fact that you don't know this, A is what you morally should do. Or, consider a standard decision-theoretic view: you should do whatever act has the highest expected utility. There can surely be close calls here; nevertheless, what you should do is decided not by what you can know about expected utility but what it is. And even independent of specific theories, there is no principled reason to think there can't be close calls about what you should do.

If there are close calls about what you should do, and so cases in which you should do something even if you don't know you should, what should we say about criticizability? Does it follow 'should' or not? Either way, the argument for rejecting KJ in favor of KP is undermined. If criticizability does not follow 'should', then it is no block to KJ even if you are not criticizable in close calls. And if criticizability does follow 'should' then any mechanism that can be used to explain why you seem less criticizable in close call 'should' cases can also be used to explain why you seem less criticizable in close call 'knowledge' and 'reason' cases.

We think the best thing to say here is that you can be more deserving of criticism in clear cases—in which you have the relevant higher-order knowledge—than in close call cases in which you lack such knowledge. So, if you know you should ϕ, and yet don't ϕ, you are more criticizable than if it is merely true that you should ϕ but you don't know that. And if you know that you know that you should ϕ, still more criticizable. And so on. So, in a case in which you just barely know *the ice is thick enough*— so that the ice is thick enough is just barely a reason you have—we can say that it is warranted enough to make it the case that you should walk across. If it does make it the case that you should walk across, then even if you don't know this, you deserve criticism. But we needn't be unreasonable in our criticism. You have an excuse which mitigates our negative assessment of you: you didn't know you should walk across, because you didn't know that *the ice is thick enough to hold you* was a reason you had.

Worries about close calls do not give us good reason to give up KJ in its fully obliging sense.

6 FALLIBILIST BEDFELLOWS

We close by considering a rather vague worry about principles like KJ. The idea is this: the reason that principles like KJ are even remotely appealing is because we are committed to infallibilism about knowledge and, if infallibilism is true, KJ is as well. But once fallibilism is allowed in, the rules change. Otherwise intuitive principles might well be false, but only because fallibilism itself is counterintuitive. Therefore, fallibilism provides us with a reason to reject principles like KJ.[34]

Consider, for example, the argument for *Safe Reasons*. Suppose it is granted that it is deeply counterintuitive to think that, in reasoning, we ever weigh *the ice is thick enough to hold me* against *there is a serious risk that the ice isn't thick enough to hold me*. But perhaps this is only because it is deeply counterintuitive to think that we can ever know that the ice is thick enough while knowing that the ice might not be thick enough, and *this* is because it is deeply counterintuitive to think that we can ever know that the ice is thick enough while it being *the case* that the ice might not be thick enough.

Or, consider the argument for the Unity Thesis. Suppose, again, that it is granted that it is deeply counterintuitive to suggest that we segregate reasons when engaged in practical deliberation. But perhaps this is only because we are committed to what we know having probability 1, so *of course* if we can reason from what we know to theoretical conclusions, we can reason to practical ones as well. But if knowledge doesn't have probability 1, then that allows the possibility of raising the stakes on our actions high enough that the chance that we're wrong makes a difference. We can't raise the epistemic stakes on belief in the same way (though some epistemologists might deny this). Therefore, there is a difference between practical and theoretical conclusions, and if fallibilism is true, it's a difference that makes a difference. Once we embrace fallibilism, we take on commitments to the truth of these deeply counterintuitive claims. So it should be no surprise that

[34] There are also worries not only that the plausibility of KJ depends on fallibilism being counterintuitive, but that it outright entails infallibilism. For arguments to this effect, and our responses, see Appendix II.

other deeply counterintuitive claims might be true if those claims depend on the fallibilist assumption.

Neither the Unity Thesis nor *Safe Reasons* plausibly derives its intuitive force from that of infallibilism about knowledge. That's because knowledge comes into the argument for KJ in a single premise and is not involved at all in the arguments for the Unity Thesis or *Safe Reasons*. Knowledge plays its role in the argument entirely in the very first step—the theoretical version of KR: if you know that *p*, then *p* is warranted enough to justify you in believing that *q*, for any *q*. Whether fallibilists are able to reconcile this principle with their fallibilism is of course an open question. But most presumably think they can.

No step in the argument after this point makes mention of knowledge at all. Therefore, whatever their intuitive status is does not obviously derive from the intuitive status of any claim about knowledge. But perhaps denying the Unity Thesis and *Safe Reasons* is counterintuitive only because fallibilism about *having reasons* is deeply counterintuitive—that is, because it is deeply counterintuitive that *p* can be a reason you have for ϕ-ing even if there is a chance for you that not-*p*.

Is this deeply counterintuitive? Not nearly as obviously so as fallibilism about knowledge. Recall Lewis' famous remark:

> If you are a contented fallibilist, I implore you to be honest, be naïve, hear it afresh. 'He knows, yet he has not eliminated all possibilities of error.' Even if you've numbed your ears, doesn't this overt, explicit fallibilism *still* sound wrong? (1996: 550)

Consider an analogous remark, but about having reasons:

> If you are a contented fallibilist, I implore you to be honest, be naïve, hear it afresh. 'That it's raining is a reason he has to take his umbrella, yet he has not yet eliminated all possibilities that it's not raining.' Even if you've numbed your ears, doesn't this overt, explicit fallibilism *still* sound wrong?

Not to our ears. If that's right, the source of the counterintuitiveness in the denials of the Unity Thesis and *Safe Reasons* can't just be the counterintuitiveness of fallibilism about having reasons. Nor can it be the counterintuitiveness of fallibilism about knowledge, because those principles aren't about knowledge at all, nor is the concept of knowledge involved in the arguments for them. The most natural source for the counterintuitiveness of their denials is that the principles are true.

But it is wrong in any case to think that allowing fallibilism (about reasons or knowledge) 'changes the rules'. At any rate, fallibilists should hope to find a way that we can allow fallibilism in the door without changing all the rules. For 'the rules' are intuitively right, so if fallibilism requires them to change, they constitute a compelling case against fallibilism. For example, an infallibilist might say that only infallibilists can resist the madness of clashing conjunctions like 'I know, but there's a chance I'm wrong.' Only infallibilists can resist the madness of segregating reasons, because if we can only have reasons for which we have probability 1, then (obviously) there will be no epistemic weakness to stand in the way of *p* justifying you. Only infallibilists can resist the madness of weighing *p* against *it might be that not-p*, because only infallibilists can require that *p* is a reason you have only when it's false that it might be that not-*p*.

If what we've said here and in Chapter 1 is right, though, fallibilists can resist all of this madness as well. Fallibilists can save themselves from the madness of clashing conjunctions by saying that knowledge that *p* is incompatible only with a significant chance of error and by cashing out significance in terms of whether the chance of error stands in the way of *p* being properly put to work. They can save themselves from the madness of segregating reasons by accepting the Unity Thesis, and from the madness of weighing *p* against *it might be that not-p* by accepting *Safe Reasons.*

The principles defended here therefore do not undercut fallibilism, either about knowledge or reasons. Quite the contrary.

4

Justification

1 FROM KNOWLEDGE TO JUSTIFICATION

It is a bitterly cold night and your car has broken down in the middle of nowhere. You need to find shelter and time is running out. After walking for hours, by the light of the full moon, you finally clearly see a barn, about 50 yards to the right. Off to the left, about 500 yards away, is another barn. You think, 'Finally! There's a barn nearby on the right! I'll stay there,' and head to the nearer barn on the right.

If you *know* that there's a barn (nearby on the right), then you are justified in heading to the right. You are *not* justified in heading to the left. Time, after all, is running out. But vary the case minimally by supposing you're Gettiered. The structure on the right is a barn, but the structure on the left is a façade. In this case, you remain justified in heading to the right. Vary the case again by supposing that there is no barn at all on the right—it's just a façade—though it is indistinguishable from a barn, and looks just as much a barn as the structure on the left. You are still justified in heading to the right, even if the structure on the left *is* a barn. Had you known that the evidence you possess is misleading, you would of course not have been justified. But given what you have to go on, you are justified.

Suppose, finally, that not only is there no barn on the right—just a façade—but you haven't formed a settled belief on the matter, although the barn façade is vivid and clear and indistinguishable to you from a real barn. You may irrationally fail to believe what the evidence points to, but this doesn't affect whether you are justified in heading to the right—whether heading to the right is the thing you are justified in doing; if you were justified with the belief, you are justified without it. If these are the only changes made to the case, you remain justified throughout in heading to the right.

Notice that we could have begun the sequence of 'subtractions' from knowledge with belief first, or with truth first, and it would have made no difference. It looks like no combination of *truth, belief,* and *the absence of Gettier-like luck*, when subtracted from the original case in which you have knowledge, makes a difference to what you are justified in doing, so long as your justification for the proposition *there's a barn* is held fixed. So, it seems that bearing some justificatory relation to this proposition—a justificatory relation necessary for knowledge—is sufficient for you to be justified in reacting accordingly.

What justificatory relation has these features? We need not specify the relevant justificatory relation independently of the concept of knowledge. Whenever you know, you obviously have what we may call *knowledge-level justification*, i.e. justification strong enough, so that shortcomings in your strength of justification do not stand in the way of your knowing. (Mirroring our discussion of sufficient warrant, we can put it this way: if *p* is knowledge-level justified for you, then *p* is *justified enough* to be known by you.)[1] When *p* is knowledge-level justified for you, then, you are justified in responding accordingly.

What justifies you in so responding? We would like to say that, when *p* is knowledge-level justified for you, then it is *p* itself that justifies you in

[1] We want to allow that *p* can be knowledge-level justified for you even if *p* is false. Plausibly, whenever *p* is knowledge-level justified even though false, *p*'s justification could be strengthened in such a way that also suffices for the truth of *p*. Therefore, it seems, whenever *p* is putatively knowledge-level justified but false, *p*'s justification can be varied in such a way that *p* comes to be true and, thus, *p* comes to be known. In short, by varying *p*'s justification, we can vary whether *p* is known. By our counterfactual condition on standing in the way, doesn't this entail that weaknesses in *p*'s justification stand in the way of *p* being known, or that *p* is not justified enough to be known? If so, then *p* is not knowledge-level justified. It follows that no false proposition can be knowledge-level justified.

However, this is not the right construal of the counterfactual condition. The counterfactual condition requires that it be possible to vary whether *p* is known by varying *p*'s justification and holding all other relevant factors fixed. When it is varied whether *p* is known only by varying *p*'s justification in such a way that *p*'s truth-value also varies, then it is not the case that all other relevant factors have been held fixed. Therefore, there is no argument from our counterfactual condition to the conclusion that only truths can be knowledge-level justified. Similar considerations apply to Gettier situations: it does not follow from our counterfactual condition that only propositions believed by subjects in unGettiered situations can be knowledge-level justified. That's because it is not possible to vary whether the subject knows by varying only the subject's justification and holding all other relevant factors fixed (e.g. whether the belief is based on a falsehood). The lesson of the Gettier examples is usually taken to be that there is a fourth condition on knowledge—in addition to the truth, belief, and justification conditions. Varying justification in a Gettier case might affect whether this fourth condition is satisfied. But it is only by doing so that knowledge is varied. When the violation of that fourth condition is held fixed, variations in justification are as impotent with respect to knowledge as they are when falsehood is held fixed.

responding accordingly. On this view, when it is knowledge-level justified for you that there's a barn, whether it really is a barn or not, whether you are Gettiered or not, your justifier in each case is the same—it's *there's a barn*. What remains the same throughout the subtractions is that *there's a barn* justifies you in reacting appropriately. If so, then this 'subtraction argument', when generalized, supports the conclusion that what is knowledge-level justified is warranted enough to justify, i.e.

($J^K J$) If you have knowledge-level justification that p, then p is warranted enough to justify you in ϕ-ing, for any ϕ.

In addition to the subtraction considerations, the same general argument we gave in defense of the claim that what you know is warranted enough to justify—of KJ—can be converted, without loss of plausibility, into arguments supporting $J^K J$. The only change in the argument needed to derive $J^K J$ is to replace the *knowledge*-reason principle for belief (KR for belief) with one for knowledge-level justification:

($J^K R$ for belief) If p is knowledge-level justified for you, then p is warranted enough to be a reason you have to believe q, for any q.

This is a strengthening of KR for belief, but it is plausible. If your justification for a proposition is knowledge-level, then if it isn't among your reasons for belief, it's not because it isn't warranted enough. The move from KR to $J^K R$ nevertheless does raise certain objections, which we discuss in Section 2. Here we only note that the argument for KJ can be transformed into one for $J^K J$ with a single plausible modification.

Usually the justification condition on knowledge is simply said to be *being justified in believing*. The standard assumption is that such justification is justification good enough for knowledge, that is, in our terminology, that justification in believing is equivalent to knowledge-level justification. Since this assumption will be important in this and especially the next chapter, we'll give it a name:

(The Equivalence Thesis) p is knowledge-level justified for you iff you are justified in believing that p.[2]

[2] The reason we call this a standard assumption is that it seems necessary to defend the common practice in much of the literature on the analysis of knowledge of simply including 'S is justified in believing that p' as the justification condition on knowledge. Thus, the very idea of a JTB+ account of knowledge, where J is *justified in believing* presupposes the Equivalence Thesis.

The right-to-left direction of the Equivalence Thesis and $J^K J$ together yield the conclusion that what you are justified in believing is warranted enough to justify, or:

(JJ) If you are justified in believing that *p*, then *p* is warranted enough to justify you in ϕ-ing, for any ϕ.

If JJ is true, then not only is fallibilist purism false of knowledge, it is false of justification for believing (and even if JJ is false because the required direction of the Equivalence Thesis is false, fallibilist purism is still false of knowledge-level justification). The argument proceeds just like the earlier argument against fallibilist purism about knowledge.[3]

Is JJ true? In this section, we've given two arguments supporting the move from knowledge to justification:

The *subtraction* argument

(S1) If you know that *p* then *p* is warranted enough to justify (i.e. KJ).

(S2) Holding fixed knowledge-level justification while subtracting from knowledge any combination of *truth, belief,* and *being unGettiered* makes no difference to whether *p* is warranted enough to justify.

Therefore

(S3) If *p* is knowledge-level justified, then *p* is warranted enough to justify (i.e. $J^K J$).

The *direct* argument

(D1) $J^K R$ for belief is true.

(D2) The Unity Thesis and *Safe Reasons* are true.

Therefore,

(D3) $J^K J$ is true.

And, from both (S3) and (D3) we can derive JJ using the relevant direction—the right-to-left direction—of the Equivalence Thesis, which holds that *p* is knowledge-level justified for you iff you are justified in believing *p*.

The right-to-left direction of the Equivalence Thesis has been called into question, on the grounds that belief is a relatively non-committal state of

[3] Assume JJ and fallibilism about justification for believing. Then there is some Low/High pair that falsifies purism. The construction of Low and High proceeds exactly as before: simply replace 'fallibly knows' with 'is fallibly justified in believing', *mutatis mutandis.*

opinion, and that it takes less to be justified in believing than it takes to have justification good enough for knowledge. We will postpone a full discussion of this worry until the next chapter, in which we look in some depth at the notion of belief. Here we will simply assume that the Equivalence Thesis is true. The goal of this chapter is to address worries about the move from affirming conditionals about knowledge to affirming conditionals about justification (2) and to explore whether something even stronger is plausible for justification—a biconditional version of J^KJ and JJ (3).

2 WORRIES ABOUT THE MOVE FROM KNOWLEDGE TO JUSTIFICATION

2.1 Worry #1: falsehoods can't justify

Both the direct argument and the subtraction arguments dismiss any factors relevant to knowledge that aren't relevant to knowledge-level justification. The direct argument makes such factors irrelevant to whether *p* is a reason you have for believing. The subtraction argument makes such factors irrelevant to whether *p* is a justifier. But are such factors really irrelevant? Here, we discuss whether truth is irrelevant. The discussion, however, should apply equally well to Gettier-conditions.

Consider again your search for shelter in the bitterly cold night. We claim that, if you know that the structure on the right is a barn, then the *fact* that it is a barn is warrant enough to justify you in heading to the right.[4] In

[4] We noted in Chapter 3 that some philosophers maintain—implausibly in our view—that facts or propositions can never be motivating reasons or justifying reasons. Such *mental state* theorists should agree with a slightly revised version of the claim we will argue for in this section. We will argue that falsehoods can justify, i.e. can be justifying reasons. Our argument can be recast as an argument that false belief states can justify, just as they can motivate.

In general, mental state theorists will want to recast the theses we are defending in this chapter as follows. JJ becomes:

> If you have a justified belief that *p*, then your belief that *p* is warranted enough to justify you.

And J^KJ becomes:

> If you have a knowledge-level justified belief that *p*, then your belief that *p* is warranted enough to justify you (and similarly for their converses).

For you to have knowledge-level justified belief that *p* requires that *p* be knowledge-level justified for you, but also that you believe that *p* and that your belief that *p* be properly based. The arguments we give in this chapter can be converted, with mostly minor changes, into arguments for these mental state recastings of our principles.

previous chapters, though, and earlier in this one, we have said that when you know the proposition that *p*, then *it*—the proposition itself—can justify you. Can propositions ever justify? It sounds odd to say so.[5] But this oddity isn't crippling, at least if we stick with only true propositions. Perhaps true propositions justify you, in a derivative sense, if and only if the corresponding facts justify you in the primary sense.[6]

However, the claim that what you are justified in believing can justify implies that *falsehoods* in some cases are warranted enough to justify, since you can be justified in believing false propositions. In some of these cases, nothing else will stand in the way of the false proposition justifying. Therefore, if what you are justified in believing can justify, then falsehoods sometimes do justify. This is counterintuitive, and not just because it is odd to speak of propositions, rather than facts, justifying. Even if we replace 'propositions' with 'considerations' or 'states of affairs', the oddity remains: if a consideration is false or a state of affairs doesn't obtain, then it doesn't seem to be a

[5] Dancy (2000: 114–17) argues that true propositions can't be reasons you have for action. On going theories of propositions, propositions, true and false ones alike, are abstract objects. No abstract object is a reason for you, in the barn example, to head to the right. There is a large literature in the interface between metaphysics and philosophy of language devoted to discussing these sorts of worries. Notice that arguments like Dancy's could be given to show that *facts* can't be reasons for action: no non-mereological complex of objects and properties is a reason. And the same is true of other relevant philosophical entities: tropes, particularized properties, events, etc. This might make one wonder whether the argument proves too much. Perhaps it is good enough for a non-mereological complex of objects and properties to be a reason for it to have a certain existence condition; in the case of the barn example, the existence condition would be this: the complex exists iff there is a barn nearby on the right. But if this is sufficient in the case of facts, it would seem that a proposition, if true, could deserve to be called a reason insofar as it is true iff there is a barn to the right; for given that the proposition has this truth-condition and is true, there is a barn nearby on the right. Alternatively, these considerations might incline one to a non-referential view of that-clauses. The idea would be that the that-clause in 'My reason for heading to the left was that there was a barn there' would not refer to anything which could then be said to be an entity which is a reason. For further discussion of worries about referential accounts of that-clauses, see King (2002), Moltmann (2003), and McGrath (2005).

[6] One might worry that if facts are individuated more coarsely than true propositions, then facts aren't justifiers. This would be a reason to take (true) propositions—or facts isomorphic to them—to be the fundamental justifiers. On standard coarse-grained views of facts, the fact that Superman lives in Metropolis *is* the fact that Clark Kent lives in Metropolis, even though the same is not true of the corresponding propositions. Lois, suppose, has no clue that Superman lives in Metropolis, but does know that Clark lives in Metropolis. That Clark lives in Metropolis might justify her in getting out of Metropolis for a while. If it is the fact that Clark lives in Metropolis that justifies her in getting out of Metropolis for a while, however, then on the view of facts we are considering the fact that Superman lives in Metropolis justifies her in getting out of Metropolis for a while. The latter is implausible. But it seems unavoidable if only facts can be justifiers and facts are individuated more coarsely than true propositions. (Thanks to Masashi Kasaki for helpful discussion on this point.)

candidate justifier. Suppose you are aware that not-*p*. Then it is not proper to assert something of the form (1) when challenged about a previous action:

(1) What justified me in doing what I did was that *p*.

For example, you can't properly say, after learning that the structure on the right is a mere façade, 'What justified me in heading to the right was that there's a barn'. Why should it be improper to say this if it is perfectly true? The simplest explanation is that falsehoods, by whatever name, are never justifiers. And if they aren't, then it is clear where the subtraction and direct arguments for J^KJ go wrong: subtracting truth can make a difference to whether a proposition justifies you, even holding justification fixed ((S2) in the subtraction argument is false). Likewise with respect to reasons you have: knowledge that *p* might provide warrant enough to make *p* a reason you have for belief, but justification doesn't. Justification doesn't entail truth, and falsehoods can't be reasons you have; (D1) in the direct argument is false.

Even when it isn't proper to assert something of the form (1), however, it can be perfectly sensible to claim that you were justified in doing what you did. When you headed to the right, you were justified in doing so, and not because of some complicated weighting of reasons. You had a clear reason. But what was it, if not *there's a barn nearby on the right*? One proposal is that the justifier is the fact that you thought or believed that there was such a barn. Generally, even when you are aware that not-*p* and cannot properly assert (1), it is still perfectly appropriate to assert (2):

(2) What justified me in doing what I did was that I thought that *p*.

(2), however, doesn't plausibly express a truth about what justified you in doing what you did. Except in rare cases, facts about what you think aren't particularly good reasons to do or believe things which the fact that *p* would be a good reason to do or believe. Suppose that there's a barn and that you think this. Then, on the view under consideration, you have two reasons to head to the right: viz. the fact that there's a barn nearby on the right and the fact that you think this. It seems clear that the latter is a different and much weaker reason. In making your decision, you wouldn't think of it as relevant at all, unlike the former. Yet if, contrary to all your evidence, it isn't a barn, you would be no less justified in heading to the right. Facts about your thoughts or beliefs, then, don't seem to do the needed justificatory work; we need to look elsewhere.

Perhaps what justifies you when *p* is false is not the proposition *p*, but whatever *facts* justified you in believing *p* in the first place. Suppose that you see a barn on the right, think, 'There's a barn', and decide to head to the right. In fact, you're right. What justifies you in heading to the right is the fact that there's a barn. Your counterpart, in an otherwise identical situation, sees what is in fact a barn façade and thinks 'There's a barn'. He, too, heads to the right and is justified in doing so—just as justified as you. What justifies him in heading to the right? If falsehoods can't be justifiers, then what justifies him is not that there's a barn over there nor, as we saw above, is it the fact that he *thinks* there is. Rather, it's whatever facts justified him in believing this proposition. And he might indeed say, after the episode is over, for instance:

(3) What justified me in heading to the right was that there was a barn-shaped structure nearby to the right.

Can such justifiers take up the slack left by the loss of the justifier *there's a barn*?

What's clear is that both you and your counterpart, when you head to the right, act on the basis of a belief that there's a barn, and not on the basis of a belief that there's a barn-shaped structure. We can assume that you didn't even have explicit beliefs about the shape of the structure. (This is confirmed in other perceptual cases, such as Bernard Williams' gin/petrol case: you decide to drink on the basis of the belief that there is gin in the glass, not on the basis of a belief that there is clear liquid in the glass.) But *bases* for action hook up with reasons for which you did what you did, i.e. with *motivating reasons*. Motivating reasons are specified by that-clauses, just as justifiers are. And, clearly, motivating reasons *must motivate*. But how can that-*p* be said to motivate? As far as we can see, only by being the content of a mental state—in this case, a belief—that is your basis for action. So it looks as though if we are to find a motivating reason for your counterpart in the barn case, the only candidate is *there's a barn*. Anything further back in the justificatory chain wasn't the content of an operative belief.

Notice that it is exactly as improper to say 'The reason for which I headed to the right was that there's a barn' when you are aware that it wasn't a barn as it is to say 'What justified me in heading to the right was that there's a barn'. So, given the foregoing considerations, either this impropriety isn't due to falsehood or the concept of motivating reason simply has no application when you act from false beliefs. We are strongly inclined to embrace the first horn of this dilemma.[7] This strategy receives further support from Dancy (2000: ch. 6). As Dancy notes, even when you are aware that not-*p*, you may properly cite that-*p* as a motivating reason so long as you add an appropriate side-comment, e.g. an *As*-parenthetical:

(4) My reason for doing what I did was that *p*, as I thought at the time.

Here the *As*-parenthetical does not modify the whole preceding sentence. (4) doesn't say that you thought at the time that your reason for doing what you were doing was that *p*. Even if true, that's not the point of (4). (4) says that you thought at the time that *p*. Nor does the *As*-parenthetical help to specify the content of your reason. Rather, its function seems to be to cancel any implication that the reason specified is true.[8] If something of the form (4) is true in the cases of acting from false beliefs, then (5) below is true in such cases as well, at least when the motivating reason was a justifying one:

(5) What justified me in doing what I did was that *p*, as I thought at the time.

This seems a promising account of why, although falsehoods can be justifying and motivating reasons, it is improper baldly to cite one as such. In doing so, you misleadingly imply that *p* is the case.[9]

We expect these considerations won't convince everyone. It is worth pointing out, then, that we can save something very much like JJ, even if we concede that only facts or truths can justify. For if you are justified in believing that *p*, but *p* fails to be a justifier only because it is false, it is not at all because you are not *justified enough* in believing *p*. You are not warranted enough, of course, because truth-value is among the truth-relevant factors

[7] For a useful further discussion of some of these issues, see Schroeder (2008).

[8] The same effect is obtained by 'The reason for which I did what I did was that *p*, though of course *p* turned out not to be the case'. See Dancy (2000: 132).

[9] Such an account would be less promising if, after being apprised of the fact that not-*p*, we found it correct to say: 'What I said earlier was false: that *p* didn't justify me in doing what I did'. But this statement is highly peculiar. The use of 'that *p*' in these reason-specifying or reason-denying contexts, we speculate, might bring with it a cancelable or defeasible presupposition that *p*. Compare: 'My reason was that *p*, as I thought at the time' with 'I have not stopped beating my wife; mind you, I never started!'

that contribute to strength of epistemic position, and as we're using 'warrant', your strength of warrant is simply your strength of epistemic position. What is needed, minimally, is a bump up in your warrant, provided by the truth of *p*. So, we have:

> (JJ—Weak Version) If you are justified in believing that *p*, then *p* is justified enough to justify you in ϕ-ing, for any ϕ.

The weak version of JJ is supported by an argument nearly identical to the one we used for the original JJ. The only difference is that 'justified enough' replaces 'warranted enough'. And the weak version, too, gives us the denial of fallibilist purism about justification for believing, just as JJ does, and by means of a nearly identical argument. It seems the weak version gets us the same key results as the stronger JJ, but without committing us to the position that falsehoods can justify. Nonetheless, because there is a good case for the claim that falsehoods do in some cases justify, our discussion hereafter will explicitly concern only the original JJ. We return to the issue of false justifiers, and generally to the relations between reasons there are, reasons-had, and motivating reasons, in Chapter 6.

2.2 Worry #2: externalism

Some epistemologists—call them radical externalists—think that knowledge does not require justification.[10] Whether you know is a matter, not of justification, but of your objective relations to the truth—reliability, counterfactual sensitivity, etc. If radical externalists are right, it seems you could know a proposition to be true while being justified in believing that it is false. One of BonJour's (1985) crystal ball cases is like this. Norman looks at the crystal ball and reliably believes that the President is in New York, and he is. We can assume that Norman has ample reasons—the sort of reasons *we* normal folk have—to believe the crystal ball is unreliable and no reason to believe it is reliable. None of this matters to whether he knows, if radical externalism is true. Assuming all the relevant objective relations to the truth are in place, he knows, and it is simply immaterial that he is ignoring powerful counterevidence. This is a clean and simple view: knowledge is one thing, justification another; the two can vary *wildly* from one another.

[10] These include Armstrong (1973), Dretske (1981), Nozick (1981), and Plantinga (1993).

According to radical externalists, justification for believing requires having some fairly strong justification for *p* while having knowledge-level justification does not. So, radical externalists' primary target should be the principle that what is knowledge-level justified can justify (i.e. J^KJ).[11] If radical externalists are right, this principle seems to be false, even when restricted to belief. You can have knowledge-level justification for *p* while having strong *justification* for not-*p* and very weak justification for *p*. But if you have strong justification for not-*p* and only weak justification for *p*, it is hard to see how *p* could be warranted enough to justify—presumably if *p* is to justify, your justification for *p* must be at least good and your justification for not-*p* at least not good, and so a warrant profile including this justificatory balance strongly in favor of not-*p* would not be strong enough for *p* to justify. So, it seems the radical externalist must reject J^KJ. Because J^KJ was the crucial premise in our argument that what you are justified in believing can justify, i.e. for JJ, radical externalists will accordingly resist that *argument*, although they might well find other reasons to accept its conclusion. Indeed, they might endorse a direct argument for JJ similar to the ones we have given for KJ and J^KJ, which take as their first premises a claim connecting justification for believing to the possession of reasons.

Can radical externalists hold on to KJ? We don't think so. Suppose, for *reductio*, that both KJ and radical externalism are true. Then there is a (possible) subject who knows *p* with strong justification for not-*p* and at best extremely weak justification for *p*. By KJ, *p* is warranted enough to be a justifier for this subject. By radical externalism, the subject has a true belief which meets the relevant externalist conditions. Each of these factors—truth, belief, and the externalist conditions—is such that subtracting it makes no difference to whether *p* is warranted enough to justify. But, if all these are subtracted, the subject is left with nothing in the way of warrant that could allow *p* to justify. Yet the subtractions don't affect whether *p* is warranted enough to justify the subject, and since it is warranted enough to justify in the case of knowledge, it is still warranted enough to justify when all is gone. Contradiction. The radical externalist cannot accept KJ, even in its theoretical restriction. Or, as we would put the point, KJ shows that radical externalism is false.

A less radical externalist might well claim that, even though knowledge that *p* is compatible with not being justified in believing that *p*, it isn't compatible

[11] They will also, presumably, reject the Equivalence Thesis: on their view, knowledge-level justification is far easier to achieve than justification for believing.

with having good undefeated counterevidence to *p*. Such externalists might hope to accept KJ. They might say that knowing that *p* requires a lack of *sufficient counterevidence* to *p*, and lacking sufficient counterevidence to *p* by itself is sufficient to make it the case that *p* is able to justify. This attempt to save KJ is implausible, because lacking such counterevidence isn't good enough. Take *p* to be: *my child will be a boy.* Suppose you lack sufficient counterevidence to *p* (you lack sufficient evidence either way). Does *my child will be a boy* justify you in taking boy-appropriate actions, such as telling all your friends that you're going to have a boy? We think not.

What of *moderate* forms of externalism, forms that allow that knowledge requires justification but which understand the justification involved itself externalistically? The moderate externalist would dispute our claim, at the beginning of this chapter, that subtracting the conditions relevant to 'being Gettiered' would make no difference to whether a proposition was warranted enough to justify. For these moderate externalists, whether the Gettier conditions (or some subset of them, including, e.g. reliability) are satisfied might very well make a difference to whether the subject is knowledge-level justified. However, the moderate externalist has no reason to dispute the subtraction argument—or, at least, an argument very much like it. She will only disagree with us about which subtraction series can terminate with a case of knowledge-level justification.

Nor do moderate externalists have any special reason to question the direct argument through the Equivalence Thesis for JJ. Moderate externalists try to make sense of justification for belief externalistically, and there is no reason for them qua moderate externalists to deny that what is known, or even what is justified, is warranted enough to justify. It is plausible, as we've seen, to think that justification for action depends on justification for belief, and there is no reason moderate externalists should want to insist otherwise.

Moderate externalists who accept JJ, however, do commit themselves to counterintuitive claims about action. To illustrate, consider a moderate externalism according to which whether your belief that *p* is justified is determined solely by whether your belief was delivered by a reliable belief-forming mechanism. Traditionally, philosophers have worried that this view gives the wrong verdicts in cases in which two subjects have the same internally available reasons for *p*, but who differ in terms of their reliability. It seems wrong to say that one is justified in believing and the other isn't.

Externalists can respond to these worries in two ways. First, they can just report that they don't find it intuitive that the two subjects differ with respect to justification. Second, they can claim that the relevant counterexamples pump intuitions about some strong deontological justification, which is something like *freedom from epistemic blame*. Such a conception seems to presuppose a problematic doxastic voluntarism and in any case is not closely connected with knowledge and so is not the target of their account of justification.

Such is how the dialectic goes when JJ is not in the picture. We leave it to the reader to evaluate the moderate externalists' responses. But consider how significantly less plausible they are when considering similar counterexamples when JJ is in the picture. Moderate externalists who accept JJ not only have to say that two subjects who differ only in how reliable they are can differ in what they are justified in believing. They also have to say that the subjects can differ in what they are justified in doing. This is counterintuitive. Do the same responses that radical externalists can invoke in the theoretical case apply to the practical case as well?

First, moderate externalists can, as in the belief case, just report that they don't find it intuitive that two subjects with the same internally available reasons, who differ only in their reliability, are justified in doing the same things. We expect few will stake much on such a reply, not the least because the intuition they're denying is so plausible. But what of the second response? In the belief case, the externalist worried that the counterexamples pumped intuitions about a deontological conception of justification for believing that A requires doxastic voluntarism and B is not the sort of justification relevant to knowledge. But the worry about doxastic voluntarism has no traction at all when it comes to what subjects are justified in doing, because actions can obviously be voluntary. And, when it comes to B, it is harder to specify, in the case of action, what alternative to the deontological conception of justification the externalist has in mind. There is no such thing as the *justification for action required for knowledge*.

We don't take this case to seal the deal against moderate externalism, but it does display how our principles make it difficult to separate too sharply views about the justification of belief from views about the justification of action.

2.3 Worry #3: JJ entails infallibilism

KJ does not entail infallibilism, though the combination of KJ and fallibilism entails impurism about knowledge. Impurism may be a hard pill to swallow, but it is not trivially false. What seems trivially false, though, is the denial of the following principle

(Justified) If S is justified in believing *p*, then anyone who is at least as well justified in believing *p* as S is also justified in believing *p*.

This principle seems guaranteed to be true simply by the fact that 'justified' is a gradable adjective.

JJ doesn't entail that Justified is false. But as we noted, JJ, together with fallibilism, rules out purism, and so rules in the possibility of variation in whether a subject is justified in believing something holding fixed strength of epistemic position, and in particular holding fixed strength of justification. So, if fallibilism is true, JJ seems to require the falsity of Justified. But the denial of Justified isn't just implausible (one might think); it's trivially false. So, JJ doesn't merely lead to counterintuitive consequences when combined with fallibilism; it entails infallibilism.[12]

Principles like Justified certainly seem trivially true of other gradable adjectives:[13]

(Tall) If S is tall, then anyone who is at least as tall as S is also tall.

(Flat) If X is flat, then anything at least as flat as X is also flat.

The standards for being flat or being tall, of course, might vary with context. But assuming that instances of Tall and Flat are each uttered within a single context, it seems they are each true, and trivially so. Why think Justified is any different?

In general, we can speak of being justified *simpliciter* in doing or believing something as well as being justified *to some degree* in doing or believing something. It was a binary notion we had in mind in the last chapter in

[12] This sort of concern is raised by Ram Neta (2007*b*).

[13] For this reason, we cannot accept the simple solution Sosa (2007: 97 n. 2) offers to a similar worry about his claim that 'a performance is apt only if its success is *sufficiently* attributable to the performer's competence'. His worry is that this claim 'leads to the awkward result that one of two performances can be more apt than the other, without either one being apt'. If this claim is awkward, then it is more awkward still if, paralleling Justified, one of two performances can be more apt than the other, while only the less apt performance is apt.

Sosa responds to this worry by comparing aptness to 'such threshold-dependent categories as that of being tall, large, heavy, etc.', noting that '[t]hese are all cases in which x can be more F than y without either x or y being F'. But even if this response succeeds in defusing the awkwardness of Sosa's claim, it needs some work if it is to defuse the 'more awkward' parallel to Justified.

using the locution 'p justifies you in ϕ-ing'. There we noted that 'justifies' could be given either an obligating or a permitting reading.[14] But, regardless of which of these one chooses, how do the binary notions—understood in terms of 'should' or 'is permitted'—hook up to graded notions of justification? Our proposal is this: you are $\text{justified}_{\text{binary}}$ in ϕ-ing iff you are $\text{justified}_{\text{graded}}$ well enough in ϕ-ing that you should (or: are permitted to) ϕ. Thus, you are $\text{justified}_{\text{binary}}$ in believing that p iff you are $\text{justified}_{\text{graded}}$ well enough in believing that p that you should (or: are permitted to) believe that p.[15]

Now, suppose we unpack Justified in accord with our proposal. We arrive at:

> (Justified Enough) If S is justified well enough in believing that p so that S should believe that p, then anyone who is at least as well justified in believing p as S is also justified well enough so that that person, too, should believe that p.[16]

This is no more trivially true than is either of:

> (Tall Enough) If S is tall enough to do her job, then anyone (say S*) who is at least as tall as S is tall enough to do *her* (S*'s) job.

[14] That you should believe entails that you should not withhold belief and should not disbelieve. It might be also taken to entail a positive obligation to believe, but some take issue with this entailment. Jon Kvanvig (forthcoming, 2009), for example, has argued that even when you shouldn't withhold or disbelieve, it might not be obligatory to believe. It might remain not obligatory because you have simply not given the matter any thought. Were you to give the matter thought, your strength of justification might ensure you wouldn't be rational to disbelieve or withhold: you'd have to believe. But prior to giving it thought, you aren't violating any obligations in not believing.

We are happy to concede this point, as well as a second: if, though you are justified in believing that p, you nonetheless withhold on or disbelieve that p, you might fail to be blameworthy. You might so fail because doxastic voluntarism is false and one isn't blameworthy for something one was unable to control. Still, to be justified in believing entails that believing is the attitude to have of the three attitudes. One way to cash out what this means is as a conditional of the sort Feldman uses to characterize a version of what he and Conee call 'Evidentialism': 'if S has any doxastic attitude at all toward p at t and S's evidence at t supports p, then S epistemically ought to have the attitude toward p supported by S's evidence at t' (Conee and Feldman 2004*a*: 178). Using Feldman's strategy, 'of the three attitudes, you should believe' is equivalent to, 'if you have any attitude at all, you should believe'.

[15] How the graded notion of *S is* $\textit{justified}_{\text{graded}}$ *in* ϕ-ing should be cashed out will depend on ϕ. In the case of belief, the most natural approach is to appeal to degree of propositional justification as a basis for degree of justification for belief.

[16] We opt for the obligating reading rather than the permitting one. This is mere stipulation, though an important one, as we will see when we turn to the defense of the Equivalence Thesis, in Chapter 5.

(Flat Enough) If X is flat enough for the purpose it is put to, then anything (say, X*) at least as flat as X is also flat enough for the purpose *it* (X*) is put to.[17]

Justified, then, construed as we are construing it—as Justified Enough—is not trivially true. And if it isn't, the case for claiming that JJ entails infallibilism is undermined.

For all we have argued, there might be some ordinary concept of binary justified belief which is independent of *being justified enough so that one should (or is permitted to) believe*, in the same way that the ordinary concept of *tall* is plausibly independent of the concept of being *tall enough to do one's job*. If so, then our principle JJ is not about that concept. But the concept we have described is surely one that is central to much epistemological discussion and is certainly not foreign to ordinary thought. We're happy to stipulate a reading for JJ in terms of that concept.

3 A BICONDITIONAL FOR JUSTIFICATION

3.1 Can the unjustified justify?

Because falsehoods can justify, the converse of KJ—that if p is warranted enough to justify you in ϕ-ing, for any ϕ, you know that p—is false. This obstacle does not stand in the way of the converse of JJ. Therefore, though we can't get a biconditional version of KJ, perhaps we can for JJ. Perhaps, if p is warranted enough to justify you in ϕ-ing, for any ϕ, then you are justified in believing that p. Though the converse of JJ doesn't bear on our case against fallibilist purism about justification for believing, it is of independent philosophical interest.

If p is warranted enough to justify you in ϕ-ing for any ϕ, must you be justified in believing p? At least regarding belief, an assumption of this sort is familiar from formulations of the epistemic regress problem, and of course the claim that if p is warranted enough to justify further beliefs then you are justified in believing p is *stronger* than the claim that if p is warranted

[17] Justified Enough is still more plausible than either Tall Enough or Flat Enough, even if it isn't trivially true. Why? Our diagnosis is that its plausibility just amounts to the plausibility of purism. To deny the conjunction of JJ and fallibilism simply because that conjunction entails the denial of Justified Enough is just to deny the conjunction because it entails impurism. This may be worth doing. But we leave until Chapter 7 discussion of such choices.

enough to justify any ϕ then you are justified in believing p. So, we will focus, throughout this section, on the theoretical case—on ϕ restricted to believings.

When considering the source of the justification for some ordinary, inferentially justified belief—say, that Clinton won more delegates than Obama on Super Tuesday—we start by giving the reasons we inferred it from. We can then ask about the justificatory status of those reasons. Here is BonJour's canonical (1986) continuation of the story:

> *Prima facie*, there seem to be only four basic possibilities with regard to the eventual outcome of this potential regress of epistemic justification: (i) the regress might terminate with beliefs for which no justification of any kind is available, even though they were earlier offered as justifying premises; (ii) the regress might proceed infinitely backwards with ever more new premise-beliefs being introduced and then themselves requiring justification; (iii) the regress might circle back upon itself, so that at some point beliefs which appeared earlier in the sequence of justifying arguments are appealed to again as premises; (iv) the regress might terminate because beliefs are reached which are justified—unlike those in alternative (i)—but whose justification does not depend inferentially on other empirical beliefs, and thus does not raise any further issue of justification with respect to such beliefs. (97 ff.)

This is an epistemic regress *problem* because each of the various options appears to have insuperable difficulties. In particular, regarding option (i), BonJour remarks that 'if this alternative were correct, empirical knowledge would rest ultimately on beliefs which were, from an epistemic standpoint at least, entirely arbitrary and hence incapable of conferring any genuine justification' (98).

BonJour's case against option (i), then, is that if a belief were not itself justified, it would be 'incapable of conferring any genuine justification'. For a belief to be capable of conferring genuine justification, it must itself be justified. Call this *BonJour's principle*. It is not the converse of JJ (even restricted to belief—through the end of 3.1.2 this qualifier will be omitted unless otherwise noted). JJ is about justification in believing, not justified belief. But presumably the regress problem is not simply a problem for justified belief. If it's a problem at all, it's a problem for how we get justified in believing anything, whether we believe it or not.

This is not just a coincidence. It is suggested by the relation between your being justified in believing that p and your belief that p being justified. p can justify you in believing q, even if you don't believe q. And p can justify you in believing q even if you believe q and your belief that q is unjustified. Your belief that *q* might not be based on *p* and in fact might be based on some unjustified belief, for the belief might stem from wishful thinking, prejudice, etc. But, if *p* justifies you in believing *q*, and you base your belief that *q* on *p*, then your belief that *q* is justified. More officially:

> (Connecting Principle) Your belief that *p* justifies your belief that *q* iff *p* justifies you in believing that *q* and your belief that *q* is based on your belief that *p*.[18]

Epistemologists differ on how to understand the basing relation. But there is broad agreement that justified belief is connected to being justified in believing in the way specified.

The connecting principle is plausible, and so is BonJour's principle. If these could be used to argue for JJ's converse, we would have a strong case. We *can* argue as follows. Suppose you are not justified in believing that *p*, but you nonetheless believe that *p*. Can *p* justify you in believing that *q*? Suppose it can. It seems perfectly possible for a belief that *q* to be based on your unjustified belief that *p*. Therefore, by the connecting principle, your belief that *p* justifies your belief that *q*. This violates BonJour's principle. So, if both BonJour's principle and the connecting principle are true, it follows that:

> *p*, when believed, justifies you in believing *q* only if you are justified in believing that *p*.

This is still not quite JJ's converse, though. JJ's converse says that no proposition—believed or not—can justify you in believing something unless you are justified in believing it. To derive JJ's converse, we need a separate argument for thinking that the restriction 'when believed' can be removed *salve veritate*.

It might seem obvious that no such argument will be forthcoming. Surely, there can be facts which make you justified in believing something even if those facts themselves are beyond your ken, and so even if you aren't justified in believing they obtain. Whatever one says about the facts that make you justified in believing certain propositions—whether one goes internalist or externalist—those facts can make you justified simply by their obtaining.

18 One might think that the right side of the connecting principle isn't sufficient for the left side because, for your belief that *p* to justify your belief that *q*, it is required, in addition, that your belief that *q* be based on your belief that *p* justified you in believing that *q*. This requirement is plausible, however, only if *p* does not itself justify you in believing that *q*. For, if *p* alone justifies you in believing that *q*, then the justifier for *q* does not include the fact that *p* justifies you in believing that *q*. It is implausible, then, that you would need to base your belief that *q* on this irrelevant fact.

We do not deny this. When we speak of *p* justifying you, we have in mind of course its being a justifying *reason* you have, and this is a very different notion than that-*p*'s being a justification-maker, being that in virtue of which you are justified. As Jack Lyons (2008: 465–6) points out, we might say that, for Descartes, the fact that you clearly and distinctly perceive that you exist is what justifies you in believing that you exist, and we might also say that it's the fact that you think which on the Cartesian view justifies you in believing that you exist. But when we make these two claims about the Cartesian view, we are using 'justifies' in two different ways. When we say that the fact that you clearly and distinctly perceive that you exist justifies you in believing you exist, we are talking about the fact in virtue of which you are justified in thinking that you exist. When we say that the fact that you think justifies you in believing you exist, we are talking about your justifying reason for thinking you exist. Descartes is not saying that your *reasons* for thinking you exist have anything to do with clear and distinct perception, and nor is he saying that the fact that you think is what makes it the case that you are justified in believing you exist.[19]

We might worry about justification-makers and justifying reasons being so distinct when it comes to single beliefs. If what makes your belief justified is independent of your justifying reasons, then we might wonder what your justifying reasons are contributing. But a justification-maker can be about the possession of a justifying reason. So, e.g. on a reasonable interpretation of the Cartesian view, what makes it the case that you are justified in believing you exist—at least when you're entertaining the *cogito* argument—is the fact that you clearly and distinctly perceive that you think and that you clearly and distinctly perceive that if you think, you exist. But justification-makers can be independent of justifying reasons, especially if it's possible for beliefs to be made justified in the absence of any justifying reasons. For example, perhaps the fact that your belief was delivered by a reliable process makes the belief justified even if you have no justifying reasons for the belief. There is still a difference between a belief made justified in that way and a belief that is justified by a reason.

So, epistemologists of all stripes will want to make such a distinction. A justifying reason you have is something you are in a position to put to work as a basis for belief; a justification-maker needn't be. A justifying reason can

[19] In Lyons' terminology, the relevant distinction is between evidential justifiers and metaphysical justifiers (465).

be false; a justification-maker can't be. The existence of justification-makers which you are not justified in believing does not, by itself, pose an obstacle to JJ's converse, since justification-makers need not be justifying reasons. JJ's converse, specified appropriately, says only that if p is warranted enough to be a justifying reason you have for believing q, then you are justified in believing p.

There are two remaining obstacles to removing the 'when believed' proviso and accepting the biconditional version of JJ.

3.1.1 Givenism

It is almost orthodoxy in epistemology that you can be justified in believing something in virtue of the fact that you have certain sorts of experiences, i.e. that such facts figure in justification-makers. The view is shared by epistemologists as diverse as Conee and Feldman (2004*a*), Huemer (2001), BonJour (2001), Fumerton (2001) and (1995), Sosa (1991), Pollock (1986), and Goldman (1979). But this is not *givenism*, at least as we will be using that term. According to givenism, experiential states do not, or do not merely, help to make it the case that you are justified in believing certain propositions; they are themselves justifying reasons you have.

When givenists say experiences are reasons they usually illustrate what they mean by saying that certain sorts of experience-to-belief transitions amount to *reasoning* and not mere causal processes. But if such a transition can be reasoning, there must be something like a good argument, abstractly conceived, which is recoverable from the transition and recoverable in such a way that the transition can be seen as your reasoning from the premises in that argument to the conclusion. One can find corresponding abstract arguments not merely for paradigm cases of belief–belief transitions but for certain transitions involving beliefs and intentions (e.g. means–end inferences such as 'I'm going to achieve E; the only way to achieve E is if I do M, so I'm going to do M'). Givenism stands or falls with the question of whether there are good arguments corresponding to the relevant experience–belief transitions.

If givenism is true, then, isn't JJ's converse false? For won't there be justifying reasons you have which are such that you are not justified in believing them? Not necessarily. To have a counterexample to JJ's converse, we need something of the form that-p—a proposition—to be warranted enough to be a justifying reason for you even though you aren't justified in believing it. If the 'good arguments' the givenist takes to correspond with experience–belief transitions do not associate experiences with premises of the form that-*p*, then there is no conflict with JJ's converse.

Alan Millar (1991), for example, who has worked through this problem for givenism thoroughly, agrees that for the experience–belief transition to amount to reasoning, there must be a corresponding abstract inferential structure, or at least something close enough: Millar calls them 'quasi-inferences' (116). They have experiential *types* as premises—e.g. a visual red-apple type of experience (for him this is understood as *the type of visual experience one typically has in the relevant conditions when in the presence of a red apple*)—and propositions about how things are—e.g. there is a red apple before me—as conclusions.[20] These are not really inferences, but they are close enough because they are, in a sense, truth-preserving, and possession of the concepts involved in quasi-inferences guarantees that one is disposed to undergo the corresponding experience–belief transition. Our aim isn't to evaluate this account, but merely to point out that it is fully consistent with JJ's converse. Experiential types are not themselves propositions. So, while an experience token or type might be said to be a reason for Millar, in having such an experience one does not have anything of the form that-*p* as a reason.

A 'good argument' corresponding to the experience–belief transition can't match an experience with a premise *about that experience*: in forming a belief in response to an experience as of something blue, you don't reason from *I am having an experience as of something blue.* If it did, then it seems perfectly legitimate to demand that you be justified in believing it: the force of the givenist response to the converse of JJ was that there might be justifying reasons that you are not justified in believing because they are not the sorts of things that admit of belief. (Of course, a fact of this form might be a justification-maker; but that's not the sort of view under discussion here.) In short, either the givenist construes the givenist justifying reasons non-propositionally—in which case they don't present a counterexample to JJ—or propositionally—in which case the givenist response that you need not be justified in believing them is not persuasive.

But perhaps, counterintuitively, if non-propositional contents of experience can serve as justifying reasons without being themselves justified, there

[20] Millar also includes among the premises a proposition about the absence of defeating conditions.

are propositional contents of experience that can.[21] Of course, once we allow this, we might as well allow all sorts of other propositional contents—even ones that aren't contents of experience—to serve as justifying reasons without being themselves justified. It is this general—and bolder—response to JJ's converse that we turn to next.

3.1.2 Hinge propositions

Philosophers in the Wittgensteinian tradition argue that there are so-called 'hinge propositions' that serve as prerequisites for our being justified in believing anything at all even though they themselves are not known, nor are things we are justified in believing.

Hinge propositions include propositions as diverse as '2 + 2 = 4' (Wittgenstein *On Certainty*: §455), 'Other human beings have blood and call it "blood" '(§340), 'I am in England' (§421), 'Motor cars don't grow out of the earth' (§279), and, of course, 'There are physical objects' (§35). One thing that unifies these propositions, it is claimed, is that they are not themselves supported by evidence. To be supported by evidence, the evidence in their favor would have to have more to be said in its favor than the hinge propositions themselves, which is impossible. But, despite their lack of support, they are immune from doubt:

> That is to say, the *questions* we raise and our *doubts* depend on the fact that some propositions are exempt from doubt, are as it were like hinges on which those turn. (§341)

[21] One way this might be fleshed out is by claiming that in responding to the experience by forming the belief you are reasoning from the content of the experience, which is not itself about your experience, but about the world. When you believe that this is blue on the basis of an experience as of something being blue, the corresponding inferential structure is: *this is blue, therefore this is blue.* This is often interpreted as McDowell's (1993) view, at least in rough outlines (though he would reject the label 'givenist'), so we will call it the 'standard' interpretation. We cannot enter into a full discussion of McDowell here, but notice that on other interpretations of McDowell, according to which the experiential state itself justifies the belief, but without providing anything like a proposition or content that fits into an inferential structure, there is no longer any conflict with JJ's converse. On the standard interpretation, however, the strategy fails. We see two problems here. The less serious of the two is that this inferential structure is trivial and so it is hard to see how, if the experience–belief transition amounts to reasoning from p to p, one can *become* justified in the belief that p in undergoing the transition, which any givenist must say does happen. Second, though, if p is a reason you have to believe that p, as the present account requires, then it is extremely hard to see how it could ever be overridden. If among your reasons for believing that this is blue is *this is blue*, then no propositions about the abnormal lighting conditions, etc. is going to defeat it. On the view being considered, then, when you have an experience with the content *this is blue*, you automatically have a justifying reason to believe that this is blue. And that is false.

> But it isn't that the situation is like this: We just *can't* investigate everything, and for that reason we are forced to rest content with assumption. If I want the door to turn, the hinges must stay put. (§343)

Hinge propositions present an obstacle for the converse of JJ if they can justify beliefs without being themselves justified. It is not obvious from §§ 341 and 343 alone that hinge propositions serve as justifying reasons for dubitable beliefs rather than as necessary presuppositions for doubt. There are other, more plausible, potential roles for hinge propositions that would not put them at odds with the converse of JJ, even assuming that they are not generally justified or known.

For example, the holding fixed of hinge propositions may be a prerequisite for other propositions to be justified, but their being held fixed wouldn't make them justified, and nor could *they* be justifying reasons for other beliefs. On this sort of view, the holding fixed of hinge propositions is an essential enabling condition for one to be justified in believing anything. A close alternative is to think of the holding fixed of hinge propositions as more than a mere enabling condition, and as indeed part of the justification-maker for justified beliefs, though again without being either justified themselves or capable of serving as justifying reasons.

These two interpretations of the justificatory relevance of hinge propositions are plausible interpretations of Wittgenstein. But neither presents any difficulty for the converse of JJ, which requires that any proposition that is warranted enough to be a justifying reason for belief is justified. If hinge propositions play either of these two roles, then even if they can't be justified, they do not falsify the converse of JJ. To falsify the converse of JJ, hinge propositions would need to be justifying reasons for belief. We think this is a less plausible interpretation of Wittgenstein, because it would saddle him with the view that we have a huge class of reasons for otherwise dubitable ordinary beliefs to which we don't ever appeal to justify those beliefs in any ordinary language game. When would we have opportunity in ordinary discourse to justify even a dubitable assertion with the claim that motor cars don't grow out of the earth or, even, the claim that there are physical objects?

Even if hinge propositions can be justifying reasons, they only present a counterexample to JJ if they are not in those instances justified. Some interpreters of Wittgenstein (e.g. Pritchard (2001) and Hazlett (2006)) think that hinge propositions do, in fact, enjoy positive epistemic status and are knowable and/or justified, respectively. But the more standard interpretation is that the hinges do not and cannot enjoy positive epistemic status. For many interpreters, the reason that the hinges cannot enjoy such status is that they are not themselves propositional. According to Danièle Moyal-Sharrock (2003), for example, our objective certainty about hinges

> is not a *coming-to-see* type of certainty; it is not of the order of knowing, justification, reason or reflection, and is therefore immune to mistake, doubt, or falsification—for where no epistemic route was followed, no epistemic fault is possible. It is a nonpropositional, ungrounded certainty which manifests itself ineffably *in* what we say and do. To be certain, here, means to *be unwaveringly and yet thoughtlessly hinged* on something which *enables* us to think, speak or act meaningfully. (131)

And, from Avrum Stroll (1994):

> [W]hat Wittgenstein is calling *hinge propositions* are not ordinary propositions at all. Such concepts as being true or false, known or not known, justified or unjustified do not apply to them, and these are usually taken to be the defining features of propositions. (146)

The textual evidence in Wittgenstein seems strong. For example:

> Giving grounds, however, justifying the evidence, comes to an end;—but the end is not certain 'propositions' striking us immediately as true, i.e. it is not a kind of *seeing* on our part; it is our *acting* which lies at the bottom of the language game. (*On Certainty*, §204)
>
> As if giving grounds did not come to an end sometime. But the end is not an ungrounded presupposition: it is an ungrounded way of acting. (§110)

It does not strictly follow from these oft-quoted passages that the hinges are not propositional, nor does it follow that they are not justified. What follows is only that, if they are propositional and justified, what justifies them is not any sort of evidence, including *a priori* intuition, nor is it merely nothing at all, but rather a certain way of acting. Nonetheless, there are enough philosophers who either take Wittgenstein as denying that the hinges are justified, or argue this way themselves that it is a position worth taking seriously.

Again, if the only reason that hinges cannot be justified is that they are not propositions, then they do not constitute a counterexample to the converse of JJ, which is explicitly about *propositions* that can justify. To make for a genuine counterexample to the converse of JJ, the Wittgensteinian must say that hinge propositions are genuine propositions, which can be among your justifying reasons even though you aren't justified in believing them. We'll suppose that something enough like this is the Wittgensteinian view.

If hinge propositions can be justifying reasons, then, in reasoning from them, they can justify beliefs. In reasoning from them you either believe them or you don't. Suppose you believe them. Then, we have a problematic result: although you believe hinge propositions you aren't justified in believing them. How could something you believe but aren't justified in believing justify you in believing other things? We can't demand of beliefs that they confer an epistemic status on other beliefs that they aren't able to instantiate themselves. Suppose, on the other hand, that in reasoning from hinge propositions, you don't believe them. You must be related to them by some mental state or attitude in order to reason from them. The question, then, is whether we can make sense of how this state—call it a *holding-fast* if you like—could be anything other than a belief.

Wittgensteinians typically do not speak of the hinges as things you have any sort of justification for—not justification in believing, certainly, but not even justification for holding fast. As Wittgenstein says: 'My *life* consists in my being content to accept many things' (§344). It seems to be the fact that you are *content* to accept or hold fast the hinges rather than the fact that you are *justifiably* content to do so which allows the hinges to play their justificatory role. But this is problematic if, as we are assuming, the hinges are propositions and holding-fast is a mental state or attitude (as it must be if you are to reason from hinge propositions). For then there are other related attitudes you in principle could have to a hinge proposition (and which you might well have later in your life, when the 'river-bed' shifts): you could *hold its negation fast* and you could *withhold your holding-fast* from the proposition. If you are in no sense *justified* in holding fast a hinge proposition rather than in holding fast its negation or withholding on both, it is very hard to see how the fact that you hold it fast allows it to justify. If you managed to hold fast the negation of *other human beings have blood*, you surely couldn't acquire justified beliefs by reasoning from it.

More recently, though they do not mention Wittgenstein or the term 'hinge', Gilbert Harman and Brett Sherman (2004) argue that 'what one knows can and usually does rest on assumptions one *justifiably* takes for granted without knowing them to be true' (493, emphasis added) and without being justified in believing them to be true. Whereas Wittgensteinian hinges are not justified in any sense, Harman and Sherman's 'takings-for-granted' can be justified (which is not to say that Wittgenstein couldn't be interpreted in a way that makes him closer to Harman and Sherman).

But what is the justificatory role of the proposition justifiedly taken for granted? They write:

> Sam knows he owns a car that is presently outside in front of his house. It seems intuitively correct to us that Sam's knowledge rests on various assumptions that he does not know but justifiably takes for granted... He is justified in taking it for granted that he is not dreaming, but that does not mean that, having taken that for granted, he knows that he is not dreaming. Nor, having taken it for granted, is he then justified in believing he is not dreaming. (493)

Here it is not clear that Harman and Sherman want to say that *I am not dreaming* is what justifies Sam in believing that he owns a car that is presently outside in front of his house. If they don't, then their account of 'taking for granted' does not present a difficulty for the converse of JJ. For their account to present a problem, we have to take it that that *I am not dreaming* can (partly) justify Sam in believing that he owns a car that is presently outside in front of his house. Strictly, the entire justifying reason would be a conjunction of justified beliefs and propositions justifiedly taken for granted of the form 'I parked it there last night and it hasn't been stolen and I'm not dreaming, etc.'. This conjunction must itself be justifiedly taken for granted: it surely is not justifiedly believed, according to Harman and Sherman, for many of the conjuncts are only justifiedly taken for granted, not justifiedly believed.

Call propositions which, when we justifiedly take them for granted, can justify us in believing other things, 'assumptions'. We want to raise three worries about this maneuver.

First, assumptions seem awfully similar to beliefs. They are mental states that can move one to form beliefs, to form the appropriate intentions, plans, etc. Unlike what we normally call 'assumptions' (or, for that matter, 'takings for granted') these assumptions can't be justified merely because they simplify reasoning. So, e.g. in calculating the velocity of a falling body, you might 'assume' that it isn't subject to air friction. You are perfectly justified in that 'assumption'. But surely this can't justify you in *believing* consequences like *there are no molecules in the air to provide resistance.* Like beliefs, and unlike what we in ordinary life often call 'assumptions', the relevant assumptions seem to be justified only if the proposition in question is sufficiently epistemically probable (this can be seen by thinking about the gambles you would be rational to take). We will focus in more detail on belief in the next chapter, but we can even now say that we see every reason to call Harman and Sherman's assumptions 'beliefs'.

Second, according to the assumption maneuver, if you justifiably assume *p*, *p* can justify you in believing *q*, even though you aren't justified in believing *p*. But *q* might entail *p*, and you might know it does. Can you really be justified in believing something, know it entails something else, but not be justified in believing that something else? Suppose you justifiedly believe that your car is parked outside in front of your house. You'll know that if it's parked outside the front of your house, it hasn't been stolen and driven away. So aren't you justified in believing the latter? Yet, according to Harman and Sherman, the latter is exactly one of the assumptions needed to get justified in believing the former. Therefore, you can't be justified in believing the latter.

Harman and Sherman respond to this worry by denying closure. This is of course a controversial response, and one might wonder if we have been given good reasons for biting this bullet. But they might say that denying closure is a real possibility if there are cases in which, although you are justified in believing that *p*, and you know *p* entails *q*, *p* isn't fitted to be a reason to believe *q*. So, perhaps *my car has not been stolen* isn't fitted to be a reason to believe *my car is where I parked it.* Why not? Because the latter is epistemically *prior* to the former.

So, perhaps the following requirement is plausible:

> *p* can justify you in believing that *q* only if *q* is not epistemically prior to *p*.

If this principle is true, we can see why *the car is outside in front of the house*—though justifiedly believed—can't justify believing that the car hasn't been stolen. The latter is epistemically prior to the former. We can also see why, although *the car hasn't been stolen* can justify or help to justify believing that the car is parked outside in front of the house, it can't justify believing that anyone who tried to steal the car failed, again because the latter is epistemically prior to the former.

But, now, what's to stop the latter—that anyone who tried to steal the car failed—from justifying belief in the former—the car hasn't been stolen? After all, this inference is valid:

> Anyone who tried to steal the car failed.
>
> Therefore, the car hasn't been stolen.

The premise is epistemically prior to the conclusion, or else we lose an explanation for why the inference can't be run the other way around.

Therefore, as long as you are justified in assuming the premise, it should be able to justify you in *believing* the conclusion. Does it justify you in having that belief? Harman and Sherman will say that you are justified in *assuming* the conclusion—that the car hasn't been stolen. But if this is right, you had better be justified in at least assuming the premise that anyone who tried to steal the car failed. The conclusion, after all, is equivalent to the premise. So, presumably, you are justified in assuming the premise. Why, then, are you not justified in *believing*—and not merely assuming—the conclusion? The epistemic priority requirement is no help here.

In general, the problem is that there are known-to-be mutually entailing pairs of propositions both of which are mere justified assumptions, one of which is epistemically prior to the other. If there are such pairs then, although one can appeal to the epistemic priority requirement to explain why you can't justifiably believe the epistemically prior proposition based on the posterior one, one needs some other account of why you can't justifiably believe the epistemically posterior one based on the epistemically prior one. In the absence of such an account, it is hard to see why the epistemically prior cannot provide a route to justified *belief* in the epistemically posterior. It looks like some of the so-called *mere justified assumptions* will be propositions you are justified in believing. But if some are, it is not clear why you *must* remain unjustified in believing any of them. One would have to argue that there is a foundational set of assumptions, F, that are epistemically posterior to no other propositions, the justified assumption of which would otherwise justify believing members of F. We are not optimistic about the prospects.[22]

For these three reasons, we doubt that, in the end, considerations about hinge propositions (or assumptions) pose a serious obstacle to the acceptance of JJ's converse, and so to the acceptance of the full biconditional version of JJ:

> You are justified in believing p iff p is warranted enough to justify you in ϕ-ing, for any ϕ.

As we saw in Section 1, the left-to-right direction is all that is needed to mount the argument against fallibilist purism about justification for belief,

[22] Notice that it will not help Harman and Sherman to, as Michael Williams does, make the epistemic priority relationship vary with context. (See Williams (1996), esp. pp. 123–5.) For Harman and Sherman's proposal to work, given the possibility of contextual variation in epistemic priority relations, in each context there would be have to be a foundational set of assumptions of the required sort. Again, the outlook is not encouraging.

but that the full biconditional is true is of general philosophical interest to those concerned with necessary and sufficient conditions for justification in believing.

3.2 Hawthorne and Stanley's biconditional

It is worth closing with some brief remarks on how our biconditional version of JJ compares to a similar biconditional defended by Hawthorne and Stanley in their (2008):

The Reasons-Knowledge Principle

(RK) When one's choice is *p*-dependent, it is appropriate to treat the proposition that *p* as a reason for acting iff you know that *p*.

The most obvious difference between RK and the biconditional version of JJ is that RK concerns knowledge. This is no small difference. We think when one's choice is *p*-dependent, it can be perfectly appropriate to treat *p* as a reason for acting even though one fails to know *p*, provided that one is justified in believing *p*. And this is because, when nothing non-epistemic is standing in the way (as is often the case when one's choice is *p*-dependent), if one is justified in believing *p* then *p* is a reason one has for performing the relevant action. Justification in believing that *p* ensures that nothing epistemic stands in the way (that one's warrant is strong enough), so if nothing non-epistemic stands in the way, *p is among one's reasons for action.* And if it is, it is appropriate to treat it as such.

Hawthorne and Stanley will presumably deny that being justified in believing a proposition, or even having knowledge-level justification for a proposition, is enough to ensure that *p* is warranted enough to be among one's reasons for action; the proposition must be true, and indeed known. We will not rehearse our arguments from Section 2.1 concerning whether falsehoods can be justifiers or reasons. But even if those arguments fail, Stanley and Hawthorne require more than the claim that only truths or facts can be reasons. They require it to be the case that it is always inappropriate to *treat* false propositions as reasons. But surely it is *appropriate* for such a subject who is justified in believing that *p* to treat *p* as a reason, even if it isn't a reason because it is false or because the subject is Gettiered.

In particular, as we mentioned above, it is highly plausible that if two subjects have all the same very strong evidence for *my glass contains gin*, believe that proposition on the basis of this evidence, and then act on the belief in reaching to take a drink, those two subjects are equally justified in their actions and equally justified in treating what they each did as a reason, even if one of them, the unlucky one, has cleverly disguised petrol in his glass rather than gin. Notice that if we asked the unlucky fellow why he did such a thing, he might reply with indignation: 'Well, it was the perfectly rational thing to do; I had every reason to think the glass contained gin; why in the world should I think that someone would be going around putting petrol in cocktail glasses!?' Here the unlucky subject, in our view, is not providing an excuse for his action or treating what he did as a reason; he is *defending it* as the action that made the most sense for him to do and the proposition that made most sense to treat as a reason. He is providing a justification, not an excuse.[23]

We think RK is best reformulated by replacing knowledge with justification:

(RJ) When one's choice is p-dependent, it is appropriate to treat the proposition that p as a reason for acting iff you are justified in believing that p.

Is the biconditional version of JJ just a recapitulation of RJ? JJ, of course, unlike RJ, does not limit the attitudes that believing that p can justify to actions: p, if justified, can justify ϕ-ing, for any ϕ. Hawthorne and Stanley, though, mean their principles to be paired with analogous principles concerning belief, e.g. 'Treat the proposition that p as a reason for believing q only if one knows that p', and cite as an advantage for their principle that 'it unifies the practical and theoretical domain of reasons: if it is correct, then proper reasons for belief and reasons for action have a uniform nature'. The

23 We cannot enter in any detailed way into the literature on the distinction between justification and excuses. We will only quote approvingly from a recent paper on the topic by Marcia Baron: '[T]o say that an action is justified is to say (insofar as we focus on the action, rather than the agent) that though the action is of a type that is usually wrong, in these circumstances it was not wrong. To say that an action is excused, by contrast, is to say that it was indeed wrong (and the agent did commit the act we are saying was wrong), but the agent is not blameworthy' (2005: 389–90). Much here hangs on the interpretation of 'wrong', though we would agree with Baron that wrongness must not be understood as a purely objective notion. Consider an example. If you could have made your son's violin recital but became engrossed in your work, you can offer your engrossment in your work as an excuse. In doing so, you are arguing that you deserve less blame than might be accorded you, although you concede that you shouldn't have done what you did. By contrast, suppose that your son's recital time was moved up by an hour but the email informing you of this arrives hours late, right at the time the recital is beginning. In this case, you will defend your not being there at the start of the concert as something any reasonable person in your situation would do. You would claim that you were not in the wrong and, in fact, that you were justified in the sense that it would have been wrong—silly—to show up earlier.

biconditional version of JJ combines the practical and theoretical principles into a single principle. But this is not a dramatic difference from Hawthorne and Stanley's position; it can be remedied by replacing 'acting' in the RJ with 'ϕ-ing, for any ϕ' and moving from choices to questions:

> (RJ—modified) When the question of whether to ϕ is *p*-dependent for you, it is appropriate to treat the proposition that *p* as a reason for ϕ-ing, for any ϕ, iff you are justified in believing that *p*.

This principle includes a restriction about the relevance of *p* to the question of whether to ϕ. Hawthorne and Stanley include their choice-dependence restriction in all their biconditional principles because they think there are clear cases in which what one knows is irrelevant to the choice at hand, so it would be *in*appropriate to treat the proposition that *p* as a reason for acting in such cases. The same could be said concerning whether to ϕ generally: when this question isn't *p*-dependent for you it would be inappropriate to treat it as a reason to ϕ. Notice, though, that when it is inappropriate to treat *p* as a reason to ϕ because *p* is irrelevant to the question of whether to ϕ, so long as you are justified in believing that *p*, it isn't weaknesses in your epistemic position that stand in the way—rather, it's the lack of a connection between *p* and the question at hand. But this won't reflect poorly on your warrant for *p*. We can accommodate the worry motivating the inclusion of *p*-relevant restrictions by moving to:

> (RJ—doubly modified) *p* is warranted enough to be appropriately treated (by you) as a reason for ϕ-ing, for any ϕ, iff you are justified in believing that *p*.

The switch from *p*-dependent choices or questions to 'being warranted enough' will presumably strike some as the narcissism of small differences. We don't want to exaggerate the differences, but we think they are real. One can perfectly well ask why it is true that, when and only when you are justified in believing that *p*, *p* is appropriately treated as a reason to ϕ in *p*-dependent situations and not appropriately treated as a reason in other kinds of situations. The doubly modified principle (and our JJ) explains why: it's because justification (knowledge)—in *all* situations—suffices to make *p* warranted enough to be appropriately treated as a reason to ϕ. The unmodified RJ offers no such explanation.[24]

[24] Hawthorne and Stanley level similar charges at our previously published (2002) principle—in their words, that 'S knows that *p* only if it is no problem for S to act as if *p*'. For example, they

The doubly modified principle comes close to the biconditional version of JJ. Is there any difference between them? Because *p* justifies S in ϕ-ing just in case *p* is a justifying reason S has to ϕ, then according to the biconditional version of JJ, being justified in believing *p* is necessary and sufficient for *p* to be warranted enough to be a *justifying reason* S has to ϕ. According to the doubly modified principle above, being justified in believing that *p* is necessary and sufficient for *p* to be warranted enough to be *appropriately treated as a reason for* ϕ-ing.

There is one substantial difference between *p* being a justifying reason one has to ϕ and *p* being appropriately treated as a reason for ϕ-ing. '*p* is a justifying reason you have to ϕ' admits of a reading—a reading we have adopted—according to which you *should* ϕ, whereas '*p* is appropriately treated as a reason for ϕ-ing' is more plausibly read in terms of the permissibility of treating *p* as a reason for ϕ-ing. Hawthorne and Stanley don't go on to say whether this means that ϕ-ing is merely permissible. Assuming it doesn't, their principle does not go far enough: justification for believing determines not just what we may do but what we should do. They may be right that it is too demanding for a subject to 'treat as a reason' every relevant proposition she is justified in believing, if treating as a reason requires some sort of explicit consideration. But that's just an argument for putting the principle in terms of 'justifying' rather than 'treating as a reason'.

The differences between the biconditional version of JJ and Hawthorne and Stanley's original Knowledge-Reasons principle all lean toward the biconditional version of JJ. The larger philosophical interest in the necessary and sufficient conditions for being justified in believing, then, is best served by the biconditional version of JJ.

worry that this sort of principle isn't explanatorily deep. But a deep explanation of the link between action and knowledge is not necessary to build an argument against purism (or what we there called 'evidentialism'), which is the purpose of that paper. Likewise with respect to the charge that our earlier principle gets the order of explanation wrong: there is no order of explanation entailed by the principle. It is simply a necessarily true condition (we argue) on knowledge—a necessarily true condition that entails the falsity of purism (or so we argued). It's not that a deep explanation for the truth of our (2002) principle wouldn't be nice to have, though. And that's what we think JJ—and this book—provides (through $J^K J$ and the Equivalence Thesis).

5

Belief

1 INTRODUCING PRAGMATISM ABOUT BELIEF

We are more confident of the truth of some propositions than others. You are presumably more confident that the next British prime minister will be a Conservative than a Liberal Democrat. But if you are like us, you don't believe full-stop either of these propositions. The next prime minister could easily be Labour. We should allow, then, that there is such a thing as graded belief—roughly being more or less confident of the truth of a proposition. But there also seems to be such a thing as *outright* believing, which is binary. What is outright belief? Here is Jean-Paul Sartre (1993) on the matter:

> I *believe it*; that is, I allow myself to give in to all impulses to trust it; I decide to believe in it, and to maintain myself in this decision; I conduct myself, finally, as if I were certain of it—and all this in the synthetic unity of one and the same attitude. (346)

The view of (outright[1]) belief suggested by Sartre's remarks is pragmatic; it associates believing with a disposition to rely on a proposition as a basis for conduct. Sartre himself seems to take belief to involve a disposition—or better a willingness—to rely on a proposition in *any* sort of conduct.[2] Other weaker but still pragmatic conceptions of belief take it to involve dispositions to rely on a proposition only in some aspects of conduct, e.g. in making assertions or in mentally assenting.

William Clifford (1999) used a pragmatic view of belief to argue that our beliefs fall under a certain ethical norm: because 'it is not possible so to

[1] Unless explicitly noted we hereafter use 'believes' and its cognates to stand for outright belief rather than graded belief.

[2] Other philosophers who defend roughly this view of belief include Braithwaite (1932–3), Mellor (1980), Rudner (1953), Stalnaker (1984), and Weatherson (2005). James (1962) extends the pragmatic view to what is plausibly construed as degree of belief (or credences): 'the maximum of liveness in an hypothesis means willingness to act irrevocably. Practically, that means belief; but there is some believing tendency wherever there is willingness to act at all' (242).

sever the belief from the action it suggests as to condemn the one without condemning the other' (73) those with insufficient evidence for action 'have no right to believe on such evidence' either (72). We can see, then, that a pragmatic view of belief gives us at least some motivation for adopting a pragmatic norm for belief (though we do not agree with Clifford that the norm is ethical).[3]

The clear path from a pragmatic view of belief to a pragmatic norm on believing raises the question of whether there is also a path running the other way as well. If it were possible to sever the belief from the action it suggests, why would there be any pragmatic norm on believing? But we argued for a pragmatic norm on believing in the last chapter: what you are justified in believing must be warranted enough to justify you in acting (or believing or anything else). Are we, then, committed to a pragmatism—even a Sartreanism—about belief as well?

Recall, though, that the pragmatic norm itself was a natural extension of certain 'pragmatic' principles involving knowledge and knowledge-level justification: what you know is warranted enough to justify you in action or belief or anything else; and *p* is justified enough for you to know it iff *p* is warranted enough to justify you in action or belief or anything else (KJ and $J^K J$, respectively). Therefore, whether we are committed to a pragmatic view of belief depends on two issues. First, there is the issue of whether we were right to extend our principles to justified belief, as we did in the last chapter. Second, there is the issue of whether, if our epistemic principles can be correctly extended to justified belief, it follows that belief itself is pragmatic, and if it does follow, how strongly pragmatic belief must be: must you be disposed to rely on the proposition believed in any manner of conduct, as on the Sartrean view, or only some of your conduct, as on the assertion and assent views?

We consider both issues in detail in this chapter, and conclude that we are committed to at least a weak pragmatism about belief. Therefore, we also spend some time arguing that this commitment is not something to worry about; rather, it's a strength. But there is an additional worry, as well: because there is such a clear path from a pragmatic view of belief to the pragmatic norms we favor, it might seem that our project is fundamentally about belief not knowledge, and that therefore it is not fundamentally an epistemological

[3] James (1962) runs a similar argument, as well: 'Since belief is measured by action, he who forbids us to believe religion to be true necessarily also forbids us to act as we should if we did believe it to be true' (257 n. 4).

project, but a project in the philosophy of mind misleadingly characterized as epistemology. We close the chapter with a discussion of this worry.

2 FROM KNOWLEDGE-LEVEL JUSTIFICATION TO JUSTIFIED BELIEF

In the last chapter, we made an assumption which, if true, shows how our pragmatic principles about knowledge and knowledge-level justification extend to justified belief. We called this assumption *the Equivalence Thesis*:

> (The Equivalence Thesis) p is knowledge-level justified for you iff you are justified in believing that p.

That is: you are justified in believing something iff you are *justified enough* to know it, or in other words, iff no weaknesses in your justification stand in the way of your knowing it. If the Equivalence Thesis is true, then the pragmatic principle we endorsed about knowledge-level justification is true of justified belief, too. That is, Biconditional JJ is true:

> (Biconditional JJ) You are justified in believing that p iff p is warranted enough to justify you in ϕ-ing, for any ϕ.

We will not defend in any detail the left-to-right direction of the Equivalence Thesis. With the notable exception of radical externalists, whom we considered in the last chapter, few would suggest that it takes more justification to justifiably believe than it does to know. But the right-to-left direction is controversial. We are all familiar with remarks such as 'I believe the meeting is next Tuesday, but I don't know it is', or 'I believe my lottery ticket is a loser, but I don't know it is'. Doesn't the right-to-left direction of the Equivalence Thesis demand too much justification for justified belief?[4] In the last chapter, we deferred discussion of this issue. We now take it up.

[4] With only the left-to-right direction, we can conclude, from our epistemic principles, that *if p is warranted enough to justify you in ϕ-ing for any ϕ, then you are justified in believing p.* And this is not particularly surprising. For one thing, if p is warranted enough to justify you in beliefs on its basis, then p itself should be justified for you, and that seems to require that you are justified in believing it. Moreover, it is unclear that, by adding fallibilism about justified belief—i.e. the thesis that justification for belief that p is compatible with a chance that p is false—we can derive *impurism* about justified belief. But we can with the right-to-left direction, and that is one reason why it is important to consider whether the right-to-left direction is true.

Suppose you have a ticket in a sufficiently small lottery, such that you do not have knowledge-level justification that the ticket is going to lose. Despite this, you might believe that the ticket is going to lose. But you certainly aren't required to believe that the ticket is going to lose. It is *permissible* to withhold on that proposition. This is intuitive in its own right. And it makes good sense in general: if you lack knowledge-level justification for *p*, then if you can grasp *p*, the proposition *p* is open to reasonable doubt.[5] When *p* is open to reasonable doubt, then it is permissible not to believe it (and if you can't grasp *p* it is of course permissible not to believe it). So, the following seems like an acceptable lemma:

(Lemma A) If you lack knowledge-level justification for *p*, then it is permissible not to believe that *p*.

Note how much weaker this lemma is than some other principles currently in vogue. It falls short, for example, of the claim that knowledge is the norm of belief. It even falls short of the claim that if you don't have knowledge-level justification for *p*, then it is impermissible to believe that *p*. So we think that this lemma should be friendly to a wide range of epistemological perspectives.

The contrapositive of Lemma A entails that if it is impermissible not to believe that *p*, then you have knowledge-level justification that *p*. This is equivalent to the claim that if you *should* believe that *p*, then you have knowledge-level justification for *p*. The conception of justified belief we are working with is:

(Lemma B) You are justified in believing *p* iff you should believe *p*.

It follows, then, from Lemma B and the contrapositive of Lemma A, that if you're justified in believing *p*, then you have knowledge-level justification for *p*. And that's just the relevant direction of the Equivalence Thesis.[6]

[5] As allies in this claim we cite Conee and Feldman's (2004*a*: 296) conception of knowledge-level justification.

[6] In the last chapter, because of objections raised by Kvanvig, we endorsed a weaker conception of justified belief, according to which you are justified in believing *p* iff of the three attitudes of belief, withholding, and disbelieving, belief is the one that you should have with respect to *p*. We can argue for the Equivalence Thesis using this weaker conception in much the same way we argued for it using the stronger one, though the lemmas are more complex. In place of Lemma B we have the conception of justified belief just mentioned. In place of Lemma A, we have this:

> If you aren't knowledge-level justified in *p*, then it's not the case that of the three attitudes, belief, withholding, and disbelief, belief is the one you should have with respect to *p*.

3 'I BELIEVE IT BUT I DON'T KNOW IT'

If the Equivalence Thesis is true—if justified belief requires just as much justification as knowledge—why would we say things like 'I believe it but I don't know it'? When we say such things aren't we precisely taking ourselves to have a justified belief which isn't justified enough for knowledge?

Again, justification for belief, as we are understanding it, is an obliging notion: if you are justified in believing something, you should believe it, or at least should believe it rather than withhold or disbelieve. When we make remarks such as 'I believe the train leaves at one o'clock, but I don't know it does', we are not suggesting that our belief is *required*, that it is one we *should* have, but only that it is one that it is *okay* for us to have, that it is permissible, even though we lack justification good enough for knowledge. When you deny yourself knowledge-level justification for *the train leaves at one o'clock*, you are denying that your justification is strong enough to make it the case that you *should* or *must* believe that it leaves at one o'clock. We see no problem for the Equivalence Thesis in 'I believe it but I don't know it'.

Consider instead: 'I don't know whether it's true, but it would be irrational not to believe it'. This sort of statement, if it were intuitive, would be problematic for the Equivalence Thesis. At least it would be some reason to think that there is a form of outright belief of which the Equivalence Thesis is false. We would say, first, that this statement hardly has the plausible ring that 'I believe it but I don't know it' has, and second, we would repeat our argument for the Equivalence Thesis: 'I'm withholding judgment, because I just don't know yet' and 'I'm suspending belief, because I just don't know yet' can be successful defenses of your not believing.

What if one brought 'believe' into focus by stress or by adding appropriate qualifiers or both? Consider 'I don't know whether it's true but it would be irrational not to at least *believe* it is true'. We will delay full consideration of such guarded uses of 'believe' until Section 6.

Here's the reasoning for this lemma. Suppose you aren't knowledge-level justified with respect to *p*. Then either you can't grasp *p* or you can. If you can't, then it isn't true that of the three attitudes belief is the one you should have; rather, of the three attitudes there is none you should have. If you can grasp *p*, then of the three attitudes, you are either permitted to withhold or permitted to disbelieve, and so it follows that it's not the case that of the three attitudes belief is the one you should have with respect to *p*.

4 IF JUSTIFIED BELIEF IS PRAGMATIC, IS BELIEF PRAGMATIC, TOO?

We have argued for:

(Biconditional JJ) You are justified in believing that *p* iff *p* is warranted enough to justify you in ϕ-ing, for any ϕ.

What can or must belief be if Biconditional JJ is true?

Consider what is sometimes referred to as *Lockean belief*, which amounts to having a high credence for *p*, higher than some threshold less than 1 and presumably greater than 1/2.[7] If belief is Lockean, then to be justified in believing something is to be justified in having a credence higher than some threshold less than 1. Now, whether you are justified in having such a credence is fixed by what credence you are justified in having. If you are justified in having a credence of .9, and if belief is having a credence of .85 or greater, then you are plausibly justified in having a credence of .85 or greater; thus, on the Lockean account, you are justified in believing. Since epistemic probability for *p* fixes which credence you are justified in having toward *p*, epistemic probability for *p* also fixes whether you are justified in having a Lockean belief that *p*. Assuming that no factors other than epistemic probability matter to whether you are justified in having a Lockean belief, it follows that *purism* is true of justified Lockean belief. That is: if two subjects have the same strength of epistemic position for *p*, then they are alike with respect to whether they are justified in having a Lockean belief that *p*. Moreover, since it is clearly possible to be justified in having a Lockean belief without having probability 1 for the proposition believed, *fallibilism* is true of justified Lockean belief. So, fallibilist purism is true of justified Lockean belief. But we showed that if JJ is true, then fallibilist purism is false of justified belief. It follows that if JJ is true, belief is not Lockean. And if this is true of JJ, it is true of Biconditional JJ.[8]

[7] Defenders of this view include Kyburg (1970), Foley (1993), and Sturgeon (2008). Sturgeon (141–2) suggests that the threshold might depend on context, but what he seems to have in mind is a sort of contextualism about 'believe'—roughly, that 'believe' in a context of use can be associated with different confidence level thresholds. But this is not the sense of 'fixed' we have in mind. The threshold is fixed in our sense only if the following is true *across contexts of use*: there is some c such that S believes that *p* iff S has credence in *p* greater than c.

[8] In keeping with a more irenic response to the worry about 'I believe it but I don't know it', we could qualify this conclusion as follows: the notion of belief of which JJ is true, and which we think fits the 'outright belief role' well, is not a Lockean one.

What else might belief be, if not Lockean? Clearly, Biconditional JJ is consistent with the Certainty View of belief, which equates belief with having credence 1. But the Certainty View is problematic for obvious reasons: it threatens robust skepticism about belief (many of the things we thought we believed, we don't) and if the view is true then fallibilism about justified belief is false. We do not rule out these possibilities, but we do not wish to commit to them.[9]

The natural thought, of course, is that belief might, and even must, be pragmatic if Biconditional JJ is true—it must be essentially connected with conduct. Let us see what merit there is in this contention.

4.1 A credal variant of Biconditional JJ

Suppose there were a true normative biconditional of the form:

> You are justified in X iff you are justified in Y.

It might seem that there is a quick argument to a claim about how X is related to Y. That is, just drop the 'are justified in's from both sides to get:

> You X iff you Y.

Assuming that this argument form is valid, we might think that we could just apply it to Biconditional JJ. Drop the normative operators from both sides and get a principle linking belief with ϕ-ing, for all ϕ.

The difficulty is that Biconditional JJ doesn't have only one normative operator on both sides. Its right side has nested normative operators, and neither one is the same normative operator as on the left side. According to Biconditional JJ, and here we make the scope of the quantifier explicit: you are justified in believing that p iff, for all ϕ, p is warranted enough to justify you in ϕ-ing. The left side is about something you are justified in. The right side is about, among other things, what aspects of p are up to snuff when considering whether p can justify you. There is no clear way to just drop normative operators from both sides.

Can we get a version of Biconditional JJ with the same normative operator on both sides? Perhaps. For, consider what it is for p to be warranted enough to justify you in ϕ-ing. Does this not have implications for (and is it not

[9] Levi (1980) argues that the skepticism about beliefs that the Certainty View commits us to is not as obviously wide-ranging as it might initially see. See Maher (1986) for a critique of Levi's position. See Chapter 7 for further discussion of the infallibilist option.

implied by) what your credences for p ought to be—what credence for p you are justified in having? We think it does. Whether p is warranted enough to justify you in ϕ-ing has implications for (and is implied by) whether you should have enough credence for p for p to be your *motivating reason* for ϕ-ing. If your justified credence that p is fixed by how warranted p is for you, then it seems like matching your credence to how warranted p is, when p is warranted enough to justify you in ϕ-ing, should give you a credence that will move you to ϕ.

Suppose *the ice is thick enough* is warranted enough to justify you in crossing it, but you aren't justified in having enough credence to motivate you to cross it. Recall that in all our principles we are giving 'justified' an obliging reading, so that something justifies you in acting iff it is a reason your having of which makes it the case that you should so act, i.e. a conclusive reason you have to so act. If *warranted enough to justify* doesn't imply *justified in having credence enough to motivate*, then the following thought ought to seem reasonable: 'I have very strong evidence that the ice is thick enough to hold me, strong enough for it to be a reason I have to cross the ice, and of course this would be a conclusive reason for me to cross it; but I need to be more confident if I am to take that as my reason.' This sounds *un*reasonable: it sounds like, in saying this, you are committing yourself to the claim that you ought to be more confident than you are. And a third-person variant makes the subject sound unreasonable as well: 'This guy won't cross the ice because he needs to be more confident it's thick enough, and yet his evidence that it's thick enough is sufficient for it to be a reason he has to cross it, and of course this would be a conclusive reason for him to cross it.' The second part of the remark seems like a criticism. If the evidence is sufficient for it to justify the action, he shouldn't need to be more confident.

So far, we have a defense of the claim that *having sufficient warrant to justify* implies *being justified in having credence sufficient to motivate.* What of the converse? Here similar reasoning can be given. The thought 'I don't need to be more confident to take this fact about the ice as my reason to cross it, but I'd need more evidence for it to be a good reason or for it to justify me' seems *unreasonable*, but it ought to seem fine if it was possible to be justified in having credence enough to motivate you without having warrant sufficient to justify you.

We don't think this case is decisive. But we think it has plausibility—enough plausibility, if the rest of the case is plausible, for us to grant that there is a version of Biconditional JJ with equivalent normative operators on both sides. But the case, as it stands, is not complete. What we have concluded so far is:

(Lemma 1) For all ϕ: p is warranted enough to justify you in ϕ-ing iff you are *justified in being such that your credence for p is high enough* for p to be your motivating reason for ϕ-ing.

But this lemma won't allow us to conclude anything from Biconditional JJ, because the right side of Biconditional JJ says that p is warranted enough to justify you in ϕ-ing, for all ϕ, whereas the left side of Lemma 1 says only that p is warranted enough to justify you in ϕ-ing, for some particular ϕ. (The universal quantifier at the beginning of Lemma 1, of course, governs the whole biconditional, not just the left side.) However, with plausible additional assumptions[10] we can argue from Lemma 1 to:

(Link) p is warranted enough to justify you in ϕ-ing, for all ϕ, iff you are justified in being such that your credence for p is high enough for p to be your motivating reason for ϕ-ing, for all ϕ.

[10] (Link) follows from Lemma 1 together with two further lemmas (we use all caps to indicate main connectives):

(Lemma 2) For *some* ϕ you are justified in being such that your credence for p is high enough for p to be your motivating reason for ϕ-ing IFF, for *all* ϕ you are justified in being such that your credence is high enough in p for it to be your motivating reason for ϕ-ing.

(Scope Interchange) For all (some) ϕ you are justified in being such that your credence for p is high enough for p to be your motivating reason for ϕ-ing IFF you are justified in being such that for all (some) ϕ your credence for p is high enough for p to be your motivating reason for ϕ-ing.

We will have nothing in particular to say about the Scope Interchange lemma, other than that we would not wish to challenge it.

What of Lemma 2? The right-to-left direction of this biconditional is trivial. What needs defense is the left-to-right direction. The best reason to accept it, we think, is that a similar claim is plausibly true of sufficient warrant to be a reason you have, and also, through the Safe Reasons principle of Chapter 3 for sufficient warrant to justify. Consider the following principle, which is a strengthened version of our Unity Thesis:

(Strong Unity) IF there is some ϕ such that p is warranted enough to be a reason you have to ϕ, THEN for all ϕ, p is warranted enough to be a reason you have to ϕ.

We think there is a case to be made for Strong Unity, although it falls well short of the case we made for Unity in Chapter 3. Suppose Strong Unity is false. Then the following sort of remark should make perfect sense: 'I have a reason to feel happy, and that is the fact that my wife is expecting, but I don't have enough evidence that she is expecting for that consideration to be a reason I have to start a college fund for the child.' But this doesn't seem to make good sense, nor does its third-person variant. If someone made this statement, one could reply, 'But if the fact that your wife is expecting is a reason you have to feel happy, why isn't it capable of being a reason you have to plan for the college fund?'

From Link and Biconditional JJ, we can derive a credal variant of Biconditional JJ with equivalent normative operators on both sides:

> (Credal Variant of Biconditional JJ) You are justified in believing p iff you are justified in being such that your credence for p is high enough for p to be your motivating reason for ϕ-ing, for all ϕ.

We allow that p can be your motivating reason for ϕ-ing even if p doesn't move you to ϕ and even if you don't ϕ at all. But, if p is your motivating reason for ϕ-ing, it must in fact weigh in your deliberations when deciding whether to ϕ. To have a credence for p high enough for p to be your motivating reason is for weaknesses in your credence to fail to stand in the way of p being your motivating reason for ϕ-ing. So, you may fail to weigh p in your deliberations about whether to ϕ, but if this failure is not due to any credal weakness with respect to p, you may well have credence for p high enough for p to be your motivating reason for ϕ-ing. When and only when you are justified in having such credence for p with respect to all ϕ, according to the credal variant, are you justified in believing p.

4.2 From the credal variant to a strong pragmatic view of belief

We will not challenge the claim that Biconditional JJ is equivalent to its credal variant. Can we derive from this a Sartrean pragmatic view of belief? Dropping the 'are justified in's from both sides yields:

> You believe p iff your credence for p is high enough for p to be your motivating reason for ϕ-ing for all ϕ.

This view imposes a pragmatic condition on belief: belief in a proposition requires having a credence for that proposition which is high enough for it to be a motivating reason for some—indeed *all*—conduct. In fact, this looks very much like the Sartrean conception of belief we considered at the beginning of the chapter. We will call it the *Strong Pragmatic View* and will call the doxastic state the view claims to be equivalent to belief *strong pragmatic belief.*

Suppose that Strong Unity is true, and suppose it remains true when 'be a reason you have to ϕ' is replaced with 'justify you in ϕ-ing'. Then given our defense of Lemma 1—which assures that sufficient warrant in p for p to justify ϕ-ing is equivalent to being justified in having sufficient credence in p for p to move you to ϕ—Lemma 2 follows.

So, we have a line of reasoning purporting to show that if Biconditional JJ is true, then a certain pragmatic view of belief is true, the Strong Pragmatic View. This might seem disconcerting, for the latter is arguably too strong. Suppose you believe, on the basis of memory, that you have Cheerios in the house. This might be your reason for not planning to get more at the store. But suppose that you are also in a life-or-death situation with respect to another proposition, say our old favorite *the ice is thick enough*. Your credence in the Cheerios proposition isn't high enough for that proposition to justify you in crossing the ice—you need a higher credence. (This is a little funny, since the two propositions are unrelated, but we can imagine the following *two* criticisms of your crossing the ice 'because you have Cheerios in the house': (1) the latter has nothing to do with crossing the ice; (2) the latter isn't warranted enough.) And suppose you have the credence you should have in the Cheerios proposition. Then it seems we have the following situation: you believe the Cheerios proposition but it doesn't have the credence it needs to move you to cross the ice. If this is possible, then the Strong Pragmatic View is false. And it seems clearly possible. So, if the Strong Pragmatic View follows from Biconditional JJ, that seems like a good reason to reject Biconditional JJ.[11]

As we mentioned above, we will not challenge the claim that Biconditional JJ is equivalent to its credal variant. What we deny is that the latter requires the Strong Pragmatic View of belief. The problem is the inference from:

> You are justified in X iff you are justified in Y.

to

> You X iff you Y.

This inference form is in general invalid, even if we add that the premise is necessarily true. Consider an example with 'should':

> You should refrain from torturing baby Joey iff you should refrain from torturing any baby.

That seems true. But

> You refrain from torturing baby Joey iff you refrain from torturing any baby.

[11] One might suspect the same worry is trouble for KJ. Do you stop knowing that you have Cheerios in the house if it isn't warranted enough to justify you in crossing the ice? We delay consideration of this objection to Chapter 7.

need not be true. Since we are using the generalized 'you', this is false if no one tortured baby Joey but someone tortured some baby.

Or, consider an example involving justified belief. Suppose it were true that:

(Assertion) You are justified in believing p iff you are justified in asserting that p.

It hardly follows that you believe p iff you assert that p. What would follow is only that, in believing p and failing to assert p, you're doing something wrong (either in the belief or in the assertion).

We think the same story can be told about the purported inference from the credal version of Biconditional JJ to the Strong Pragmatic View. For all the credal version entails, belief might only amount to being such that there is some ϕ such that your credence is high enough in p for p to move you to ϕ. Or belief might amount to being such that for some restricted class of ϕ, your credence in p is high enough for p to move you to ϕ. Or belief might not be pragmatic at all. So long as it's true that you *should* be in the relevant weaker doxastic states iff you *should* have strong pragmatic belief, belief might be one of the weaker doxastic states and not strong pragmatic belief. And, given the assumptions used in the previous section, this can be true.[12]

[12] Here is the explicit reasoning. Call the view that you believe that p iff there is some ϕ such that your credence in p is high enough for p to be your motivating reason to ϕ *the Weak Pragmatic View*. Suppose this view is true. Suppose also that our Lemma 2 and Scope Interchange are true (see n. 10). The argument is then this. Attaching 'justification' operators to both sides of the Weak Pragmatic View, we have:

(i) You are justified in believing that p iff you are justified in being such that there is some ϕ such that your credence in p is high enough for p to be your motivating reason to ϕ.

Now, by Scope Interchange, we can move to

(ii) You are justified in believing that p iff there is some ϕ such that your credence in p is high enough for p to be your motivating reason to ϕ.

and by an application of Lemma 2 we have:

(iii) You are justified in believing that p iff for all ϕ, you are justified in being such that your credence in p is high enough for it to be your motivating reason for ϕ-ing.

and then with one more application of (Scope Interchange) on the right-hand-side of (iii), we arrive at the credal version of Biconditional JJ.

What this argument plausibly shows is that the credal version of Biconditional JJ could be true even if belief were not *strongly pragmatic*. A similar derivation is possible beginning from

4.3 If justified belief is pragmatic, must belief be at least *weakly* pragmatic?

The truth of JJ, we have seen, does not require that belief be strong pragmatic belief. But does it require that belief be at least weakly pragmatic, where by this we will mean that that believing requires there being some ϕ such that one's credence in p is high enough for p to move one to ϕ?

Here again, we know of no decisive argument. But we register this worry: if belief isn't at least weakly pragmatic, why is justified belief pragmatic? More carefully: if belief in p has no implications for p's having sufficient credence to move you, why should justified belief have implications for p's being warranted enough to justify you in anything let alone everything? If belief that p requires that p have sufficient credence to move you to ϕ for some ϕ or to some restricted set of ϕ, we can see how this could be, given appropriate assumptions about the normative demands 'reverberating' from one ϕ or a restricted class of ϕ to all ϕ. But if belief doesn't require even this limited pragmatic condition, we are left asking how justified belief could have the pragmatic condition it has.

Here is another way of putting the same concern. Suppose you should believe the ice is thick enough to hold you. Then if JJ is true, and assuming its credal version is true as well, you should have credence in this proposition sufficient for it to move you to cross the ice. Now suppose believing the ice is thick enough to hold you is perfectly compatible with this proposition's lacking the credence necessary for it to move you to cross the ice. So believing it is thick enough to hold you doesn't guarantee your having high enough credence for crossing the ice, but your being justified in believing it is thick enough does guarantee that you should have high enough credence for ice-crossing. Of course, if belief required having credence sufficient for it to move you to do, think, feel something else, other than ice-crossing, we could see why you should have credence sufficient for ice-crossing, insofar as the normative demands reverberate from the something else to ice-crossing. But if there is nowhere for these normative demands to get started, how do they apply to anything and everything, including your crossing the ice?

views of belief which associate it with credal sufficiency for a restricted class of ϕ. The only change is that Scope Interchange will need to be true for restricted universal quantifiers, which seems unproblematic assuming Scope Interchange as formulated is true.

5 THE MAIN CONTENDER: THE LOCKEAN ACCOUNT

If outright belief were Lockean, then we would not be right to extend our pragmatic principles to justified belief. But, we pointed out, Lockean belief fares poorly against the requirement that lack of knowledge that *p* entails permissibility to fail to believe that *p*. We now want to argue that Lockean belief scores poorly on a number of other desiderata on an account of outright belief. In the next section, we turn to worries about the pragmatic view.

Consider the following apparent facts about outright belief:

> *The truth standard.* If you believe *p* and *p* is false, then you are mistaken about whether *p*, and if you believe *p* and *p* is true, then you are right about whether *p*.
>
> *Transparency.* Strength of justification for *p* is directly proportional to the strength of justification you have for believing *p*.
>
> *Resolution.* If you believe that *p*, then your mind is made up that *p*.

These three features of belief, especially when taken together, provide good reason to be unhappy with the equation of outright belief and Lockean belief. We consider each in turn:

The *truth standard.* Consider a standard Lockean View under which belief is a matter of having a credence greater than some degree $d < 1$. Suppose d is .98. If you have a .99 credence for *p*, and *p* turns out to be false, it does not follow that you were wrong about whether *p*. If you are told: 'Ha, so you were wrong about whether *p*, weren't you?' you could reasonably say in your defense: 'Look, I took no stand about whether *p* was true or not; I just assigned it a high probability; I assigned its negation a probability, too.' It is not clear that more sophisticated variants of the Lockean View of belief do any better, even views under which belief is a thick credence extending up to 1 on the confidence scale. If you assign a thick confidence of <.99, 1> to *p*, and *p* turns out false, are you necessarily mistaken about whether *p*? This seems doubtful. You assigned a (lower) thick credence to its negation, too: <0, .01>.[13]

13 Suppose you assign the same (low) credence to each of the propositions that express, of all the tickets in a 100-ticket lottery, that they will win. Do you end up right about 99 of the tickets and wrong about 1 of them? Or can you rightfully say, 'I wasn't right or wrong about any of them. I never took a stand'?

It is also interesting that in high-stakes cases, subjects may have very high credences for a proposition, *p*, but still say the likes of 'I don't want to be wrong that *p*' and then proceed not to rely on *p* in their actions. For instance, one might say 'I don't want to be wrong in thinking it's a local', and then proceed to check further to 'make sure'. This usage is some evidence that ordinary folk are thinking of a belief state that isn't Lockean belief but is more closely tied to action.

Transparency. Slightly increasing your evidence for *p* doesn't necessarily make you justified in believing *p*, but it still weighs in favor of believing *p*: your justification for believing *p* increases. If you buy a ticket in a very large lottery, you are not justified in believing you'll win (notice: *win*, not *lose*), even though you have more justification for believing you'll win than you did before. But it seems false that when your evidence for *p* slightly increases that it weighs even weakly in favor of having a very high credence for *p*. When you buy a ticket in a very large lottery, your justification for having a very high credence for *p* increases not at all: you have no justification at all for Lockean credence. Similarly, anyone who has only fair-to-middling evidence for *p* has fair-to-middling justification for believing *p*, but not for giving *p* a high credence. Strength of justification for having a Lockean credence doesn't vary with strength of propositional justification in the way that it should if belief were Lockean credence.

Of course, as you get slightly more evidence for *p*, you become justified in having a higher credence than you did before, and you might become more justified in having some particular credence, c. But this is not to say that there is some other, very high credence, which you become more justified in having when you get a very small increase in otherwise negligible evidence.

Resolution. If you outright believe that *p*, your mind is made up that *p*. But, here again, this doesn't seem to be true for Lockean credence. Consider a person who is searching hard for more evidence, given just how much is at stake for her, and who stays up late at night worrying. Is this person's mind made up? Not in any natural sense. But, consistent with all this, the person might have a Lockean credence.

Some readers will be suspicious: is it really surprising that when we apply commonsense ideas of correctness, reasons for belief, and 'having one's mind made up' in conjunction with technical notions like credences, our intuitions go awry? If not, then these commonsense features of belief pose no serious difficulty for the Lockean View. But, recall, that the Lockean

View is a view about belief—outright belief—which is not a technical notion but one present in ordinary thinking. The Lockean might be trying to give us an explication of belief, in Carnap's sense, rather than conceptual analysis. But we have to judge the account against others, such as the Pragmatic View, in part[14] by how well it does accommodating the relatively uncontroversial features of belief. And the Lockean View does rather poorly on this score.

Taken together, the three features—*The Truth Standard, Transparency,* and *Resolution*—suggest a picture of belief in a proposition as involving *commitment* to the proposition as true, just as intention is commitment to the proposition as *to be made true*. Sufficiently strong pragmatic views of belief seem consistent not only with this picture but even with the key idea of commitment to a proposition as true. When p has the credence it needs to move you—to be the reason for which you act, believe, etc.—that is a clear way of being committed to p as true.

Consider the Strong Pragmatic View. Suppose believing p requires that p have the credence sufficient for it to be a basis for any action, intention, plan, belief, feeling to which p is relevant. If p has the credence it needs to move you, then you are prepared to put p to work as a basis for what you do, believe, etc.—to do, believe, etc. as would be required were p true. If p turns out to be false, then it is not implausible to conclude, as the truth standard requires, that you were wrong about whether p. As for transparency, even slight increases in justification for p seem to require some increase in justification for having a credence high enough to put p to work, just as even slight increases in justification for thinking that an act would be good require some increase in justification for having the motivation necessary to intend to bring it about. And it is very plausible that having such a credence suffices for having your mind made up that p. When you believe, the difference between complete certainty that p—credence 1—and the credence you have is idle in a way captured by the Strong Pragmatic View. So the resolution property applies, too.

However, some weaker pragmatic views score well, too, which is a good thing since the strong view is too strong. Consider the view that belief doesn't require credal sufficiency to move you to any ϕ, especially wildly unrelated ϕs, but does require credal sufficiency to move you to any relevant or connected

[14] We also have to judge it, as well as the Pragmatic View of belief, against more formal constraints on the relation between belief and credences (for example, Bayesian constraints). We discuss these issues in Section 8.

or perhaps salient ϕ. So if you believe you have an extra box of Cheerios, you need to have credence necessary for it to be a motivating reason you have for not planning on buying more at the store, say, but you needn't have credence necessary for unrelated actions, such as crossing the frozen pond. It is not easy to specify exactly what the appropriate restriction is, and we will not pursue the matter in any detail, but the idea would be to restrict 'ϕ' to actions, beliefs, plans, feelings, etc. to which the question of whether the given proposition is true is germane (leaving open whether what is germane is a highly subjective or objective matter). On such a pragmatic view, we think the idea of belief as commitment to the truth is preserved, and therefore that three desiderata—the Truth Standard, Transparency, and Resolution—are satisfied.

We do not claim that the three desiderata we have discussed are the only ones on an account of outright belief. Any good account of belief must account for its explanatory relations to action, for instance, but it seems the Lockean account will not outperform all pragmatic accounts on this matter. Still, haven't we so far left out of the picture a desideratum on which the Lockean view scores much more highly, the psychological counterpart to purism about justified belief? Call it

> *Stability.* Two subjects with the same credence for *p* are also alike with respect to whether they believe *p*.

Don't pragmatic views sacrifice *Stability*?

By itself, no pragmatic view entails the falsity of *Stability*, any more than JJ entails the falsity of purism about justified belief. One must add fallibilism to JJ, and one must add the corresponding claim—that it is possible to believe something having credence less than 1—to any pragmatic view. We remain neutral throughout the book on the question of fallibilism as well as whether belief requires credence 1.

But isn't it a mark against pragmatic views that those who think belief is compatible with a credence less than 1 can accept them only by giving up *Stability*, just as it is a mark against our epistemic principles that fallibilists can accept them only if they give up purism? We discuss the latter claim at some length in Chapter 7. Concerning the former, we grant that pragmatic views restrict one's options for accommodating *Stability.* But it is not clear how much weight we should give *Stability.* Mary and John, in Cohen's airport case, will presumably be prepared to say, 'Smith doesn't know the plane stops in Chicago'. But will they be equally prepared to say, 'Smith doesn't believe it stops in Chicago'? Will Smith be prepared to say, of Mary and John, that they believe the plane stops in Chicago? Or consider temporal shifts. If you haven't changed your credence for *the bank is open tomorrow*, but the stakes have risen dramatically, is it clearly wrong to say, 'Well, I did believe it was open tomorrow but now I really don't'? It is hard to see that it is.

6 LINGUISTIC PROBLEMS FOR THE PRAGMATIC VIEW

If belief is a commitment to a proposition as true, a commitment that engages all relevant action, intention, assent, etc., then what is going on when we say the likes of:

> I believe the train leaves at one o'clock but I'm going to call to check.
>
> I believe I wouldn't get the flu but I'm getting a flu shot just in case.

To have a label for such remarks, call them instances of 'I believe it but I'm not going to act on it'. Such remarks are not far from, and may be defended or explained by explicit appeal to instances of 'I believe it but I don't know it'. In Section 3, we noted that the widespread use of the latter doesn't undermine the Equivalence Thesis because it doesn't suggest that one would be irrational not to believe. And, the same would go for the claim that 'I believe it but I'm not going to act on it' undermines JJ. JJ is about justified belief—about what you should believe—and there is no implication that you should or must have the belief in such remarks. However, the threat to pragmatic views of belief is more direct. If the pragmatic view of belief is true, then it is hard to see how 'I believe it but I'm not going to act on it' could be true, particularly since it is often used to mean 'I believe it but I'm not confident enough to act on it', which seems to assert that one has a belief that p and that one's credence in p is not high enough for p to be a motivating reason for action, which is impossible if the pragmatic view is true. Appeal to permissions will not avoid the problem the way it avoids the problem for JJ and the Equivalence Thesis.

But consider:

Dialogue 1:

A. I believe the train leaves at one o'clock.

B. Then why are you calling Amtrak?

A. It might leave earlier. I don't know.

B. Do you believe it *does* leave at one o'clock or just that it's *likely* it leaves at one o'clock?

A. That it's likely.

In Dialogue 1, A is not willing to assert simply that the train leaves at one o'clock but only that she believes this. This seems peculiar if belief were commitment to the truth. But under pressure to clarify from B, A replies that what she believes is not that it *does* leave at that time but that it is likely that it does. A is committed to the truth of something, alright, but not the proposition that the train leaves at one o'clock. What A is committed to is that it is likely that it leaves then.

Now, is A 'pulling back' from her original statement, in saying that what she believes is that it is likely? Compare a second dialogue:

Dialogue 2:

[A and B are in the supermarket shopping]

A. There's no need to buy Cheerios, we have an extra box at home.

B. You believe we do have them.

A. Yes.

B. Do you believe that we *do* have them or just that it's likely we have them? Little Toby has to have his Cheerios.

A. It's not just likely we have them. We do have them. I made a point to check before we left the house. I want a divorce.

In this second dialogue, A holds her ground. We do have them—that's what A believes—not merely that it's likely. This is in clear contrast to the first dialogue.

Obviously, these are only two dialogues, though there is nothing particularly unusual or special about them. But we think Jonathan Sutton (2007) is right that in some cases 'believe that *p*' is used to indicate commitment not to *p* itself but to the proposition that *p* is probable. In fact, if you are asked whether *p*, and you reply not with '*p*' but with 'I believe that *p*', this seems to indicate not merely that you do have a commitment to *p*'s being likely but that you don't have a commitment to *p* itself, the latter being cancelable—you can say 'I believe that *p*, and it is *p* which I believe not merely that it is probable'.

So, the Sutton strategy is a plausible way to cope with the hedged uses of 'believe', found in 'I believe it but I'm not going to act on it', as well as 'I believe it but I don't know it' and their third-person counterparts. Belief is a commitment, but a belief attribution may attribute belief not in the specified proposition but in the proposition that it is probable.[15] Why, though, if belief is fundamentally committal, in the way the pragmatic view captures, is it possible by saying 'I believe *p*' to indicate that you don't have belief that *p* but only that *p* is probable?

If you aren't committed to the truth of *p*, and belief is commitment to the truth of *p*, how can it be possible to say felicitously 'I believe that *p*'?[16] Compare the case of intention. One would *think*, initially, that just as outright belief is a commitment to a proposition's being true so outright intention is a commitment to making a proposition true. If you believe that *p*, you are settled on the truth of *p*, and if you intend that *p*, you are settled on making it the case that *p*. But notice the apparent propriety of:

> I intend to finish the job by next month, but don't be surprised if I don't

said by a workman remodeling one's home. Notice, also, that if asked, 'Will you finish the job by next month?', the workman might reply, 'I'm not saying that. I'm saying I intend to.' Why would there be this hedged use of 'intend' if intention is commitment to making a proposition true, to making something the case?

We suspect that whatever term was invented with the explicit stipulation that it denotes a commitment of the relevant kinds would acquire this sort of

15 Isn't belief that *p* is probable the same as Lockean belief? And so, aren't we in effect conceding that Lockean belief is a kind of outright belief? There are reasons to doubt that belief that *p* is probable is Lockean belief, because it seems one could have a Lockean belief that *p* without having a belief about the probability of *p*. However, suppose we put this aside. If belief that *p* is probable is Lockean belief, then isn't Lockean belief a form of outright belief?

We are neutral between two replies. First, we might insist that the only relation of outright belief is the committal relation. But even supposing that to outright believe that *p* is probable in this committal sense amounts to having a Lockean belief, what follows? Only that outright believing certain propositions, of the form *p is very probable* (or something of the sort), is the same as having credence in *p* which exceeds a certain threshold. It doesn't follow that in outright believing that *p is probable*, you outright believe *in any sense* the proposition *p*.

A more conciliatory reply is to allow that there is a perfectly good sense in which, assuming that you are committed to the truth of *p is probable* and assuming that this amounts to having a Lockean credence, you can be said to outright believe that *p*. It is not as if the two senses of 'believe' are entirely unrelated, or even equally basic. Rather, the basic sense is the committal sense, but there is a derivative sense in which Lockean credence suffices for counting as 'outright believing' a proposition *p*, even if you aren't committed to the truth of *p*.

16 In some cases, of course, an outright assertion of *p* might be impolite, as when delivering comments on a paper you say 'I believe the author neglects the fact that ...' rather than 'The author neglects the fact that ...'. But in many cases in which the more hedged use of 'believe' is appropriate, politeness is not an issue. If asked, 'But is *p* true? Yes or no?' you would, in some cases, not reply 'Yes' but rather 'Look, I believe it is true; that's all I can say; I can't say it *is* true.'

hedged use. In the cognitive case, there is reason to think that even the words and phrases 'sure', 'certain', 'positive', 'fully believe', and others which can be used to express genuine commitment to the truth of *p*, have this hedged use. If asked, 'Did you turn off the gas?' you might not want to go as far as to say 'Yes, it's off' as to say any of:

> I'm sure I did, but maybe I should go back and check.
>
> I'm certain, but we won't really know until we get back.
>
> I fully believe I did, but let's call the neighbor just in case.[17]

The same goes for 'fully intend':

> I fully intend to be there by noon, but if I'm not, just go on without me.

By using a word which marks a threshold of commitment along a dimension, we can communicate that our position along the dimension isn't quite high enough to meet the threshold. Why should this be the case? The best hypothesis, in our view, is the indirection involved in reporting a commitment rather than expressing it—the choice to focus attention on the having of the state rather than on the aspect of the world the commitment is about—can make the audience ask: 'Why is he speaking about his state rather than the world? Does he really have the state?' And this, we suspect, can give rise to the hedged use in which you are understood precisely not to have the committal state but to be committed only to something weaker: *p is probable* or *I will try to make p true.*

Richard Moran (2001) points to an illuminating passage in Sartre (1993):

> [T]he very word 'to believe' [is] a term utilized indifferently to indicate the unwavering firmness of belief ('My God, I believe in you') and its character as disarmed and strictly subjective. ('Is Pierre my friend? I do not know; I believe so.') (Sartre 1993: 346)

Moran remarks, 'for Sartre, self-consciousness of one's own belief involves a distancing of one's self from the perspective of the declaration or endorsement of one's belief' (Moran 2001: 78).

So, we think that a view under which outright belief that *p* is commitment to the truth of *p* is not refuted by facts about our hedged use of 'believes'.

[17] What about 'absolutely certain'? Perhaps some will think 'I'm absolutely certain but maybe I should go back and check' is infelicitous. We are inclined to disagree (having said those sorts of things before). But even if this is infelicitous, absolute certainty is more than commitment to the truth of *p* requires, at least assuming that the Certainty View is too strong.

Even if a word were explicitly defined in a committing way, there is every reason to think that it would acquire a hedged use. And since, as we saw in the preceding section, a pragmatic view of belief does well in capturing this committal notion of belief, we see no difficulty in the hedged use of 'believe' for the pragmatic view.

7 BELIEF AND ACCEPTANCE

It might seem that on pragmatic views of belief, belief merely amounts to, or at least requires, what L. J. Cohen (1989), Bratman (1992), and Stalnaker (1984) call *acceptance.* To accept that *p*, according to Cohen, is to 'have or adopt a policy of deeming, positing, or postulating that *p*—that is, of going along with that proposition ... as a premiss in some or all contexts for one's own and others' proofs, arguments, inferences, deliberations, etc.' (Cohen 1989: 368).[18]

Now, if pragmatic views *did* equate belief with acceptance, or even did imply that acceptance requires belief, they would be wrong. Bratman gives a number of convincing cases that acceptance is possible in the absence of belief. Here is one. For the purposes of determining the maximum cost of a construction project with many subcontractors, to see if you can afford to do the project all at once or spread it out over time, you might accept that the costs for each subcontractor will be at the top of the estimate range. But you don't believe this. Following Cohen (1989: 369), a defense attorney might well believe his client is guilty but still organize his thinking about how to prosecute the case around the contrary assumption. In Cohen's view, the attorney accepts that his client is innocent despite the fact that the lawyer doesn't believe his client is innocent.

You can certainly fail to believe that *p*—and even believe or know that not-*p*—but use *p* as a premise in a certain specialized deliberation or reasoning. But we need to make sure to clear up exactly how *p* is used as a premise in that deliberation. We must not confuse the 'deeming, positing, and premising' involved in acceptance with *credal sufficiency to be a motivating reason.* When you decide to go ahead with your construction project after calculating costs based on your acceptance that the subcontractors' final bills will be at the top

[18] This is a stipulative definition of 'acceptance'. It may not accord well with the ordinary use of the term.

of the estimate range, what consideration is it that moves you to action? What is your motivating reason? Is it *the construction project will cost $X*, where X is the final calculated amount, or even the fact that it will cost approximately $X? No, what moves you is *the construction project will cost at most $X*. But this is something you believe.

Furthermore, Bratman seems to think that acceptance is distinctively connected to *practical* reasoning and action,[19] but clearly there is acceptance in theoretical reasoning as well. In the course of computing a rough estimate of the velocity of a falling body, you might *accept* the claim that there is no air friction, a claim you know to be false, and so use this in your reasoning. If asked about how you can use this as a premise, you might reply that it is simplifying and that it makes no essential difference to the final estimate you are seeking. Bratman's project-costs case can be altered so that it is merely about theoretical as opposed to practical reasoning. You might, for whimsical amusement, calculate the maximum costs of the complicated project you know you can't afford. The best way to do the calculation might be to use *the costs will be at the upper end of the estimate ranges for each subcontractor* as a premise in your reasoning.

So, whether the reasoning is practical or theoretical, you can use the negation of what you know for certain purposes (though, as noted, we must be careful about what it is to 'use' the negation). Again, you know air creates friction when a body is accelerated through it and yet you accept the negation of this proposition for the purposes of determining a rough estimate of the velocity of a falling body. This is entirely consistent with your credence in *there is air friction* being high enough for this proposition to be your motivating reason. Certainly, it is a basis on which you form further beliefs. But it also the basis on which you adopt certain intentions and plans (e.g. those having to do with your hang-gliding hobby). More to the point, it is perfectly consistent with your failure to use *there is air friction* in a particular bit of reasoning that *there is air friction* has the credence sufficient to be a basis on which you do that very reasoning. Even if you had credence 1 that there is air friction, which you arguably in fact do, you would still have left it out of your calculations. Therefore, the Pragmatic View is consistent with the contention that you

[19] Bratman appeals to the relation of acceptance to action, through practical reasoning, in responding to the suggestion that acceptance is just supposition.

can 'accept' that not-p in the sense Bratman and Cohen have in mind while believing that p.

8 THE BAYESIAN CHALLENGE

According to Bayesian epistemology, belief is fundamentally a graded matter rather than a binary one in this sense: fixing a subject's graded beliefs is enough to fix her binary or outright beliefs, but not vice versa. A natural conclusion to draw from this is that the justification of graded beliefs is more fundamental than the justification of outright beliefs, again at least in the sense that fixing the justification of the former is enough to fix the justification for the latter, but not vice versa.[20]

Bayesian epistemologists may disagree about whether there are outright beliefs at all (Jeffrey 1992), and even if they do accept such beliefs they can disagree about how precisely the two sorts of belief are related. But they will reject any view under which your outright beliefs can float free of your total state of graded opinion, as well as one which takes the justification of outright beliefs to float free of the justification of graded opinion.

Our project, like most projects in mainstream epistemology, focuses on the epistemology of outright belief, on justification for believing, and on knowledge. It is not uncommon for Bayesians to grumble about this focus. After all, as they see the psychology and the epistemology, all the real action concerns graded belief. Focusing on outright belief, to the exclusion of graded belief, doesn't merely sideline the more fundamental reality, it risks mistakenly treating outright belief and its epistemology as fundamental and thereby drawing incorrect conclusions about outright belief.

For instance, a mainstream epistemologist might think, as many have, that outright beliefs must answer to the laws of logic, because logic has normative force over our doxastic lives. But if this leads one to hold that your beliefs must be consistent if you are to be rational, one is forgetting that there is an alternative: logic might well have its normative force on our doxastic lives in

20 Epistemologists accepting Bayesianism as we are understanding it include, among many others, Christensen (2004), Jeffrey (1983) and (1992), Levi (1980), Kaplan (1996), and Maher (1993). The phrase 'the Bayesian challenge' is Kaplan's. Most philosophers calling themselves Bayesian epistemologists would also insist that Bayesian epistemology requires that your credences, to be rational, satisfy the probability axioms. This saddles Bayesian epistemology with a number of difficulties orthogonal to our purposes in this chapter, and so we set this issue aside here.

the first instance by constraining our graded beliefs. Its normative force, such as it is, for outright belief might merely reflect outright belief's dependence on graded belief, and not support the strong claim that outright beliefs must be jointly consistent on pain of irrationality. This, at least in broad strokes, is one of the main points for which David Christensen (2004) argues.

Mainstreamers often brush off such worries on the ground that whatever is being said about outright belief can be extended *mutatis mutandis* to graded belief. For instance, evidentialists might suggest that their talk of doxastic attitudes fitting the evidence extends to graded beliefs (they, too, can fit the evidence), and coherentists might point to the extensions of logical and explanatory coherence for graded beliefs. In many cases it will be reasonable to think the extension won't introduce fundamental changes, but only complicate the picture.[21] The rationale for focusing on outright belief is simply that the added complications of telling the full Bayesian story are beside the particular epistemological point being made. If the issue is whether the justification for beliefs is evidentialist or externalist, one *could* couch the debate in terms of graded belief, but why bother? Mainstream epistemologists, in short, can say that their remarks about outright belief are helpful simplifications of the 'real' theory—the version applied to graded belief.

Can *we* give the Bayesian epistemologist this sort of friendly brush-off? Here is an argument the Bayesian might make that we can't. Purism is true, the Bayesian might say, of justification for credences. Surely Locke was right to instruct us to *proportion* our belief to the evidence. If there are such things as outright beliefs, the question of how their epistemology relates to the evidence is perhaps more complicated than this, if only because outright belief cannot be proportioned. But given that the evidence bears in a graded manner on propositions, (i.e. that it supports propositions (for you) more or less), and given that your credences should match the evidence, then your credences should be proportioned just as the evidence is: purism should be true of them.

We, however, have argued that, pending the fate of fallibilism, purism about justified belief—about 'S is justified in believing that *p*'—might well be false. The Bayesian will press us: given that purism is true of the justification for graded beliefs, and given that the justification for outright beliefs is fixed

[21] There are wrinkles in some cases: what should reliabilists say about the 'reliability' of credence-producing processes? (See Goldman (1999) but also DePaul (2004).)

by the justification for graded beliefs, then won't purism have to be true of the latter as well? And isn't it our neglect of graded belief that is leading us to take impurism seriously in the case of outright beliefs? The Bayesian will resist any brush-off from us. What we're saying about justification for outright belief doesn't extend to graded belief. So there is a real question whether our main claims are compatible with the main tenets of Bayesian epistemology. If they aren't compatible, then we must make a serious attempt to argue against the Bayesian view.

We concede the correctness of purism about justification for credences. So, we cannot avoid the Bayesian worries by extending our 'pragmatist' conclusions to the epistemology of credences. We need to answer the challenge directly. We need to show that pragmatic views of belief, combined with the assumption that belief is possible in the absence of credence 1, is compatible with Bayesian epistemology. Is it? Or does belief, on this conception, 'float free' of graded opinion? True, having a certain credence *for p* doesn't fix whether you believe that *p*. The supervenience can't take this sort of atomistic form. But this is true of other views of belief accepted by Bayesians, e.g. Kaplan's (1996: 109–11) Assertion View, according to which you believe that *p* iff 'were your sole aim to assert the truth (as it pertains to *p*), and your only options were to assert that *p*, assert that not-*p*, or make neither assertion, you would prefer to assert that *p*' (109).[22] Kaplan points out that having as your sole aim asserting the truth about whether *p* is consistent with having different value weightings for asserting *p* when *p* is false and not asserting *p* when *p* is true. Thus, he concludes that two people could have the same credence with respect to *p* while differing in whether they believe that *p*. (What is more, a single person might have different weightings with respect to different propositions, so that she attaches the same credence level to two different propositions but only believes one of them.[23])

Kaplan claims his account 'radically dissociates' belief from credences, but the dissociation isn't as radical as he suggests. It is plausible that fixing the totality of your credences across all propositions thereby fixes the totality of your Kaplanesque beliefs: two subjects with the same total credence state with respect to all propositions will be alike with respect to their total

22 See also Maher (1986) and (1993: ch. 6).

23 We might avoid this somewhat counterintuitive result—though there are counterintuitive consequences no matter where one turns in this area. See the discussion of intra-subjective purism in Chapter 7.

outright belief state. (This would mean understanding preferences in terms of credences. We could avoid that assumption by saying that the totality of your credences together with the totality of your preferences fix what beliefs you have.)

We see no reason why the same couldn't hold under pragmatic views of belief, assuming that belief is possible without credence 1. Whether your credence for *p* is high enough for *p* to be a motivating reason for a certain range of ϕ may not be fixed by your credence for *p*, but there is no good reason to think it wouldn't be fixed by your entire set of credences, perhaps plus preferences—the complete Bayesian corpus. This corpus includes credences and preferences about the options available, their outcomes under various conditions, etc. There seems to be no threat of any Bayesian-unfriendly supervenience failure any more than for Kaplanesque beliefs. In fact, there seems to be no reason why token credences couldn't *be* token beliefs under the Pragmatic View. Assuming credence 1 isn't necessary for belief, then whether a token credence is a belief could vary depending on one's other credences and preferences. The property of being a belief would be a contingent and in some cases temporary property of a credence.[24]

Nor, on pragmatic views, need the justification of outright belief float free from the justification of graded belief. The acceptance of Bayesian epistemology does not commit one to the atomistic view that whether you are justified in having a belief that *p* is fixed by how high a credence in *p* you are justified in having. The justification of belief whether *p* must, for the Bayesian, be fixed by justificatory facts concerning the total Bayesian supervenience base consisting of credences and preferences. But if belief is pragmatic, justification for belief could be fixed in this more holistic way. So, if changing stakes always reflect themselves in some of your justified credences—if, that is, perceived stakes are what matter rather than actual stakes—we can see how the justification for outright belief that *p* could vary with stakes even though the justification of your credences is purist.

Pragmatic views, here again, are in the same boat as Kaplan's Assertion View. Just as the question of whether you are justified in Kaplan-believing that *p* is not fixed by your justification for having certain credences with

[24] This view is endorsed by Weatherson (2005: 420). However, notice that even if token credences (and only token credences) are beliefs, it doesn't follow that being justified in believing that *p* amounts to being justified in having credence level c toward *p*, even if the token instance of c is the token belief that *p*.

respect to *p*, but *is* fixed by this together with other factors acceptable to the Bayesian (e.g. justification for credences toward value propositions, or perhaps rationality of the utilities associated with getting truth and avoiding falsehood), the same goes for being justified in (pragmatic-)believing that *p*, if belief doesn't require credence 1. As far as we can see, there need be no epistemological danglers, either for us or for Kaplan.

Bayesians will naturally want some motivation for thinking that there are important doxastic states other than credences. And here, just as Kaplan cites reasons why it might be important to mark out a doxastic state which meets the conditions of his Assertion View (146), one could make a similar case about pragmatic views. Roughly the importance might be as follows: if belief doesn't amount to credence 1, then belief marks a movable yet important confidence threshold in relation to relevant sets of actions, intentions, feelings, etc.; if you believe that *p*, your credence is high enough so that it doesn't stand in the way of the proposition being your basis for the actions, intentions, feelings, etc. relevant in your situation.[25] If you know that Jill's credence for the proposition that the ice will hold her is .95, you don't know if that's credence enough for her to rely on in her situation; if you know that she believes it is thick enough, you do know she will rely on it.

Therefore, we see no obstacle from Bayesian epistemology to accepting a pragmatic view of belief.

9 IS IT ALL ABOUT BELIEF?

We have given reason for thinking that if justified belief is pragmatic, so is belief. But if this is so, the concern arises whether it is the pragmatic view of belief doing all the work—that our principles about justified belief and even our principles about knowledge may well be true, but even if they are, they are not of distinctively *epistemological* interest.

For instance, Brian Weatherson (2005) and Dorit Ganson (2008), responding to Fantl and McGrath (2002), have independently argued for a certain epistemologically deflationary vision of our project. They agree that we

25 This would help blunt Christensen's (2004: 97) argument that binary belief marks a threshold no more important than the size thresholds marked by 'large dog'.

succeed in our goal of calling into serious question the purist thesis we called *evidentialism*:

> (Evidentialism) If two subjects have the same evidence for/against *p* then either both or neither are justified in believing that *p*.

But they think that we overstate the epistemic significance of the result. We have not, as we claimed to, shown that there is a pragmatic condition on justification. Why not? The final principle we defend in that paper seems to be exactly that:

> (PC) S is justified in believing that *p* only if S is rational to prefer as if *p*.

The consequent is indeed pragmatic. But it takes more than this for there to be a pragmatic condition in any important sense. Here is Weatherson:

> First, imagine a philosopher who holds a very simplified version of functionalism about belief, call it (B)
>
> (B) S believes that *p* iff S prefers as if *p*
>
> Our philosopher one days starts thinking about justification, and decides that we can get a principle out of (B) by adding normative operators to both sides, inferring (JB)
>
> (JB) S is justified in believing that *p* only if S is justified to prefer as if *p*.
>
> Now it would be a mistake to treat (JB) as a pragmatic condition on *justification* (rather than on belief) if it was derived from (B) by this simple means. And if our philosopher goes on to infer (PC) [i.e. S is justified in believing that *p* only if S is rational to prefer as if *p*] from (JB), by replacing 'justified' with 'rational', and inferring the conditional from the biconditionals, we still don't get a pragmatic condition on *justification*. (Weatherson 2005: 417–18)[26]

One can see the point here. Compare Weatherson's derivation of JB to a similar derivation of:

> (NB) S necessarily believes that *p* iff S necessarily prefers as if *p*.

[26] Note that Weatherson is *not* arguing that our principle PC might be derived from the very same principle about belief: if S believes that *p*, then S is rational to prefer as if *p*. This would be a bad argument. As we observed in Chapter 3, just because you believe something doesn't make you rational in acting or preferring on its basis, because your belief might itself be unjustified. And even supposing the replacement *did* preserve truth, there is no way to derive PC from the corresponding principle about belief. After all, being justified in believing something doesn't entail believing it.

NB follows trivially from Weatherson's pragmatic notion of belief. This hardly shows that there are pragmatic conditions on necessity. Of course, it does show that there are pragmatic conditions on necessary belief—and they are different conditions than there are on belief. Believing that *p* requires only that the believer prefer as if *p*, whereas necessarily believing that *p* requires necessarily preferring as if *p*. Likewise, even if Weatherson's JB isn't a pragmatic condition on justification, it is surely a pragmatic condition on being *justified in believing*. But, justification *simpliciter* isn't an epistemic notion in any case. Actions, intentions, desires—all can be justified. Being justified in believing is the notion relevant to epistemology. And this is the very notion that, even in Weatherson's JB, admits of a pragmatic condition. So taken as an argument that JB doesn't constitute a pragmatic condition on something epistemic, Weatherson's argument fails.

One might still feel that, if the source of the pragmatic condition is simply the pragmatic character of belief, there is something epistemologically unimportant about the pragmatic condition on justification in believing. We shouldn't be so quick to indulge this feeling, however. After all, the pragmatic condition entails the falsity of fallibilist purism, which is of considerable epistemological importance. It's hard to see what epistemological importance could amount to if not the entailment of highly controversial and substantive epistemological positions.

Let us take Weatherson's conclusion, then, not as a conclusion about the epistemological unimportance of principles like PC, but as a conclusion about the relation of pragmatic conceptions of belief to those principles. Two questions, at least, need to be distinguished. First, there is the question of whether there is a Weathersonian derivation of some or all of our main epistemic principles—JJ, JJ's converse, KJ, etc. More specifically, is there a sound derivation which takes a pragmatic account of belief as a premise and relies on no substantive epistemological claims in the derivation of the conclusion? Second, given any derivation of our epistemic principles from a pragmatic account of belief—whether it is free of epistemological substance or not—we can ask whether the derivation shows that the pragmatic account of belief is the explanatory ground for the epistemic principle. We'll deal with each kind of question in turn.

Is there a sound Weathersonian derivation from any pragmatic account of belief to some epistemic principle? Weatherson does not himself endorse his quoted derivation of our PC from his B. And we think he is right not to.

B, according to which S believes that *p* iff S prefers as if *p*, is a poor theory of belief. To show this, we indulge in a brief examination of our (2002) principle, which seems to be where the 'prefer as if *p*' locution originates. We unpacked 'S is rational to prefer as if *p*' as: for all states of affairs A and B, it is rational to prefer A to B iff it is rational to prefer A&*p* to B&*p*. If we subtract 'rational to' from 'prefer as if *p*', what do we get? This: for all A and B, one prefers A to B iff it is *rational* to prefer A&*p* to B&*p*. That's what preferring as if *p* is. It is a partially normative state. It is the state of aligning your preferences in the way it is rational to align your *p*-conditional preferences. So, it is hopeless, we think, to identify belief with preferring as if *p*. Just because you believe *p* doesn't mean that your *p*-conditional preferences are rational. We should not expect you, then, to align your unconditioned preferences with your *p*-conditioned ones just because you believe *p*.[27]

So, B won't do. Nor, we think, will the Sartrean view, which we called the Strong Pragmatic View. It won't do because it is too strong. But what about the pragmatic account of belief for which we expressed sympathy—the view that you believe iff your credence is high enough for *p* to be your motivating reason for ϕ-ing, for all ϕ suitably connected to *p*? Might it allow for a plausible epistemologically uncontroversial derivation of some of our epistemic principles?

Consider first our principles about knowledge and knowledge-level justification, for instance, Biconditional $J^K J$:

> (Biconditional $J^K J$) You have knowledge-level justification for *p* iff *p* is warranted enough to justify you in ϕ-ing, for any ϕ.

This cannot itself be derived from a pragmatic theory of belief in Weatherson's way, nor can its converse. Knowledge-level justification is propositional justification, and so one cannot correctly speak of someone being knowledge-level justified in believing that *p*. The best one could do is to derive Biconditional $J^K J$ from the pragmatic notion of belief by first deriving Biconditional JJ

[27] An example: suppose you believe (*p*) John is away from his home. Suppose you also, quite irrationally, prefer robbing his home given he's away to not doing so. (Invent your own preferred story about why this is so. Perhaps you have excellent reason to think you'll be caught and imprisoned.) We expect you to go rob the house, because we can expect that you prefer robbing it to not. Do you prefer as if *p*—as if John is away from his home? No! To prefer as if *p* would be to prefer not robbing his home to robbing it, because *given that he isn't at home* it is rational to prefer not robbing the home to robbing it.

(Biconditional JJ) You are justified in believing *p* iff *p* is warranted enough to justify you in ϕ-ing, for any ϕ

and then using the Equivalence Thesis, which equates justification for belief with knowledge-level justification, to get Biconditional $J^K J$. There are two problems with this.

First, the Equivalence Thesis is a controversial, even if widely accepted, principle about the relationship between knowledge-level justification for *p* and justified belief. Its substance presents itself in two ways. First, it rules out the possibility that there are justifications for belief that can override 'epistemic' justifications, e.g. pragmatic justifications. If such pragmatic justifications were possible, then it should be possible for you to have knowledge-level epistemic justification for *p*, but have stronger countervailing pragmatic justifications for withholding on or disbelieving *p*. You are knowledge-level justified, say, in believing that your brother is guilty but your pragmatic reasons for not believing him guilty outweigh any epistemic reasons, any reasons rooted in your evidence or propositional justification for his guilt. In such a situation, you would have knowledge-level justification but fail to be justified in believing your brother is guilty. This is ruled out by the Equivalence Thesis.

Of course, not everyone is as unsympathetic to the possibility of pragmatic justifications for believing as we are.[28] There are cagey ways to maintain commitment to the Equivalence Thesis, primarily by appending 'epistemically' to 'justified' in the consequent. Even so modified, however, it is a substantive principle. It is denied by externalists who think that the justification *p* must enjoy for you to be able to know that *p* is fairly minimal (or non-existent). Such externalists might easily embrace a more internalist requirement on the justification for believing and say that for it to be the case that you should believe that *p*, you must have quite a bit of justification for so believing. And it would be denied by Lockeans about belief who accept our principles about knowledge.

28 Here are two reasons to be unsympathetic. First, it would seem that if there can be practical reasons for or against belief they would sometimes make it the case that you should believe something for which you had a very low degree of propositional justification. But even if we were threatening your life to believe that Dukakis was elected in 2000, it would be rationally permissible to continue to believe that he wasn't. Second, and more importantly, if there could be practical reasons for belief then you could justifiably conclude that *p* on the basis of some practical reason to believe *p*, and so there should be good arguments corresponding to your reasoning, but no argument of the form *Believing p would have such and such good results, therefore p* is a good one (except, of course, in unusual situations in which *p* is about the results of believing itself).

The Equivalence Thesis is not all one needs to derive Biconditional J^KJ from a pragmatic view of belief. Slapping on justification operators on both sides of a biconditional of the form

> (Pragmatic Belief) You believe that *p* iff you have enough credence in *p* for *p* to be your motivating reason for ϕ-ing, for all relevant ϕ

only gets us what we called in Section 3.1 the 'credal variant' of Biconditional JJ. To get Biconditional JJ, one needs the lemmas we identified earlier. Consider, again, Lemma 1:

> (Lemma 1) For all ϕ, you are *warranted enough* in *p* for *p* to justify you in ϕ-ing iff you are *justified in being such that your credence for p is high enough* for *p* to be your motivating reason for ϕ-ing.

This links the notion of being justified in having a high enough credence to move you with the *epistemic* notion of being warranted enough to justify you. Lemma 1 is plausible, but it is hardly epistemologically trivial. Once again, it might be false if what justifies you in having credence for *p* high enough for *p* to be your motivating reason includes factors other than the justification *p* enjoys for you—e.g. if there are pragmatic justifiers for your credence levels or if justified credence levels (and not propositional justification) takes into account your reliability. Therefore, Biconditional JJ does not follow in an epistemologically trivial way from a pragmatic notion of belief.

So, not only is there no Weathersonian derivation of our principles about knowledge, such as Biconditional J^KJ, but there is no such derivation of our principle about justified belief: Biconditional JJ can't be derived from a pragmatic theory of belief without substantive epistemological assumptions.

What about the explanatory issues? One might argue as follows. First, begin with:

(1) It's because a pragmatic view of belief is true, that you are justified in believing that *p* iff you are justified in being such that your credence for *p* is high enough for *p* to be your motivating reason for ϕ-ing, for any ϕ.

Next, one might claim that the only thing that can make *p* warranted enough to justify you is that you are justified in being such that your credence for p is high enough for p to be your motivating reason. (This is to read Lemma 1 asymmetrically.) One then concludes that if (1) is true, so must be (2):

(2) It's because a pragmatic view of belief is true that you are justified in believing p iff p is warranted enough to justify you in ϕ-ing, for any ϕ.

(2), in effect, says that it's because a pragmatic view of belief is true that Biconditional JJ is true. Here it doesn't matter that we got to (2) from (1) only with the help of a substantive claim; all that matters is that the substantive claim—about the explanatory priority of *having sufficient credence to motivate* over *being warranted enough to justify*—is true.[29]

Supposing this argument succeeds, one might hope to show that all of our principles are true ultimately because belief is pragmatic. Starting with (1), one would make the substitutions corresponding to each substantive claim about explanatory priority needed in the derivation. So, to argue for:

(3) It's because a pragmatic view of belief is true that Biconditional $J^K J$ is true (i.e. you have knowledge-level justification for p iff p is warranted enough to justify you in any ϕ),

one would begin with (1), proceed to (2) as we have, and then substitute *p is knowledge-level justified for S* for *p is warranted enough to justify S* in (3), on the grounds that the latter is explanatorily prior to the former. The hope would be that one could give a similar argument.

The problem is that the explanatory priority claims needed for the substitutions are implausible. Consider the substitution needed to go from (1) to (2). Why should you have high enough credence in p for it to be a motivating reason, when you should? The answer, we think, is, *because p is warranted enough to justify you.* The same goes for the substitution needed to go from (2) to (3). It is plausible to think that what makes you justified in believing p, when you are, is that your justification for p reaches to the level required for knowledge (recall that we are employing an obligating notion of justification: you should believe because your justification rises to knowledge-level).

More generally, the justification for our doxastic attitudes is grounded in the justification we have for the objects of those attitudes, rather than vice

29 Other lemmas are needed, of course, as we saw in Section 4.1.

versa.[30] This fact about explanatory order at once undermines the attempt to explain the truth of Biconditional JJ and Biconditional $J^K J$ in terms of the Pragmatic View of belief and supports our dialectical strategy—of drawing conclusions about belief's being pragmatic from premises about pragmatic conditions on justification and knowledge.

30 Here we again claim as allies Conee and Feldman (2004*a*), who offer a notion of justification that makes justification for doxastic attitudes 'turn entirely on evidence' (83).

6

The Value and Importance of Knowledge

1 THE VALUE OF KNOWLEDGE

Sometimes it's good to know. An adequate theory of knowledge might be expected to explain why. Perhaps this is easy: it's sometimes good to know, because knowing can have good consequences. If a patient has early-stage lung cancer, it would be good for her physician to know this, because the patient would immediately be given life-saving treatment. If a gambler could know ahead of time which teams would win, he would be able to place his bets accordingly.

However, in many cases, it seems that knowing has good consequences only because knowing involves true belief, and true belief, more fundamentally, has the good consequences. One might wonder whether knowing ever has good consequences that can't be chalked up to those of true belief. If Timothy Williamson (2000: 62–4) is right, it does. The fact that a person knows can non-derivatively account for her achievement of good results. That the burglar knows there are diamonds in the house accounts for the persistence of his belief and his perseverance in the search after the obvious hiding places are eliminated, and so accounts for his finding the diamonds at last. That his belief is true isn't good enough, not even that it is a justified true belief. Knowledge has a kind of stability that these states in general do not have. However, even if Williamson is right that knowing can have good consequences which don't derive merely from those of subcombinations of its components, some philosophers have wanted more.[1]

Jonathan Kvanvig, who, along with Duncan Pritchard, is largely responsible for the 'value turn' in epistemology, presumes that knowledge is valuable 'by its very nature' (Kvanvig 2003: xiv). It is not merely valuable, but valuable anywhere—and in every possible world in which—it is found. A particular

1 Williamson himself denies that knowledge has proper components. But the point can be recast as a point about insufficient but necessary conditions.

knowing might lead to bad results in a particular case, and so be *ultima facie* disvaluable, and for this reason Kvanvig is careful to add a 'prima facie' rider in the formulation of his presumption: knowing is anywhere and everywhere *prima facie* valuable (roughly, in the absence of other value-relevant factors, knowings are valuable). No account that ties the value of knowledge merely to its good consequences can make good on this presumption because it at best explains the contingent value of some cases of knowledge.

Kvanvig himself thinks that the necessary value of knowledge can be defended: knowledge is necessarily valuable insofar as it includes as a component true belief, because true belief is necessarily valuable (2003: 204). True belief is valuable anywhere it is found because true beliefs are intrinsically good, at least *prima facie.* (Any particular true belief may, of course, have extrinsic properties that override the intrinsic good.) This is not the end of the story, though. Kvanvig thinks that even a cursory examination of the history of epistemology in the Western tradition, starting with Plato's *Meno*, will make it plain that epistemologists have assumed something more than the value—even the necessary value—of knowledge. When Socrates asks why knowing the way to Larissa is better than merely having true opinion about the way to Larissa, he is assuming that knowledge is not merely valuable, but that it is *more valuable* than mere true belief, and he wants to know why. Generalizing from Socrates, contemporary epistemologists might naturally want to know why knowledge is not merely valuable, but *distinctively* valuable, i.e. more valuable than any subcombination of its components. Again, according to Kvanvig, the presumption is not merely that knowledge happens as a matter of contingent fact to be distinctively valuable, it is distinctively valuable by its very nature, and necessarily so. Knowings, wherever found, will, at least *prima facie*, have some value in addition to any value contributed by subcombinations of its components. Knowledge must be distinctively valuable as such. At least, that's the presumption Kvanvig finds in the history of Western epistemology.

Is knowledge distinctively valuable (as such)?[2] Here Kvanvig (2003: ch. 5) is skeptical. Knowledge can be shown to be more valuable than true belief, because knowledge includes justified true belief, which is more valuable than true belief, but knowledge is not more valuable than justified true belief. If we look at the leading candidates for specifying the anti-Gettier condition, it is hard to see the ad hoc sprawl they add to

[2] We often allow 'as such' to go implicit.

JTB as adding any value (here he echoes Williamson 2000: 62). Kvanvig does not deny that one can find in the literature theories of knowledge which *do* represent knowledge as distinctively valuable (e.g. some infallibilist accounts), but unfortunately, in his view, such accounts get the extension of knowledge wrong. So, if Kvanvig is right, knowledge is not distinctively valuable. And he takes this to have a real practical upshot: epistemologists should devote less attention to knowledge and more to epistemic statuses that are of distinctive value, such as justification and, in particular, understanding.

Kvanvig's arguments have not gone without criticism. Michael DePaul (2009) thinks that Kvanvig's case against distinctive value requires the problematic principle that 'ugliness' of the analysis entails that the analysans lacks value.[3] In a separate review, coauthored with Stephen Grimm, DePaul (2007: 501–4) denies that epistemologists have assumed that knowledge is distinctively valuable. We will be concerned here, however, with one of Kvanvig's seemingly less ambitious, positive arguments that knowledge is valuable, even if it isn't distinctively valuable, because knowledge includes true belief, which is valuable. We think that the issue is not so straightforward and that perhaps true belief and knowledge are not valuable at all or at least not very valuable—as such. This might seem to raise serious worries if one agrees, with Kvanvig, that epistemologists should not devote so very much attention to epistemic relations that are not very valuable (let alone distinctively valuable).

2 THE VALUE OF TRUE BELIEF

Let's grant, with Kvanvig, that if true belief is valuable, knowledge is as well. Is true belief valuable?[4]

[3] We ourselves think that Kvanvig's argument about the Gettier proposals shows, at best, that the various Gettier plugs do not mark value spikes, so to speak, not that they lack value. So, for instance, Kvanvig remarks that it would clearly be valuable to be such that there are no unpossessed undermining defeaters, but that being immune from misleading defeaters seems less clearly valuable (2003: 130). One might reasonably reply that being immune from misleading defeaters *is* valuable, even though it doesn't represent a value 'spike'. But being distinctively valuable doesn't require that knowledge represent a value spike. It could well be that there are superior states—such as JTB + the non-existence of unpossessed defeaters, misleading or otherwise—which are considerably more valuable than knowledge. Knowledge could still be more valuable than any proper subcombination of its components.

[4] Kvanvig suggests but does not endorse the claim that belief and truth both have value. However, as DePaul and Grimm point out (2007: 502–3), there are too many beliefs and truths that seem to

The stock objection is that true beliefs about trivia are without value, e.g. a true belief about the phone number of some random person, or the number of grains of sand at some beach. The stock *reply* is to say that such true beliefs have value, but not very much, and so they are easily overridden, say if truly believing a piece of trivia clutters your mind or distracts you from some more worthwhile pursuit. So, it might be *ultima facie* disvaluable to have such trivial true beliefs. Still, their existence does add some small value to the world.

We think the stock objection is not so easily put to rest, and that ultimately something like it carries the day. To explain why, we need to clarify what it means to speak of a relation as valuable. A standard approach takes a property or relation to be valuable just in case states of affairs of its instantiation are valuable. Thus, a relation **R** is valuable if and only if states of affairs of the form *x***R***y* are valuable. Notice the use of the bare plural in this account—'states of affairs'. Does 'states of affairs' mean 'all states of affairs' or something weaker, such as *most* or *many* or '*in the normal case*'? The standard approach can be developed in any of these ways. (Kvanvig, as we have noted, thinks the presumption found in the history of Western epistemology is a very strong one—that knowledge and true belief are valuable anywhere and everywhere they are found, across possible worlds, that they are valuable as such.) Applying the standard account, then, we have:

> (The Value of Relations as Such—Standard Approach)
>
> A relation R is valuable (as such) iff, necessarily, all states of affairs of the form *x*R*y* are valuable, at least *prima facie*.[5]

Kvanvig thinks knowledge is valuable insofar as true belief is—insofar, on the above account, as it's necessary that all states of affairs of the form *S truly believes that p* are valuable, at least *prima facie*. The stock objection depends on the intuition that when *p* is a piece of trivia, states of affairs of the form

have no value whatever. Having the capacity to form beliefs might be of value to human beings, they grant, but this doesn't entail that every belief has value, even *prima facie*. The same holds, if anything more clearly, for the truth of propositions. Kvanvig also mentions the possibility of arguing that while neither belief nor truth have any value, true belief does, because it is an organic unity in G. E. Moore's sense.

[5] Could a relation's instantiations be necessarily valuable even if the relation isn't, in an intuitive sense, valuable as such? Suppose the relation of loving is valuable as such. Is the following relation also valuable as such: *loving or being jointly such that 2 + 2 = 4*? Probably not. But these complications won't matter to our argument.

S truly believes that p are not valuable *prima facie*. If this intuition is correct, then true belief is not valuable.

We concede that, strictly speaking, the stock objection fails, because the stock reply is perfectly defensible: such states of affairs *are* valuable *prima facie* even if they have very little—and easily overridden—*prima facie* value. But the objection points to a deeper problem. When we naively think about 'the value of' true belief, and even if we explicitly set aside instrumental value, we typically have in mind true beliefs about matters of some importance, such as about fundamental issues in biology, physics, religion, philosophy, ethics, etc. True beliefs about such matters seem to be valuable *prima facie* in all possible worlds. But here the content of the true beliefs intrudes, skewing our value judgments. Because the content is important, we judge that the true belief is very valuable. The stock objection makes vivid the importance of factoring out any value influence from the content of the true belief, for that influence is irrelevant. In fact, the amount of value associated with true belief as such seems best judged by considering true beliefs about trivia, precisely because these beliefs factor out any value-contribution from the content of the belief. The trivial content neither adds value nor subtracts it; it allows us to see through to the value of true belief.

The need to factor out any contribution from the content of the true belief should have been clear in any case.[6] Suppose *p* describes some horrible situation, say immense suffering of innocents. It then looks as though the

[6] This need is recognized in the so-called 'isolation tests' recommended by, among others, Plato (in the *Meno*), Sidgwick (1884), and Moore (1993). We can distinguish between 'negative' isolation tests, such as those that Moore attributed to Sidgwick, and 'positive' isolation tests, such as those employed by Moore. Negative isolation tests attempt to ascertain the value of a part of a composite by asking how much the value of the composite is decreased when that part is imagined absent. If the value is lost, the entire value of the composite is chalked up to the 'absent' part. Positive isolation tests attempt to ascertain the value of a part of a composite by asking how much value remains when the rest of the parts are imagined absent. So, to use Moore's (1993: 240) example, consider the composite that is the pleasure you get listening to Beethoven's Fifth Symphony. While it is plausible, Moore argues, that the mere hearing of the symphony, without any attendant pleasure, is without value, it would be wrong to conclude, as Moore claims Sidgwick does, that the value of the composite is entirely due to the value of the pleasure. For, Moore points out, mere pleasure, without any corresponding consciousness of, say, something beautiful, is likewise plausibly without value (or, at least, has less value than the composite). For a similar distinction, see Santas (2001: 43).

The test we eventually endorse, below, is not strictly an isolation test, because we do not simply isolate the value contributed by true belief by abstracting away the content of the belief. Imagining a true belief without content is somewhat beyond our cognitive abilities, but others may have better luck. Rather, we use a 'replacement' test in which we imagine a true belief in what is arguably a neutral content.

addition of the state of affairs *S truly believes that p* will add immense suffering to the world, with the consequence that whatever good the state of affairs adds is completely swamped by the bad it adds. Is this state of affairs itself *prima facie* good? On the usual rough test, no, because in the absence of other value-relevant factors—where 'other' refers to factors independent of the state of affairs itself—the state is bad! It is part of the state of affairs itself, not something independent of it, that there is immense suffering. Does this imply that true belief isn't valuable as such? It does, if we follow the standard approach to the value of relations as such which simply looks at the value of each and every possible instantiation.

We therefore need to revise the standard approach, by insisting on the explicit factoring-out of any possible value contribution from sources other than the relation itself. We recommend the following account:

> (The Value of Relations as Such—Revised)
>
> A relation **R** is valuable (as such) iff, necessarily, if a state of affairs is an **R**-ing state of affairs—one of the form x**R**y—the fact that it is an **R**-ing state of affairs *prima facie* makes it valuable.[7]

This revision helps us not merely with the case of true belief, but with other problematic relations which seem to be of value as such, e.g. the relation of *taking pleasure in*. (If you think this isn't valuable as such, substitute love, friendship, aesthetic contemplation, etc.) Some *taking-pleasures-in* are, even *prima facie*, disvaluable, e.g. someone's taking pleasure in causing immense suffering. But this doesn't mean that *taking pleasure in* isn't valuable as such. For even when we consider *S takes pleasure in causing immense suffering*, we can still see that the fact that this is a *taking-pleasure-in* state of affairs *prima*

[7] One well-known test for whether a state of affairs being of the R-ing sort makes it valuable is W. D. Ross's (2002). And Ross is quite explicit that in testing for the value of knowledge (and true belief), he needs to factor out other independent values. He says, 'It seems clear that knowledge, and in a less degree what we may for the present call "right opinion," are states of mind good in themselves. Here too we may, if we please, help ourselves to realize the fact by supposing two states of the universe equal in respect of virtue and of pleasure and of the allocation of pleasure to the virtuous, but such that the persons in the one had a far greater understanding of the nature and laws of the universe than those in the other. Can anyone doubt that the first would be a better state of the universe?' (138–9). Ross is trying to isolate the value contributed to a state of affairs by the instantiation of knowledge and right opinion. We think he errs only in neglecting a particular independent source of value—namely, the content of the knowledge or right opinion. Once that is held fixed, we think that adding true belief (or knowledge) to a universe results in a better state of the universe.

facie makes it valuable. The state nonetheless isn't valuable because of other value-relevant properties it has, e.g. that it is a state of affairs which includes immense suffering.[8]

By appealing to this modified approach to the value of relations, we can defend the value of true belief as such from alleged counterexamples in which the content of the true belief is a proposition whose truth is very disvaluable. Combine this with the stock reply to the stock objection about trivia and it seems we have a solid defense of the value of true belief as such. The only hitch—and it is a big one—is that in preserving the value of true belief as such we have to concede that it is minuscule. Once we factor out any value contribution that depends on the content of the true belief, and we zero in on the mere fact that a state of affairs is of the *true believing* sort, then it is plain that this fact can't confer anything more than minuscule value. If it contributed more, then the *prima facie* value of states of affairs in which you truly believe some piece of trivia would be great. The stock objection fails, but not by much.

The same sort of argument can be applied to justified true belief, as well, and even directly to knowledge. It starts to seem that knowledge is of very little value as such: the mere fact that a state of affairs is a knowing contributes little good. If you add up lots of knowledge, the mere fact that they are knowings confers only minimal value on each (e.g. think of adding up vast stores of knowledge of the contents of telephone books). Even if we assume none of this value is defeated—the knowings don't clutter minds, etc.—the total amount of good added by the fact that these are knowings is still very little.[9] More to the point, the value contributed merely by truly believing or knowing can't be sufficient to explain why epistemologists are so concerned with knowledge or true belief: for the value contributed by these things is minuscule, and is swamped by many other concepts in the vicinity that

[8] There might be other reasons the state isn't valuable. For example, it might be an additional value that pleasure be derived from a state of affairs in proportion to the value of the state of affairs—much as Ross thinks that, in addition to the values of pleasure and virtue, there is a value of pleasure being allocated in proportion to virtue. This mechanism will allow us to conclude, we think intuitively, that there is *something* valuable about the pleasure S gets from causing immense suffering while also concluding that there is something disvaluable about it—something disvaluable over and above the immense suffering that S causes.

[9] One cannot avoid these problems by scaling back to the view that, although true belief and knowledge aren't valuable, they do at least *prima facie* make the believer better off. Here, too, it all depends on the content of the beliefs. It is not the fact that your true belief *is a true belief* that makes you significantly better off, but the fact, e.g., that it is a true belief about how to live your life.

epistemologists are quite unconcerned with. Should epistemologists, then, *be* so concerned with knowledge and true belief?[10]

3 FROM VALUE TO IMPORTANCE

Suppose the negative conclusions from the previous section are borne out. Knowledge is only minimally valuable, at least as such. Does this imply anything about how we should do epistemology? Shouldn't we focus on more valuable states? This might not be easy. The state of *understanding* as such likely won't be much more valuable (think of understanding trivial phenomena). Nor will justification. Should epistemologists instead investigate states which are of real value, such as *knowing truths about matters of importance*? Perhaps this should recommend to us something like *wisdom* as the primary epistemological subject.

The tight connection between the value of knowledge and the worth of focusing on it is implicit in much of the literature on epistemic value. Here is Kvanvig's opening salvo:

> The history of epistemology centers on the concept of knowledge, especially on the difficult questions of whether knowledge is possible and, if it is, how much of it there is. A presupposition of this inquiry is that whether and to what extent we have knowledge is deeply important. Philosophers reflect on the nature and extent of knowledge not simply because they have free afternoons to fill but (also) because questions about what we know and how we know it touch on the deeply significant questions about the relationship between mind and world and the possibility of success in determining what is true and what is not. In a word, knowledge is valuable, and philosophers reflect on what we know because they share this viewpoint. (2003: ix)

One can imagine something roughly similar in a book on other concepts, e.g. those of necessity, property exemplification, existence, or causation. But the last line would have to be modified. Necessity, property exemplification, etc. are not valuable, and metaphysicians know that. Nothing about the value of

[10] Granted, a relation which isn't very valuable as such can serve an indispensable role as part of an organic unity. The mere fact that L is a law might not add much value to the world, and the mere fact that a person, in believing that L is a law, believes something true, might not add value either, but the fact that the person truly believes something with the content *L is a law* might add some genuine value, and so some value that isn't merely aggregative. But the point about organic unities cuts both ways. Suppose you are assisting someone in a crime. The mere fact that you are doing this has disvalue, as perhaps does the mere belief that you are doing so, but these disvalues don't simply aggregate when you truly believe you are assisting someone in a crime.

these properties and relations is presupposed by metaphysical inquiry into the corresponding concepts. These are concepts of properties which have little to do, in particular, with us. But even when a concept picks out a property that bears on us, inquiry into it doesn't presuppose that the property is valuable to instantiate. So, for instance, we study reference, intentionality, perception, belief, desire, intention, and action. Perhaps there's something of value in our ability to refer, to take as an object of thought, to perceive, believe, etc., though it's unlikely that there is anything valuable, even *prima facie*, in all or even most cases of referring, thinking, etc., let alone in all possible such cases. We doubt that any claim about the value as such of instantiating these properties and relations is a presupposition of our inquiry, let alone the distinctive value as such of instantiating them. What is presupposed is that the concepts are worth investigating.

One way concepts can be worth investigating is for there to be great value in instantiating the properties they pick out. But this is only *one* way. A concept might be worth investigation in a number of other ways. For instance, apparently obvious truths stated using the concept might lead to extremely surprising conclusions (think of skeptical arguments), in which the mistake made would seem to be something a philosopher could discover by scrutinizing that concept. That would justify philosophical investigation of the concept. Second, a concept might be worth investigating because it is simply interesting in itself. For example, knowledge seems to require something of a knower, the world, and their relations, and it might simply be interesting just what these requirements are, just as it is interesting just what is required to perceive an object, and this is the sort of thing a philosopher is well placed to investigate.

The concept of knowledge is worthy of investigation for both of these reasons. But does any of this suggest that the concept of knowledge deserves the lavish attention it has been given? Understanding, for instance, is philosophically interesting in its own right. And one can find worrisome conceptual puzzles lurking in many quarters in epistemology, by no means only when the concept of knowledge is involved. Why the special attention to knowledge at the expense of other epistemic concepts?

4 THE IMPORTANCE OF KNOWLEDGE

A concept can also be worth investigating because there are reasons for thinking it figures in principles of explanatory significance for philosophy. Let's say that when a concept does figure in such principles, it is a 'philosophically important' concept. The idea, then, is that a concept can be worth investigating because there are reasons to think it is philosophically important. For example, if Williamson (2000: ch. 9) is right about the relation between knowledge and evidence (E = K) and the relation between knowledge and assertion (assertion is that speech act such that the explanatorily basic rule is to assert only what you know), then knowledge figures in explanatorily significant principles. Even if Williamson turns out to be wrong that knowledge is valuable (because stable), his project will have made good on what seems to us to be the initially more plausible presumption that knowledge is important.

Most theorists trying to find *value* for knowledge typically focus on backward-looking conditions—where the belief came from, whether it was the exercise of a virtue, etc.—to locate the relevant value. However, the pragmatic principles we've endorsed in previous chapters suggest refocusing attention on forward-looking conditions. Our slogan, after all, is that when you know something you can put it to work. We made this more precise in our principle KJ, viz. that what is known can justify, i.e. is warranted enough to justify you in ϕ-ing for any ϕ. KJ connects knowledge to the broad notion of justification, which applies not only in relation to belief but to action and intention and any other ϕ such that you can have a reason to ϕ.[11] KJ is an important philosophical principle, if true. So, if KJ is true, then perhaps knowledge gets at least part of its importance from the fact that it figures in KJ.

However, one might still ask whether KJ provides grounds for claiming any *distinctive* importance for knowledge. If it doesn't, and generally if there is no good reason to think knowledge is distinctively important, we might wonder whether Kvanvig's negative conclusion about the distinctive value of knowledge carries over to its importance. Perhaps he was wrong to focus on value rather than importance, but if knowledge can be shown not to be of distinctive importance, won't he still be right to bid us to focus our epistemological efforts elsewhere?

When the topic is importance rather than value, we need to rethink questions about distinctiveness. It would be silly to try to show that knowledge

[11] Like Kvanvig, we will mostly ignore differences between *the concept of knowledge* and *knowledge* in what follows (though those differences might be seen to be more important in the final section). Depending on one's opinions about what philosophy of the kind we're practicing investigates—concepts or properties/relations—one might take the importance to attach to the concept of knowledge or to knowledge itself (or, as we see it, to both).

is *more* important than belief, truth, true belief, justified belief, etc., whatever precisely that would mean. The question is rather whether knowledge has an importance to call its own, one which is distinctive to it.

The smoothest way to show that knowledge has such an importance is to provide some explanatorily significant true biconditional of the form K ↔ X. For no such principle, at least if it is necessarily true, could be true of anything less than knowledge or of anything more. So, for example, if all and only what you know constitutes your evidence, as Williamson argues, we have a good case for distinctive importance. We will not examine the proposals from Williamson here. Given what we have argued in Chapter 4, though, we suspect the best Williamson can claim is to have provided explanatory significant principles stating necessary conditions on knowledge, not sufficient ones.[12]

In the next section, we consider the prospects for constructing a biconditional version of KJ.

4.1 A biconditional for knowledge

In Chapter 4, we argued that false propositions can and in some cases do justify, i.e. that they can be and in some cases are justifying reasons one has. This point alone rules out simply affirming the converse of KJ, i.e. that anything warranted enough to justify is known. But there remains the possibility of supplementing the consequent of KJ—adding conjuncts to it—in such a way as to make for a true biconditional. In earlier chapters, we distinguished between something's being a reason there is for you to ϕ (call this a 'favorer' or 'favoring reason'), which must be a fact (or a true proposition), and something's being a reason you have to ϕ (a 'justifier' or 'justifying reason'), which needn't be. The former bears on whether you ought to do something in an objective sense, the latter in a less objective but still not merely subjective sense. If your doctor incorrectly tells you (through a mix-up at the lab) that your strep test came back positive (in fact it is negative and you don't have strep) and on that basis gives you a prescription, then even if you ought not in an objective sense take the prescription, in

12 One might run a 'subtraction' argument like the one we gave at the beginning of Chapter 4 on the relation between knowledge and evidence, to show that something weaker than knowledge that p suffices for p's being evidence you have. In any case, the arguments of Sections 1 and 2 of that chapter are highly relevant to whether Williamson is right that only what is known can be evidence you have.

another not-yet-subjective sense, this is what you should do. Notice that this is so even if you believe, on no good basis, that you shouldn't take the pill. Perhaps you would be somehow incoherent or irrational if you intentionally did something you believed you shouldn't do, but that doesn't make your beliefs about what you should do automatically true! What you should do in the favored intermediary sense is dependent on *the 'information' you have to go on.*[13]

Distinguishing reasons-there-are from reasons-had might seem unmotivated if the two are simply left unconnected. But there is a clear connection. When you know that *p*, then *p* can be—that is, is warranted enough to be—both a favoring reason (because true) and a justifying reason (because justified). Assuming that knowing requires believing, knowing *p* also ensures that *p* can be—has credence enough to be—your motivating reason. However, this observation doesn't yet deliver a biconditional. Having a justified true belief that *p* is enough to qualify *p* to be a reason in all these senses.

A natural next thought, in our search for a biconditional version of KJ, is to include as an extra condition the existence of a non-accidentality condition holding between these reasons—in essence, a Gettier plug. One might propose that when you know *p*, it's *because p* can favor that it can justify. However, as everyone who is familiar with the Gettier problem knows, we can rig up Gettier cases in which the truth causally explains your justification through a deviant causal chain. (Seeing a hologram of a man, you believe there is a man behind the desk, and there is, behind the hologram, and in fact the man is causally controlling the hologram through an electronic device.) But if 'because' isn't causal—or merely causal—what is it? It seems to us that the only thing to say is the less-than-helpful claim that if you know that *p*, it's not a matter of Gettier-like luck[14] that *p* can favor given that *p* can justify.

[13] Talk of 'information' here, which needn't consist solely of truths, is of course very close to talk of what evidence you have, or more generally your 'total justificatory perspective'—a perspective determined by the totality of facts about your degrees of propositional justification for various propositions.

[14] Can't we at least eliminate 'Gettier-like' here? Arguably, not. As Kvanvig (2003: 113–14) notes, to claim that knowledge is justified true belief in which it's not a matter of luck that one's belief is true given its basis *is not* to give a theory of knowledge. Consider the Havit/Nogot case. But let's suppose that Havit and Nogot are in communication via cell phone. Havit will buy a Ford at the precise moment Smith, seeing Nogot driving a rented Ford, will form the belief that someone in the office owns a Ford. Here it's not a matter of luck in at least some sense that Jones has a true belief (the whole thing was planned, etc.) but it is a matter of Gettier-like luck. Furthermore, you can know that *p* even if you are lucky in *some* sense to have gotten it right given your basis: you're lucky (in some sense) to be a human disposed to react in the right way to your evidence, etc. See

Any attitude, activity, or state for which you can have reasons can be in a broad sense *Gettiered.* Suppose you have two brothers, and that you have what would seem to be decisive evidence that your elder brother, the spendthrift and all-around family embarrassment, has been secretly diverting money from your bank account to his. You are saddened. And, as you see it, you have a powerful reason to be saddened: that a brother of yours would steal from you rather than ask for help. You in effect cite this as your reason when you say, 'I am saddened that a brother of mine would steal from me rather than ask for help.' Unbeknownst to you, it's the otherwise honorable and respectable younger brother who is stealing the money. Now, one question we could ask here is whether your claim of the form 'I am saddened that *p*' is false. Many working in the emotions literature would answer this question in the affirmative.[15] And in fact it is probably the standard view that *S regrets/is proud/is embarrassed/is saddened/etc. that p* entails *S knows that p*. But even if, as we think is plausible,[16] your earlier sadness report in the theft case was true, it still seems that it was only a matter of Gettier-like luck that that which justifies and motivates you favored doing what you did—or to put it more intuitively: it was only a matter of Gettier-like luck that *your reason* for feeling sad was *a reason for you* to feel sad.

To generalize: if ϕ-ing is something for which you might have reasons, there can in principle be cases in which it is only a matter of Gettier-like luck that your justifying and motivating reason for ϕ-ing was *a reason* for you to ϕ. This is what we are calling *Gettiered* ϕ-ing. Now for the connection to knowledge and a further biconditional. Suppose you are then saddened that your brother stole from you. Then if—and only if—you know that he did is it the case that your sadness is unGettiered, that is, it is not a matter of Gettier-like luck that your motivating and justifying reason for being saddened is a reason for you to be saddened. More carefully, this delivers a principle connecting knowledge to invulnerability to Gettierization:

(KG) You know that *p* iff: *p* can be a reason in all three senses—justifying, favoring, and motivating—and it is not a matter of Gettier-like

Pritchard (2005) for an attempt to spell out precisely what sort of luck is relevant to knowledge, and see Lackey's review (2006) for a critique.

15 See the influential discussion by Gordon (1987: 47–9). See also Unger (1975: 158) and Owens (2008).

16 Notice that, after learning all the facts, and conceding that you didn't really know that a brother of yours was stealing from you, you would not conclude 'I guess I wasn't really saddened that a brother of mine would steal from me rather than ask for help.'

> luck that p can be a favoring reason given that it can be a justifying and motivating reason.[17]

KG guarantees not only that if you know that p you satisfy the JTB conditions for p but also that any attitude, including but not limited to belief, which you have on the basis of p is unGettiered with respect to p. Knowledge that Smith owns a Ford doesn't merely protect you from Gettiered belief that *someone in the office owns a Ford*, it protects you from Gettiered envy, Gettiered pity, etc. Moreover, only knowledge can do these things. Justified true belief is not enough to protect against Gettiered ϕ-ing on the basis of p, as the case of sadness based on the Gettiered belief that a brother of yours would steal rather than ask for help exemplifies.[18]

So, KG is a biconditional for knowledge. It is explanatorily significant only if there is something important in the concept of *unGettiered* successful ϕ-ing in general—something that is missing from justified successful ϕ-ing. If there isn't, then KG will not suffice for the distinctive importance of knowledge.

We do not know how to argue for the importance of unGettiered successful ϕ-ing other than by noting that we often seem to *treat it* as important. When you learn that it was your younger brother who was stealing from you, you will regard your previous sadness as somehow misaligned with the facts: perhaps it's true that you were sad that a brother of yours stole from you rather than ask for help; but you feel your sadness wasn't really responsive to the facts, to the reasons there were. One might try to explain this by

[17] KG doesn't seem to require proper basing for knowing. The basing requirement appears to consist in a requirement that the fact that you believe p is no coincidence given that p is justified for you. An initial thought about how to accommodate this requirement is to add to the right-hand side of KJ a condition to the effect that it is not a matter of luck that p can be a justifying reason given that it can be a motivating reason. We will not pursue the question further.

[18] A referee worried whether doubting needs to be connected with knowledge in the way KG suggests. We see no difficulty in the left-to-right direction. If you know p, then p seems perfectly qualified to be a reason you have to doubt something, as well as a reason there is to doubt something, etc. (If you know that the forecast is 90% chance of rain, that this is the forecast can be your reason in all these senses for doubting it will be sunny.) Perhaps the difficulty is supposed to be with the other direction. Suppose p is qualified to be a reason in all these senses, and there is the right non-accidentality relation holding between these qualifications. Could you still fail to know? We don't see how, at least supposing that our argument for JJ in Chapter 4 is sound. If you meet the conditions on the right-hand side of KG, with respect to *the forecast is a 90% chance for rain*, and doubting it will be sunny, then you are justified in believing *the forecast is a 90% chance for rain*, and have knowledge-level justification for this proposition. And given the other conditions, you believe it, it is true, and there is no relevant Gettier-like luck. We don't see why you wouldn't know it.

Perhaps we've misunderstood the worry. Perhaps there is some worry whether KG, and indeed KJ, entails infallibilism by entailing that if you know p then you have a reason—namely, p itself—to be absolutely certain that p. We answer this objection in Appendix II.

saying that the explanation of why *a brother of yours stole from you rather than ask for help* is a reason for you to feel sad and the explanation of why this same proposition was a reason you had don't hook up in the right sort of way. It was a reason because of something about your younger brother, but you had that reason because of the misinformation about your elder brother. But, however it is explained, we feel a misalignment and register it in our emotional reactions. You are *chagrined* at your sadness.[19]

In environmental Gettier cases, there also seems to be less a misalignment than a fortunate alignment. When you learn that you bought property with a barn on it while your buddies bought adjacent properties with barn façades, you feel a sort of undeservingness when you compare your situation with theirs—that you have somehow unfairly benefited. In short, you feel *embarrassed.* The same is true when you are on the other side: you feel that you have unfairly suffered; you feel *resentful.* Of course, we have these same feelings just about Gettiered justified belief in the first place, so it's not clear that our latest biconditional, KG, adds anything fruitful on *this* score. If the arguments work well here, they'll work well just about unGettiered belief. What KG contributes is greater understanding about what the importance of knowledge consists in: not just in unGettiered justified true belief, but protection from Gettiered attitudes generally.

Kvanvig claims that these feelings, even if they are evidence of value (or, as we would rather say, importance), don't fix on Gettier-like luck alone. They show 'only the common human inclination against being duped, and one can be duped because of truths that undermine knowledge and because of truths that do not undermine knowledge' (2003: 26). He admits that, yes, when you learn that you were Gettiered, as in the first version of the Tom Grabit case (you saw Tom take the book but unbeknownst to you his mother testified, truly, that Tom has an identical Twin who is a thief), you feel embarrassment or regret for asserting what you did. But modify the case by making the defeater misleading and nothing need change:

> The police know the story is concocted; they know [Tom's mother] is an inveterate liar and will say anything to protect Tom. They also know Tom has no twin. But you don't know all this, and if you were told what the mother said, you'd be every bit as inclined to take back the assertion that Tom stole the book and to experience

[19] This point might also help demonstrate that knowledge is an essential part of states of value (and also of states of disvalue!). Though, again, knowledge as such, even if it has more value than Gettiered JTB as such, has very little value.

some embarrassment or regret for having confidently claimed it. But the defeater is a misleading one; without having been told it, it does not undermine your knowledge, because it is so obviously farcical. (26)

Kvanvig is speaking about assertion, but he presumably would generalize: the feelings of embarrassment, etc. do not track the lack of knowledge. We think they do. You feel embarrassment about your assertion 'Tom stole the book' after you get the misleading information about the mother. The fact that you feel embarrassment does not of course entail that you didn't know. The suggestion is rather that it is a reaction to your belief that you didn't know, and this is evidence that it is important to us whether we know. And you do think you didn't know in this case. What happens, though, when you learn that the defeater was misleading, because the mother is a liar, among other things? We think it isn't at all implausible to feel a kind of vindication, at least so long as you are convinced you originally knew despite the existence of the misleading defeater.

The leading idea, then, is that when you believe that your previous ϕ-ing was Gettiered, you feel a kind of emotional reaction that is lacking in cases in which you think your previous ϕ-ing is grounded in knowledge. This is certainly no proof that the link between knowing and invulnerability to Gettiered ϕ-ing which KG asserts is explanatorily significant, but it provides some grounds for hope, and so some basis for optimism that KG can secure the distinctive importance of knowledge.

4.2 A second argument for distinctive importance

Does the case for the distinctive importance of knowledge hinge on the importance of being Gettiered? If invulnerability to Gettierization in belief, action, emotion, etc. isn't of special importance, does that close the case on whether knowledge is distinctively important? We don't think so.

We have been working under the assumption that if there is an explanatorily significant biconditional of the form $K \leftrightarrow X$, then knowledge has distinctive importance, an importance to call its own. But there is a second way knowledge can have distinctive importance: there might be an explanatorily significant principle in which the concept of knowledge figures essentially.[20]

[20] The one advantage for the first strategy is that it is neutral between whether the concept of knowledge has distinctive importance and whether knowledge—the state itself—has distinctive importance. On this second strategy, at most what is shown is that the concept of knowledge has

So, suppose that $\Phi(K)$ is an explanatorily significant true principle. If the truth of $\Phi(K)$ does not derive from some explanatorily deeper principle $\Phi(F)$, where F is some knowledge-free concept, then—and arguably only then—$\Phi(K)$ reveals an importance distinctive of knowledge. Here $\Phi(K)$ need not be a biconditional. Suppose Williamson is right that all knowledge is evidence but he is wrong that only knowledge can be evidence. The principle '$K \rightarrow E$' could still reveal an importance distinctive to knowledge if this principle didn't derive from explanatorily deeper ones, e.g. ones such as '$B \rightarrow E$' or '$J \rightarrow E$'.

Does our key principle KJ—what you know is warranted enough to justify—reveal an importance that is distinctive to knowledge? There is a good case to be made, at least if fallibilism is true. We grant that KJ is not explanatorily basic. It is true because knowledge-level justification can justify. $J^K J$, we have claimed, is explanatorily deeper than KJ. But the concept of knowledge-level justification obviously is not knowledge-free, and so is no obstacle to KJ's identifying a distinctive importance to the concept of knowledge. Recall that, for us, *p* is knowledge-level justified for you if and only if you are justified well enough to know that *p*.

Suppose, however, that there is a good account of knowledge-level justification of the form:

> for *p* to be knowledge-level justified for you is for you to satisfy X(*p*),

where X expresses a knowledge-free concept, and where

> if you satisfy X(*p*), then *p* is warranted enough to justify you in ϕ-ing for any ϕ,

is explanatorily deep. Then it would seem to follow that KJ does not reveal the distinctive importance of knowledge, because KJ would derive from a deeper principle—XJ—which is knowledge-free. We cannot prove that there is no such X, but we think there is good reason to think there isn't.

One candidate for X which we can dismiss from the start is 'is warranted enough to justify you in ϕ-ing for any ϕ'. The problem is that the corresponding principle of the form 'If you satisfy X(*p*), then *p* is warranted enough to justify you' is of the trivial 'If A, then A' form, and so not at all

distinctive importance. This would be sufficient to justify the widespread epistemological interest in the concept. It is an interesting question, which we will not discuss here, whether the importance of the concept of knowledge is sufficient for grounding the philosophical interest in how much knowledge we actually have (or can have).

explanatorily deep. And since it isn't explanatorily deep, there is no fear that KJ owes its explanatory significance to it. Some other candidates for X are also quickly ruled out. X can't simply be *having some reasons to believe p, being pretty well justified*, or even *being very well justified*. None of these even get the extension of knowledge-level justification right.

One might hope that X can be *justified in (outright) believing*—that:

> you are justified in believing that p only if p is warranted enough to justify you ϕ-ing, for any ϕ

is explanatorily deeper than:

> (J^KJ) p is knowledge-level justified for you only if p is warranted enough to justify you in ϕ-ing, for any ϕ.

However, we argued in Chapter 5 that although *being justified in believing that p* is equivalent to *having knowledge-level justification for p*, the latter is explanatorily more fundamental. When you are justified in believing that p—when you should believe that p (or better, when believing, of the three attitudes, is the attitude you should have)—this is because your propositional justification for p is strong enough for knowledge that p, rather than *vice versa*. Therefore, the antecedent of J^KJ is explanatorily more fundamental than the antecedent of the proposed replacement principle and J^KJ is explanatorily deeper than the replacement principle—just as 'S is male only if S has a Y-chromosome' is explanatorily deeper than 'S is a bachelor only if S has a Y-chromosome': S is a bachelor because S is, among other things, male, not vice versa.

The term 'knowledge-level justification', as far as we know, comes from Conee and Feldman. Let us see whether they can provide the needed X. Here is their 'criminal' account of knowledge-level justification:

> A belief is epistemically justified sufficiently for knowledge, according to the 'criminal' standard that we endorse, when one has strong reasons in support of it, no undefeated epistemic reason to doubt it, and no undefeated epistemic reason to believe that one's evidence for it is unreliable (2004*b*: 296)

where a 'strong reason' in support of a proposition is a proof 'weaker than a mathematical proof, but stronger than a good reason to believe'.

Taken at face value, this proposal is somewhat vague. When do we count as having a reason to doubt? What makes a reason 'good' or, worse, 'stronger than good'? The answers to these questions seem to be that, whatever it is to have better than good reasons without having undefeated defeaters, when you are in this situation, your belief is beyond reasonable doubt—you should not doubt the proposition. You should not withhold and you should not disbelieve. Knowledge-level justification, on this account, is a degree of justification such that, when *p* enjoys it, belief is the attitude you should have, of the three attitudes. In other words, Conee and Feldman's 'criminal' account boils down to the previous account in terms of justified belief, and we have already argued that this gets the order of explanation backwards.[21]

Conee and Feldman (and Chisholm) explain knowledge-level justification in terms of the attitudes you should have toward *p*. All such accounts, arguably, will get the order of explanation wrong. Is there an alternative? There are a number of other accounts of knowledge-level justification available in the literature, e.g. Lehrer's (2000) account in terms of all objections to *p* being answered or neutralized on the basis of one's acceptance system and Klein's (1980*b*) account in terms of complete absorption of counterevidence to *p*. Let us abridge all such accounts by saying that, according to such accounts, you have knowledge-level justification that *p* when you can 'deal with' the possibility that *p* is false. Here is the difficulty confronting all such

[21] Chisholm's accounts all seem to suffer from this difficulty, though this might be the least of their problems. In all three editions of Chisholm's *Theory of Knowledge*, the level of justification associated with knowledge is dubbed *the evident*. What does it take for a proposition to be evident? In the first edition (1966), the answer given is this: *p* is evident for S if and only if believing *p* is reasonable for S and there is no proposition such that it is more reasonable for S to believe it than it is for him to believe *p*. Chisholm is answering the question 'How justified must *p* be to be knowledge-level justified?' by saying 'justified enough to make believing *p* as reasonable as believing anything'. This gets the order of explanation backwards. (A more fundamental difficulty, as Hinton (1969: 384) noted, is that this definition seems to require that nothing one knows can be more justified than anything else. This is plausible under infallibilism but not under fallibilism.) In the second edition (1977), Chisholm took the above definition to define 'certain' rather than 'evident'. He then redefined the evident as follows: *p* is evident for S if and only if believing *p* is more reasonable than withholding on *p* and any proposition which it is more reasonable for S to believe than it is for S to believe *p* is certain. Here again, knowledge-level justified for *p* is being understood in terms of reasonableness of attitudes towards *p*. (Again, there are other problems. As Wayne Wasserman (1980) noted, Chisholm's definitions entail that all non-certain evident propositions are equally reasonable to believe, i.e. equally justified, which seems wrong given fallibilism.) Finally, in the third edition (1989), Chisholm revamped the first edition definition by moving to a comparison to withholdings: *p* is evident for S if and only if believing *p* is reasonable for S and there is no proposition such that it is more reasonable for S to withhold on it than it is for S to believe *p* (11). Again, the order of explanation seems wrong: it is because *p* is justified enough for knowledge that this relation of relative reasonableness of attitudes holds, if it holds at all. (It is also unclear whether this account avoids the problem Wasserman noted with the second. Think of how very reasonable it is for you to withhold on *this fair coin when tossed will come up tails*. Is it equally reasonable for you to believe propositions about your teaching schedule next semester, the city of your birth, etc.? Unless we want to give in to infallibilism, we will presumably know some such things. So, if Chisholm is right, they must be evident, and yet by his definition it seems they are not.)

accounts, if they are to be consistent with fallibilism. Given what we have argued in Chapter 4, if fallibilism is true, then knowledge-level justification is something which can vary holding fixed the absolute degree of justification. So, what is it, then, to be able to deal with the possibility that *p* is false if, with the same absolute degree of justification, you can fail to be able to deal with it when much is at stake in your action depending on whether *p*, even though the chance of not-*p* is very, very small?

One proposal, of course, is that you fail to be able to deal with the possibility that *p* is false when that possibility stands in the way of having knowledge-level justification. But that is circular. Presumably, the defenders of these proposals will take a different line, like this: you can deal with the possibility that *p* is false when *p* is justified enough for you to rely on it, to put it to work. And the more careful answer will appeal to *p*'s being justified enough to be a justifier. In the end, in other words, one arrives at our claim $J^K J$, that *p* is knowledge-level justified for you iff *p* is justified or warranted enough to be a justifying reason you have to ϕ for any ϕ. But of course, we wanted a knowledge-free account of knowledge-level justification which is such that:

> if you satisfy X(*p*), then *p* is warranted enough to justify you in ϕ-ing for any ϕ

is true and could explain why $J^K J$ holds. Substituting the right-hand side for the left, one of course is back to a trivial conditional, and so one which can't explain $J^K J$.

We have not of course considered all possible knowledge-free accounts of knowledge-level justification. But our discussion gives us reason to think that, at least given fallibilism, there is no correct knowledge-free account which (a) is consistent with $J^K J$ and (b) can be invoked to explain $J^K J$. If, indeed, there is no such account, it looks like KJ secures the distinctive importance of knowledge.[22] Not only would KJ secure this, it would do it by connecting knowledge to an important normative status: being warranted enough to be a justifying reason, whether practical or theoretical. KJ would therefore secure the distinctive *normative* importance of knowledge.

[22] Even if there is no X to do the job we have set out, might there be an X which answers to the following conditions: (1) the conditional 'If X(*p*), then one is knowledge-level justified' is true, (2) X(*p*) isn't explainable in terms of knowledge-level justification, (3) X is knowledge-free, and (4) 'If you satisfy X(*p*), then *p* is warranted enough to justify you' is explanatorily deep? The prospects look no better here. None of the candidates for X we have considered meet these conditions.

All this assumes fallibilism. What if we give in to infallibilism? We might then say that knowledge-level justification is justification that allows for no chance of error, i.e. that X is infallible justification. The conditional

(Certainty) If *p* is certain for you (i.e. if *p* has epistemic probability 1 for you), then *p* is warranted enough to justify you in ϕ-ing for any ϕ.

would seem to be explanatorily significant. Might it be the explanatory basis for KJ, if infallibilism is true?

It would all depend on whether *p* being knowledge-level justified is explanatorily prior to *p*'s being certain for you, or vice versa. But, assuming there is an equivalence here, it is not implausible to think the explanatory order runs from certainty to knowledge-level justification. Whereas what doxastic attitude you should have with respect to a proposition seems to derive from more basic facts about how strong your propositional justification is for it, and in particular whether your propositional justification is knowledge-level, epistemic certainty is not an attitude, but rather a particular level of propositional justification. We see no essential barrier to thinking of epistemic certainty as more fundamental than knowledge-level justification, given infallibilism.

So, given infallibilism, it seems far less clear that KJ reveals any distinctive importance to knowledge (though there might still be other principles that do, e.g. our knowledge-Gettierization principle KG). We have tried to stay neutral on the question of fallibilism. But you will recall that we have argued not merely that knowledge-level justification is warrant enough for a proposition to justify; knowledge-level justification is also *required.* We have argued, that is, that Biconditional $J^K J$ is true:

(Biconditional $J^K J$) *p* is knowledge-level justified for you iff *p* is warranted enough to justify you in ϕ-ing, for any ϕ.

Notice what happens when we replace 'knowledge-level justified' with 'certain':

(Biconditional Certainty) *p* is certain for you iff *p* is warranted enough to justify you in ϕ-ing, for any ϕ.

Reflection on this biconditional should make us wonder whether knowledge-level justification really does require certainty. It is quite implausible to think hardly any propositions can justify us or can be justifying reasons we have, reasons which make it the case that we should do or believe something. It would be more implausible to think that we can never have reasons that *permit* us to act, of course. But it's implausible still to think that we could hardly ever have reasons that make it the case that we should do or believe something. If hardly any propositions are certain for us, and if Biconditional Certainty is true, then hardly ever do we have justifying reasons.

The plausibility of infallibilism, then, depends on the range of propositions that can be certain for us. If the range is wide, then we might do well to embrace infallibilism. This would have the advantage of allowing us to maintain a commitment to purism. If the range is narrow, though, perhaps we would do well to adopt fallibilism and thus deny purism. It is to this question—whether to embrace infallibilism or instead impurism—that we turn in the next and final chapter.

7

Infallibilism or Pragmatic Encroachment?

Suppose that what you know can justify you, in action as well as belief. Then, as we have argued, fallibilist purism about knowledge is false. Either you cannot know that *p* if there is a chance for you that not-*p* or else two subjects can have the same strength of epistemic position with respect to *p* even though one subject is in a position to know that *p* and the other isn't. The same holds for our principles about justification—$J^K J$, JJ, etc. If they are true, then fallibilist purism about the epistemic concepts involved in those principles is false as well. Assuming that our principles are indeed true, either fallibilism or purism (or both) is false. Which is it? In this chapter, we examine what is to be said for and against both infallibilism and pragmatic encroachment, that is, impurism due to the encroachment of pragmatic factors.

1 INFALLIBILISM?

The primary hurdle for infallibilism is the seemingly robust degree of skepticism it requires. We engage with this hurdle in the closing remarks of this section. We begin by considering whether there is independent support for infallibilism.

1.1 Arguments for infallibilism

In Chapter 1, we considered the charge that fallibilism is 'mad' (see, again, Lewis' oft-quoted invocation to 'hear it afresh'): 'I know but I might be wrong'. We discussed various aspects of this charge, concluding that fallibilists can accommodate and explain the apparent madness of fallibilism by taking knowledge to be compatible only with an idle probability of error. We will not rehearse those arguments here.

A second argument for infallibilism appeals to multi-premise closure. It's only if knowledge ensures no epistemic chance of error that competent deduction from multiple known premises can be guaranteed to secure knowledge of the conclusion. This consideration may sound powerful when we think about deducing a proposition from two or three other propositions which obviously entail it (e.g. in reasoning from p and if p, then q, to q, or reasoning from p and q to $p\&q$). But, as has been widely noted, the full version of multi-premise-closure seems doubtful if not clearly false. You might know $p_1, \ldots, p_{1000}$, but not at all feel confident that you know their conjunction, and this lack of confidence seems reasonable. The natural explanation for why it seems reasonable is that as you conjoin known premises, you accumulate epistemic risks. At the very least, it is far from clear that multi-premise closure holds in general, and so any argument for infallibilism from it will be problematic.

One might hope to find a more decisive argument for infallibilism in the work of Timothy Williamson, who is often cited as having shown that knowledge requires probability 1. However, Williamson (2000: ch. 10) is careful to insist that his account is an account of 'evidential probability', or probability on your evidence. He does argue (ch. 9), explicitly, that your evidence is what you know: E = K. If he is right about that, then probability on your evidence just is probability on what you know: the evidential probability of h for you is $P(h/e)$, where e is your total evidence. If h is part of e, then the evidential probability of h is 1. And, because E = K, the evidential probability of all known propositions must therefore be 1.

It is worth noting that there is a useful notion of *probability on one's knowledge* or some part of one's knowledge. If you sit in on a probability or statistics class, you will hear the instructor over and over again say the likes of, 'We know that there are exactly six ways the die can come up, and so the sample space includes six possible outcomes', and you'll learn different procedures for estimating one population parameter when another is 'known' vs. when it is 'unknown'. Perhaps very often what one does when one talks about the probability of events is to think about their probability on a certain body of one's knowledge. This is entirely reasonable, so long as one has no good reason to think that that the relevant body of known propositions fails to agglomerate, that is, fails to be such that one knows the conjunction of the known propositions. But often in practice this is not a reason for worry. Therefore, Williamson's account of evidential probability might very well pick out a concept that is interesting and useful in a number of ways.

But is it infallibilism? It is if and only if having an evidential probability of 1 implies having an epistemic probability of 1. Even those fallibilists who accept E = K can deny that evidential probability 1 entails epistemic probability 1. The proposition *I was born in the United States* can be part of your total evidence, and so have evidential probability 1. But you are not rational to gamble on it if the stakes are too high, and it seems lotterizable: conjoining it with similar propositions results in a conjunction whose epistemic probability is clearly less than 1. Therefore it seems that its epistemic probability is less than 1. For epistemic probability—a measure of propositional justification—is precisely relevant to rational choice between gambles, and measures aggregative risk through the conjunction of lottery-like propositions. Of course, the infallibilist might just insist that, if *I was born in the United States* really is known, then it has epistemic probability 1. But this insistence isn't motivated by Williamson's argument, but by a prior commitment to infallibilism. There is no non-question-begging way of using Williamson's argument about evidential probability to argue for infallibilism. One could consistently be a fallibilist in our sense while also subscribing to Williamson's views of evidence and evidential probability.[1] We see no independent argument for infallibilism from Williamson's work on evidential probability.

1.2 How skeptical must the infallibilist be?

The positive arguments we've considered for infallibilism are not convincing. But this doesn't mean we shouldn't accept infallibilism as opposed to denying KJ or accepting pragmatic encroachment. We need to ask just how implausible infallibilism is.

The primary obstacle to accepting infallibilism is of course skepticism. Here is Lewis (1996: 549 ff.):

> uneliminated possibilities of error are everywhere. Those possibilities of error are far-fetched, of course, but possibilities all the same. They bite into even our most everyday knowledge. We never have infallible knowledge.

What to do? Lewis says: 'if forced to choose, I choose fallibilism. (And so say all of us.)'. Lewis grants that there may be 'infallible knowledge of a few

[1] There are reasons to be suspicious of E = K. First, as Goldman (forthcoming) argues, the notion of 'one's evidence' is more closely tied to what one is non-inferentially justified in believing (or non-inferentially knows) than E = K allows. Even if you know you will be alive next year, that doesn't seem to be part of your evidence. Second, the considerations we invoked in favor of saying that your reasons can be false may well carry over to your evidence.

simple, axiomatic necessary truths; and of our own present experience', but contends that 'it is not nearly enough. If we have only that much infallible knowledge, yet knowledge is by definition infallible, then we have very little knowledge indeed—not the abundant everyday knowledge we thought we had. That is still absurd.'

Is Lewis' pessimism about the scope of infallible knowledge warranted? It is certainly widely shared. But if those propositions we are infallible about aren't limited in the way he suggests, then even if merely reading a schedule doesn't give us knowledge that this train will stop in Foxboro, we might have infallible knowledge enough. It is worth seeing just *how* skeptical one must be to be an infallibilist.

The infallibilist claims that knowledge requires epistemic probability 1. We argued in Chapter 1 that many of the propositions we claim to know in ordinary life do not have epistemic probability 1. Two considerations supported this claim: possible gambles and accumulated risk. Here we consider possible infallibilist responses to each.

1.2.1 Possible gambles

When your normally very reliable spouse tells you at 3 p.m. that he or she will be home by 5 p.m., you will likely be prepared to say, sincerely, 'I know my spouse will be home, if not by 5 p.m., then at least by 6 p.m.'. (Suppose you are asked by your child: 'Do you know when Mom/Dad will be home?' You will have no problem responding in the affirmative.) Does this proposition have epistemic probability 1 for you? If it does, it looks like it ought to be at least rationally permissible for you—assuming its probability remains 1—to accept high-stakes gambles on that proposition. For if the probability of *my spouse will be home by 6 p.m.* is 1, then the expected value of accepting a gamble that pays a penny if this proposition is true and costs you your house if it is false will be greater than that of turning down the gamble, for a penny is better than nothing. Perhaps a gain of a penny isn't enough to make it the case that you *should* take the gamble if offered, but it is presumably enough—if you care about the penny—to make it the case that you are permitted to do so.

But are you? What if we make it a gamble on your life, or your family's lives? Here you *should not* take the gamble. If so, it looks like your epistemic probability isn't 1 after all. And so, if infallibilism is true, you don't know what you claim to know. If you don't have this knowledge, then it seems you lack knowledge of many of the propositions you claim to know in ordinary life.

How might an infallibilist respond? First, following Hawthorne (2004: 178), perhaps you do have epistemic probability 1 for the proposition in question but you would lose it if you were faced with the high-stakes gambles. This response commits one to thinking that mere changes in what's at stake for you in whether *p* affect your epistemic probability for *p*. As we argued in Chapter 3, this is implausible. Probability isn't plausibly affected by mere changes in practical environment. To repeat our example: if you are offered a high-stakes bet on the proposition that this die will come up 6, that doesn't seem to lower its probability for you and it certainly does not raise the probability for you that it will come up 1–5, or any of 1–5 individually. We see no reason to think that matters are different when the probabilities approach or even reach 1, and so when it can seem plausible that, before being offered the bet, you know.[2]

Second, the infallibilist might reply that you would not be irrational for accepting the high-stakes gambles. The only reason we find it irrational is that the salience of the bad outcome is distorting our judgment.[3] If you focus enough on bad outcomes, then even if there is literally no epistemic chance that they will obtain, you will feel that you shouldn't 'risk it'. If someone really could put together a credible gamble on the truth of a simple logical truth—if *p*, then *p* and *p*, say—where the payoff is minimal but the loss if the proposition is false is immense, people would hesitate to take the gamble. (Even Hawthorne is hesitant, though he thinks hesitancy is the rational response: 'I wouldn't even bet on the law of noncontradiction at any odds, and I think myself rational on that score' (2004: 29).) It is a big 'if' as to whether anyone—an oracle, a divine being—could possibly put together such a gamble, of course, but suppose so. Would it be irrational to take it? The current infallibilist claim is that, despite people's tendency to hesitate, it is not.

We don't think this reply succeeds. Suppose you are offered a credible gamble on the falsity of the proposition about your spouse's returning at

2 Note further that in general it is impossible to isolate probability movements in the intended way unless one is willing to bite a further bullet and take inferential environment regarding a proposition *p* with probability 1 to alter the conditional probabilities of propositions on *p*. There is also the embarrassing question of how far the probability drops from 1 or rises from 0. It might seem too convenient if it drops precisely to what it must be for the expected utility of taking the gamble to be just barely lower than that of refusing it.

3 The proponent of this account might hope to find vindication in the psychological theories of decision-making, e.g. prospect theory (cf. Kahneman and Tversky 1979). As prospect theory is usually cast, one of its tenets is that people tend to weigh small probabilities too heavily in decision-making. The infallibilist might hope to show empirically that even when events have zero probabilities their salience can lead to their being given a weight greater than 0.

6 p.m. (one certainly *can* put together such a gamble): if it is false, you gain a fortune, if it is true, you lose only a penny. If it is no effort to accept the gamble, surely you can rationally take it. But if the probability that your spouse does not return home by 6 p.m. is zero, you shouldn't take it. Here no really bad outcome is salient, only a really good one—therefore, the infallibilist response that a bad outcome is distorting our judgment does not apply. Of course, one could try out the same salience theory to account for intuitions here. But does this sort of case really seem so different from buying a ticket in a large lottery? When you have a ticket in a large lottery, though, you do *not* have epistemic probability 1 for *I will lose.* Granted, the reasons supporting your belief about your spouse's return time are not or need not be 'intrinsically' probabilistic, and some philosophers have argued (e.g. Klein 1981: 195–6) that their non-probabilistic character is what allows them to give you knowledge. But this is a different question from the question of whether the reasons are good enough to give you epistemic probability 1.

The infallibilist does have a third retort, though, and this one is more persuasive: every day we in effect take gambles on the truth of propositions that are epistemically no better off than *my spouse will return by 6 p.m.* For example, we drive the kids out for ice cream (rather than staying at home and serving them some from the freezer). This is, presumably, marginally more fun for the family, but that is all. There is no important gain from the drive.[4] At the same time, taking the drive is gambling on the truth of the proposition *we will not get in an accident on our way to the ice cream parlor.* If the latter had a probability less than 1, wouldn't taking this gamble be irrational? The ice cream case is only one of a huge set of cases from ordinary life. We are gambling every time we drive in a car, and gambling with lives: our own, our family's, and those of others. We are gambling every time we cross a busy street as pedestrians or ride our bikes or get in elevators or fly in airplanes or eat in restaurants. If the probabilities here were not 1, wouldn't these gambles be irrational, at least in the numerous cases in which the payoff is minimal?

[4] There is a diminishing margin of utility of trips to get ice cream. For, there might be significant gain if you are the sort of person who has never taken a risk of the relevant sort—if you have never left the house (perhaps because of a phobia). The more you go out, the less valuable each particular going out becomes. Examples in which the value of going out is significant for a subject do not provide the sort of support for the infallibilist position that we consider here. In the examples of most use to the infallibilist, the gain from the risky venture is minimal and the potential costs awful. Yet, despite this combination of features, we take such actions all the time.

We agree that in judging the rationality of accepting explicitly offered gambles we should keep in mind the implicit gambles we accept every day. If we are going to say that accepting the explicitly offered ones in certain cases is irrational, we need to ask ourselves seriously whether this is true of the implicit ones we accept so regularly. However, while we concede this point, we think it is too quick to assume that the probability must be 1 if these mundane actions, for minimal gains, are to be rational. If the probability is sufficiently close to 1, then perhaps the risk is worth it.

1.2.2 Accumulated risk

Another reason to be suspicious of the claim that ordinary knowledge-claims like the claim that your spouse will return by 6 p.m. have epistemic probability 1 is that when we start conjoining them it seems we accumulate risk. Take all the things you claim to know in a day—$p_1, \ldots, p_n$—and conjoin them as $p_1\& \ldots \& p_n$. The latter seems not to have probability 1. But why wouldn't it if all of $p_1, \ldots, p_n$ have probability 1? Surely the relevant instantiation of the conjunction rule has probability 1 if these sorts of ordinary knowledge claims do.

Again, the infallibilist can claim, with Hawthorne, that you can lose probability 1 for a proposition by conjoining it with propositions which themselves have, unconjoined, probability 1. Hawthorne suggests this as one way of explaining how it is possible to know that your lottery ticket will lose (2004: 183–4). You can know it and have probability 1 for it, and similarly for claims about other tickets, but when you start conjoining them, you lose probability 1 for them, presumably for each of them simultaneously.[5] (Hawthorne is, in effect, treating 'inferential environment' as similar to 'practical environment': both can affect probability.)

This move is implausible when your probability for p is less than 1. When I conjoin 'The die will not come up 6' with 'The die will not come up 5', to say that the former's probability decreases would seem to require that it becomes more likely that the die comes up 6, and presumably less likely it comes up, say, 4, which is absurd. We see no difference in kind when we drive the numbers of cells in a partition up to arbitrarily large finite numbers. The move is similarly implausible when your probability for p is 1.[6] There

[5] Hawthorne's final treatment of these matters invokes the idea of 'determinacy' (2004: 184).

[6] Suppose that your probability for p would not drop when entered into a conjunction when your probability for p is less than 1, but would drop when entered into a conjunction when your probability for p is 1. How much would it drop? If a non-zero amount, then it falls below

is, in fact, a general worry that while Hawthorne is claiming that the relevant proposition p has probability 1, it seems that if he is right in his claim that both practical and inferential environment can lower this probability, p behaves exactly as if it has probability less than 1 on the relevant tests for what its probability is: propose a credible gamble on p, and the probability lowers from 1; conjoin p with other propositions like it in their source and its probability lowers.

These considerations provide a strong *prima facie* case that infallibilism brings with it at least some degree of skepticism. If it is true, then ordinary knowledge-claims like the one about the spouse's return time would seem to be false. This is a cost but perhaps it is a cost that can be borne if some large chunk of our supposed knowledge is left intact.

1.3 The cost of infallibilism

Infallibilism, it seems, will not allow us the truth of humdrum knowledge-claims (like *my spouse will be home by 6 p.m.*). What's left? According to Lewis, just a 'few simple, axiomatic necessary truths; and . . . our own present experience'. This might be unduly pessimistic. Consider the following propositions:

(1) Here's a hand. [conjoined with the relevant gesture]
(2) My 2-year-old son did not murder Nicole Brown Simpson.
(3) The country to the immediate north of the continental United States is Canada.
(4) George W. Bush was not the first president of the United States.
(5) The Red Sox did not win the last seven Super Bowls.

Now, there might be gambles on the truth of these propositions which you wouldn't accept. For example, if the gamble were a dollar versus your children's lives on whether (1) is true, you might not take that gamble, for principled reasons: you just don't gamble with your children's lives (although, again, parents do drive their children around in cars!).[7] Here, though, it's

the probability you have for propositions whose probability would *not* drop when entered into conjunctions. This is not an acceptable result. A much more appealing explanation for what is going on here is that you *don't* have probability 1 for the claims about the individual tickets. That would explain much more cleanly why, when you conjoin these claims, the probability of the conjunction drops.

[7] As we mentioned earlier, putting together a credible such gamble might well require a divine being, and one who has given much evidence of its powers.

not epistemic shortcomings with respect to (1) that are standing in the way: it's the intrinsic distaste for gambling with the lives of your children. But let's put such non-epistemic considerations aside. Is there any *risk* of losing our children's lives with such a gamble on (1), or any of (1)–(5)? It seems not.

However, perhaps this is too quick. Infallibilist knowledge of (2) and (4) may require you to accept high-stakes gambles against the possibility of certain claims about reincarnation and soul-shifting—say, that George Washington was reincarnated as George W. Bush or that O. J. Simpson's non-reductionist self was transported into your 2-year-old son. (We're letting our skeptical fantasies rip.) Infallibilist knowledge of (3) and (5) may require you to accept high-stakes gambles against the possibility that Canada and the Red Sox have covertly legally changed their status—Canada into a U.S. state, the Red Sox, prior to each of the past seven Super Bowls, into the eventual winning team in that Super Bowl. Infallibilist knowledge of (1) may require you to accept a high-stakes gamble that you are not currently living in the year 2205, when vivid virtual reality helmets are commonplace. And infallibilist knowledge of any of these propositions may require you to accept high-stakes gambles on the falsity of any number of philosophical views—say, those that entail that there are no countries, hands, teams, propositions, relations, or truth values.[8]

Would you be rational to accept these gambles? If not, and if you would on the assumption that the propositions have (epistemic) probability 1 for you, then they must not have probability 1 for you, and yet—it seems—you know them. But we don't see an obvious and decisive argument that you would not be rational to accept these gambles. If you would be—or if you wouldn't be even if the probability of these propositions were 1 for you—then they might well have probability 1 for you and, therefore, you might well know them infallibly. The point remains that the infallibility requirement comes with the cost that a great many of our humdrum knowledge claims are false. This cost has been taken by many contemporary epistemologists to be decisive. We are not so sure. Try to get someone to concede he doesn't know his spouse will be home by 6 p.m., and you will

[8] If 'not' in (2), (4), and (5) is stipulated to take wide scope, though, it is hard to see what philosophical arguments would stand in the way. Consider: *it's not the case that George W. Bush was the first president of the United States.* This doesn't entail that George W. Bush exists, that the United States exists, etc. Hard to see, but we philosophers are awfully good at devising radical arguments. For discussion of the skeptical impact of philosophy, see Bryan Frances (2005).

get your concession without too much work. Try to get someone to concede that he doesn't know that George W. Bush wasn't the first president—and good luck to you! Fallibilists have developed many strategies for making sense of our tendency to concede ignorance: contextualism, warranted assertibility maneuvers, and so on. But it is not at all obvious that infallibilists have a worse explanation: people really don't know these things, and when they say they do, they are speaking loosely, exaggerating, etc. There remains a vast storehouse of knowledge that often goes unspoken, the likes of (1)–(5) above.

So, we don't think infallibilism is out of the question. Still, speaking for ourselves, there are many propositions we can't help thinking that we do know even though they don't have epistemic probability 1 for us. If infallibilism is false, though, purism must be as well. Can that be made palatable?

2 PRAGMATIC ENCROACHMENT?

Suppose we reject infallibilism. Then, given KJ, we are committed to impurism, and in particular a kind of impurism according to which knowledge can vary with variations in pragmatic factors, holding fixed truth-related factors, that is, to pragmatic encroachment. How bad is pragmatic encroachment? We start with a kind of *tu quoque*: many epistemologists are already committed to many of the troubling consequences of pragmatic encroachment, insofar as they drive a wedge between justified belief and probability. Our aim here is not to show that the consequences of pragmatic encroachment are not troubling, but only that it does not face these troubling consequences alone.

2.1 Cognitive decision theory

A number of epistemologists, including Hempel, Lehrer, Levi, and Maher approach the question of what you are justified in accepting or believing in terms of the fundamental concepts of decision theory.[9] Acceptance is treated in the way a decision is treated in standard decision theory for acts, although one need not view acceptance or rejection as a species of action, and such 'decisions' are evaluated for justification or reasonableness in terms of their

[9] In this section we are ignoring differences between belief and acceptance.

relative 'expected epistemic utility' or 'expected cognitive value'. We thus have:

> (Cognitive Decision Theory) You are justified in believing/accepting *p* just in case believing/accepting *p* maximizes expected cognitive value, i.e. just in case the expected cognitive value of believing/accepting *p* is higher (or at least as high) as that of believing/accepting not-*p* and that of withholding belief/acceptance on whether *p*.

Now, this theory is, in a certain sense, trivialized if the cognitive value of *believing p if p* is 1 and that of *believing p if not-p* is 0, no matter what *p* is. If this is how it is for belief, presumably the same holds for withholding, and so one would say that *withholding on p if p* and *withholding on p if not-p* have the same cognitive value, greater than 0 and less than 1, no matter what *p* is. Given these assumptions, it follows that you are justified in believing a proposition only if its probability exceeds the greater of .5 and the cognitive value of withholding on *p* if *p*. (The mention of the .5 lower bound is required so that it is not more justified to disbelieve.) In other words, what one gets is a probability threshold account of justified belief, and in this sense cognitive decision theory is trivialized.

Most defenders of cognitive decision theory reject this trivialization. And one can see why it might be rejected, once one sees justified belief through the lens of expected cognitive value. Lehrer (2000) asks us to consider two statements: 'It looks to me as though there is a computer in front of me' and 'there is a computer in front of me'. About these statements he writes:

> How would one compare the reasonableness of accepting each of these statements with the objective of obtaining truth and avoiding error? The first statement is less risky, but it tells us less. The second statement is a bit more risky, but it is more informative. As a result, we can say that the risk of error is greater in accepting the second than the first, but the gain in obtaining truth is greater in accepting the second than the first. This example reveals that the objectives of obtaining truth and avoiding error are distinct and may pull in opposite directions ... The probability of a statement tells us what our risk of error is, but it tells us nothing about how much we gain in accepting it when it is true. (Lehrer 2000: 127–8)

Lehrer is claiming, in effect, that because some propositions if true are more informative than others, the cognitive value (CV) of accepting the former propositions if true is greater than that of accepting the latter if true. That is: for some *p* and *q*, CV(accepting *p* if *p*) > CV(accepting *q* if *q*), because *p* if true is more informative than *q* is if true. Of course, informativeness is only one possible ground for differences in cognitive value of true beliefs, and we should leave room for others.

We might then add to cognitive decision theory the thesis that some propositions are such that it is cognitively more valuable to believe them if true than it is to believe others if true. Lehrer thinks we should go further, though. Note that cognitive decision theory together with this thesis leaves open the possibility that you are never more reasonable to accept a less probable claim than a more probable one. It leaves this possibility open because it leaves open the possibility that increases in the cognitive value of believing a proposition if true are always offset by corresponding decreases in the cognitive value of believing that proposition if false, so that the expected cognitive value for believing a proposition in every case just amounts to its probability. But as Lehrer says, echoing William James, the objectives of gaining truth and avoiding error are distinct (as James says, they are materially different 'laws'). Lehrer suggests, like James, that the greater cognitive value in believing some propositions if true isn't always offset by a compensating lower cognitive value of believing them if false.

To accommodate this, we need to recognize that the difference in cognitive value of true beliefs is not always offset by compensating differences in cognitive value of false beliefs. And in fact we need to require more than this: we need to require that there sometimes be no compensating differences in the cognitive values of *not having the belief if it is false*. The supplemented thesis will serve as our official version of *cognitive value pluralism*.

> (Cognitive Value Pluralism) Some propositions are such that it is cognitively more valuable to believe them if true than it is to believe others if true, and there are no compensating differences in the cognitive values of not believing these propositions if false.

There is a second way in which cognitive decision theory may be trivialized (or 'radicalized' if you prefer): the values associated with withholding belief may be so high that the expected value of belief is always lower than that of withholding unless the probability of the proposition in question is 1. This would be to give up fallibilism about justified belief.

Let us call the combination of fallibilism, cognitive decision theory, and cognitive value pluralism *robust* cognitive decision theory. We want to argue for two claims about this theory. First, its division between justified belief and probability brings in its train odd consequences similar to those which pragmatic encroachers seem required to accept. Second, a significant number of epistemologists conceive of justified belief in a way that makes robust cognitive decision theory seem attractive. We will take these points in turn.

Suppose robust cognitive decision theory is true. Then it will be hard to resist the conclusion that you can be justified in believing some proposition *p* but not justified in believing another proposition *q*, even though *q* is as probable for you as *p*. We don't claim there is a strict entailment here. But the conclusion is hard to resist. If one accepts robust cognitive decision theory, one will think that the values associated with withholdings do not in every case swamp that of believing truly. Now suppose that you are justified in believing a proposition, *p*, which has probability less than 1 for you, and suppose that it is a fairly close call in the following sense: had there been just a little less cognitive value associated with believing *p* if true, and no compensating changes in cognitive value elsewhere or in the probability of *p*, you wouldn't have been justified in believing that *p*. Given cognitive value pluralism, it should be possible, consistent with your being 'barely' justified in believing *p*, for there to be another proposition, *q*, which is as probable as *p* for you, but for which the cognitive value of believing it if true is just a little less than it is for believing *p* if true, and for which there are no compensating differences in cognitive value elsewhere.

If there is such a pair, {*p*, *q*} then the same sorts of claims will come out true that are supposed to be so problematic for pragmatic encroachers. For *p* and *q* are propositions such that you are justified in believing that *p*, but not justified in believing that *q*, despite the fact that *p* and *q* are equally probable for you. In fact, by reducing the cognitive value of believing *q* if *q* a bit more in relation to *p*, it seems *q* could be more probable for you than *p* even though you are justified in believing *p* but not in believing *q*.

In a nutshell, it is difficult to see how the proponent of robust decision theory can avoid acknowledging the possible truth of utterances like:

(6) *p* is less likely than *q*, yet I'm justified in believing *p* but not justified in believing *q*.

(6) sounds wrong regardless of whether the source of the trouble is pragmatic or not.[10]

10 We do not claim that robust cognitive decision theory entails impurism. As we saw, Lehrer thinks degree of justification for believing is not the same as probability, and he does not deny that degree of justification (reasonableness) fixes whether a person is justified *simpliciter* in believing. There is a question of whether degree of justification, for him, is purist, insofar as cognitive values,

The peculiarities don't end with (6). If the measure of informativeness Lehrer has in mind is just logical strength, then there won't be changes in cognitive values over time or worlds, or across subjects. But is our interest in accepting 'major scientific claims, those concerning galaxies, genes, and electrons' (Lehrer 2000: 145) merely a matter of their logical strength? Couldn't a proposition about phone numbers of residents of Detroit have greater logical strength, or at least a logical strength not less than this? Informativeness as logical strength seems unlikely to do the job that Lehrer and cognitive decision theorists want done (and indeed Lehrer's own discussion suggests he agrees). However, once one moves away from mere logical strength, to explanatoriness, comprehensiveness, simplicity, and the like, then since these can apparently vary with your stage in inquiry or with whether or not you are engaged in the relevant inquiry, the door is opened to justified belief (and knowledge, assuming it requires justified belief) coming and going over time, across worlds, and across subjects, without any changes in probability. So, we would expect the same odd predictions about temporal and modal shifts:

(7) *p*'s epistemic probability hasn't changed between *then* and *now*, yet I am *now* justified in believing *p* but I wasn't *then* because the explanatory value of believing *p* if true is higher *now* than it was *then.*

(8) I am justified in believing that *p*, but had the question of whether *p* been of less importance in my inquiry, then even though *p* would have been exactly as likely to be true as it is in fact, I wouldn't have been justified in believing that *p*.

Further, if cognitive value can differ between subjects, we get the same problems with the transferability of justified belief which have been raised as problems for pragmatic encroachment. Imagine some proposition about the legs of a locust. Belief in this proposition, even if true, might have no special cognitive value to speak of for an ordinary layperson. But for an insect biologist, it might be of paramount importance; if truly believed it could contribute enormously to his and other biologists' understanding of insect communication. If all this is right, the following should be possible. The

in addition to probabilities enter in. But he would likely reply that informativeness, his key cognitive value, is certainly truth-related. We will not dispute the claim. So, we would withhold the label 'cognitive value encroachment' in the case of Lehrer, as well as many other cognitive decision theorists. But even if these philosophers are not committed to impurism, they are committed to the common truth of instances of (6).

layperson knows the biologist finds this proposition (*p*) to be very important and knows that the biologist will believe it even if its probability for the biologist isn't particularly high. The biologist tells the layperson that *p*. The layperson, it would seem, would not be justified in believing that *p* and could not derive knowledge on the basis of the biologist's word, even though the biologist is justified in believing *p* and perhaps even knows *p*. We are not especially sympathetic to this argument: we're not convinced of the lessons it's supposed to teach us about pragmatic encroachment. But, our point here is, if it presents a difficulty for pragmatic encroachment, it presents a similar difficulty for a robust cognitive decision theory that allows cognitive value to vary between subjects.

So, many of the same sorts of costs of pragmatic encroachment, and of impurism in general, are costs many epistemologists apparently live with. *Many* epistemologists? Why think the list goes much beyond Lehrer, Levi, Maher, and the few others mentioned? A very popular gloss on what epistemic justification is, tracing back to William James' 'Will to Believe', and repeated countless times in the recent epistemological literature (cf. Alston 2005, Riggs 2003), makes cognitive decision theory seem quite plausible. The gloss is this: epistemic justification for belief is justification which is concerned with the promotion of the twin goals of gaining the truth and avoiding error. Once this gloss is accepted, one quickly is faced with the question of whether it is the mere fact that your believing would serve the goal that makes you justified. Surely not, because then you would be justified in believing every truth. So, we must weight the cognitive values somehow, and a natural way to do this is by using epistemic probabilities of *p* and not-*p* as weights.[11] Given this weighting, it is short step to cognitive decision theory (one need only accept in addition a maximization rule for connecting expected cognitive values to justification).

Moreover, once the Jamesian gloss is accepted, we face the question of whether all truths are equally valuable to believe, cognitively speaking. One can certainly see the appeal of answering in the negative, for the reasons Lehrer gives in the quoted passage above. This way lies cognitive value pluralism. Add fallibilism and we arrive at robust cognitive decision theory, with its division between justified belief and probability and the attendant peculiarities. We do not claim that anyone who accepts the Jamesian gloss on justification is

[11] Alvin Goldman avoids this by, in effect, accepting a sort of rule consequentialism about justified belief: reliabilism.

committed to any of this. We only note that this gloss lends considerable plausibility to robust cognitive decision theory and its troubling consequences.

2.2 Justified belief, knowledge, and restrictions on kinds of evidence

Epistemologists can be burdened with many of the difficulties associated with encroachment even if they are not strictly committed to impurism. Consider a view according to which whether you are justified in believing that *p* is a function not simply of how epistemically likely *p* is for you, but the kind of evidence you have for *p*. For instance, you might hold, with Klein (1981), that intrinsically probabilistic evidence cannot deliver knowledge, because it cannot 'guarantee the truth of *p*' (175) by delivering 'complete justification'—the strength of justification required for knowledge. In this way, it might be said, we can preserve the intuition that you can't know, prior to the results being announced, that your lottery ticket is a loser, no matter how large the lottery.

As we noted in Chapter 1, Klein thinks that *p* can be completely justified even if the probability for *p* is less than 1. Notice, then, that if the lottery can be made arbitrarily large, what this view implies is that *p* can be completely justified even though *p* is less epistemically likely for you than other propositions that are not completely justified, and that *p* can be completely justified for you and not for someone else, even though you have lower probability for *p*. This view, then, is committed to the truth of propositions like (6) and (7), as well as the following counterpart of (8):

(8K) Had my evidence for *p* been of a different sort, then even though *p* would have been exactly as likely to be true as it is in fact, I would not have been justified in accepting *p*, whereas in fact I am justified in accepting *p*.

But this sort of view is compatible with purism about justification, in the strict sense in which we've defined purism. One might take the strength of your epistemic position with respect to a proposition to be partly determined by the kind of evidence you have for *p*, and one might endorse the principle that if your evidence for *p* is merely probabilistic, then your strength of epistemic position for *p* is not strong enough for justified belief in *p*. So, there is room for a purist version of the view.[12]

[12] One thing Klein must not admit, if he is to avoid impurism, is the claim that epistemic probability is a measure of justification. If he admitted this claim, he would have to reject the

Those who advocate pragmatic encroachment, then, are not alone in their commitment to the truth of propositions like (6)–(8). Their fellows will include both advocates of robust cognitive decision theory, as well as epistemologists, be they purists or not, who think that the kind of evidence you have matters to whether you know or are justified in believing. Anyone comfortable with the likes of (6)–(8) who is not comfortable with pragmatic encroachment should rethink whether their reasons for opposing pragmatic encroachment are decisive enough to outweigh the independent arguments for fallibilism and KJ.

2.3 The Neta problem for pragmatic encroachment

Ram Neta (2007*a*) raises the following 'State and Main example' as a problem for views that make knowledge come and go with practical environment:

> Kate needs to get to Main Street by Noon: her life depends upon it. She is desperately searching for Main Street when she comes to an intersection and looks up at the perpendicular street signs at that intersection. One street sign says 'State Street' and the perpendicular street sign says 'Main Street'. Now, it is a matter of complete indifference to Kate whether she is on State Street—nothing whatsoever depends upon it. So Kate does not care, and has not the slightest reason to care, whether she is on State Street; but she very much cares, and has great reason to care, whether she is on Main Street. She looks straight at the pair of street signs that say 'State' and 'Main'. The ambient lighting is perfectly normal, and Kate's eyesight is perfectly normal, and she sees both street signs equally clearly. She has no special reason to believe that either street sign is inaccurate, though she also has no special reason to think either one of them any more likely to be accurate than any other street sign. There is nothing else unusual about the circumstances. (182 ff.)

We can imagine that Kate's practical environment is such that, given KJ, she is not in a position to know that she is on Main Street. The question is: does she know that she is on State Street? What should the pragmatic encroacher say? Neta writes:

> ... does Kate know that she is on State but not know that she is on Main?

principle that sameness of strength of justification for *p* fixes whether you are justified in believing that *p*. But since your standing on truth-relevant dimensions that make no difference to strength of justification presumably makes no difference, barring impurism, to whether you are justified in believing something, to reject the claim just mentioned commits one to rejecting purism about justification for believing.

To answer this question in the affirmative is to bite a big bullet. It seems clearly wrong to say

(a) Kate knows that she is on State, but she doesn't know that she is on Main.

And it seems clearly right to deny (a). For the sake of plausibility, the anti-intellectualist [pragmatic encroacher] will want to find a way to avoid affirming (a). (183)

We agree. This is not merely an oddity. (a) seems deeply troubling. Moreover, and more seriously, Kate herself will certainly deny that she knows she is on State if she denies she knows she is on Main. Not only will she deny this, she will not believe she is on State, anymore than she believes she is on Main. The pragmatic encroacher could attribute an error here, but this is too big a concession. For this reason, we think that there is no serviceable WAM available. We agree with Neta that Kate's assertion of 'I don't know I'm on State' is true rather than false but somehow appropriate.

KJ, we grant, commits us to denying that Kate knows that she is on Main: for some ϕ, that she is on Main is not warranted enough to justify her in ϕ-ing. We're in luck, then, if KJ also commits us to denying that Kate knows that she is on State. It does so if the proposition that she is on State is not warranted enough to justify her in ϕ-ing, for some ϕ. Is it?

In Chapter 3, we offered a counterfactual sufficiency condition on p being not warranted enough to justify. p is not warranted enough to justify you in ϕ-ing if whether p justifies you in ϕ-ing can vary with variations in your epistemic position, holding fixed all other factors relevant to whether p justifies you in ϕ-ing. This test alone, however, will not tell us whether that she is on State is or is not warranted enough to justify Kate in ϕ-ing, for any ϕ. For example, does the proposition that she is on State justify her in believing that she is on Main? One factor relevant to whether this proposition justifies her in believing that she is on Main is whether there is a good inference from *I am on State* to *I am on Main*. There is no such good inference. Therefore, holding that factor fixed, no variation in her epistemic position with respect to *I am on State* will vary whether it justifies her in believing that she is on Main.

The counterfactual condition is a sufficient condition, not a necessary one. When more than one thing stands in the way of p justifying you in ϕ-ing, the condition will be violated, regardless of whether p is warranted enough to justify you in ϕ-ing. So, that the conditional is violated tells us nothing about whether *I am on State* is warranted enough to justify her in believing that she is on Main.

So far, we have no principled reason to say that Kate doesn't know that she is on State. Of course, we also have no principled reason yet to say that Kate knows she is on State. Which it is depends on whether *I am on State* is warranted enough to justify her in ϕ-ing, for some ϕ, and our counterfactual condition is neutral on this subject. This alone shows that the Neta problem does not *demonstrate* that pragmatic encroachment is committed to the wrong result in this case. But that's hardly a satisfying response. What is needed is a principled way for the pragmatic encroacher to reject (a) while denying purism.

Fortunately, there is one. In Chapter 3, we assumed without too much argument that even if p is unconnected to ϕ-ing, epistemic weaknesses in your position with respect to p can stand in the way of p justifying you in ϕ-ing. After all, if you were to ϕ on the basis of p, we can offer two criticisms: (1) ϕ-ing has nothing to do with p and (2) even if it did, you don't have warrant enough for p to base your ϕ-ing on p. This argument does not seem decisive (and we allowed that the assumption could be dropped if needed: see notes 8 and 9 of that chapter). But the assumption makes sense for other reasons, too.

Consider: if p fails to be warranted enough to justify you in ϕ-ing, for some ϕ, what that means is that some epistemic weakness in your position with respect to p stands in the way of p justifying you in ϕ-ing. Suppose, for example, the weakness that stands in the way is the degree that p falls short of certainty for you. But now consider some other proposition, q, that falls short of certainty to that very same degree. q, then, has the very same epistemic weakness that p does. If that very weakness stands in the way of p justifying you in ϕ-ing, it is at least natural to suspect that it also stands in the way of q justifying you in ϕ-ing. If the natural suspicion is right, then this suggests the following principle:

> (The Global Warrant Principle) If your epistemic position with respect to p is no stronger than your epistemic position with respect to q, then, for all ϕ, if q isn't warranted enough to justify you in ϕ-ing, p isn't warranted enough to justify you in ϕ-ing.

By hypothesis, Kate's epistemic position with respect to *I am on State* is no stronger than her epistemic position with respect to *I am on Main*. But, by hypothesis, there is a ϕ, such that *I am on Main* is not warranted enough to justify her in ϕ-ing. That is why Kate doesn't know that she is on Main. Therefore, by the Global Warrant Principle, that she is on State is also not warranted enough to justify her in ϕ-ing.

Again, the Global Warrant Principle is plausible because it incorporates the intuitive view that, when a proposition's epistemic weakness stands in the way of that proposition justifying you, it is that very feature—the epistemic weakness—that's the problematic feature. It stands to reason, then, that any other proposition with that feature would inherit the same problem. But taking this principle seriously has a rather dramatic consequence.

It predicts that, given KJ, there will be no such cases like Neta's 'State and Main'. In general, those cases involve subjects with the following features:

(i) q is not warranted enough to justify the subject in ϕ-ing, for some ϕ,
(ii) the subject is in a position to know that p,

and

(iii) the subject's epistemic position is no stronger with respect to p than it is with respect to q.

There can be no such cases, if KJ and the Global Warrant Principle is true. Given (iii) and the Global Warrant Principle, p is warranted enough to justify the subject in ϕ-ing only if q is. But, by (i), q is not warranted enough to justify the subject in ϕ-ing. Therefore, p is not warranted enough to justify the subject in ϕ-ing. By KJ, then, the subject does not know that p. This violates (ii).

What this means is that, if the stakes are ever raised on a proposition so that, for that proposition to justify you in doing something, your strength of epistemic position has to be above a certain level, it follows (from the Global Warrant Principle) that your strength of epistemic position for *any* proposition has to be above that level, in order for that proposition to justify you in doing that thing. Because knowledge of a proposition requires that the proposition be able to justify you in doing anything, it follows that if changing the stakes raises the knowledge-threshold for one proposition, it correspondingly raises the knowledge-threshold for all propositions. This is what we might call *intra-subjective purism*: whatever the minimal strength of epistemic position for knowing one proposition, you cannot know any other proposition if you are short of that minimal threshold.

One interesting result, then, is that statements such as (6) above—'p is more likely to be true than q but I'm not justified in believing p but I am justified in believing q'—won't come out true according to the sort of pragmatic encroachment that arises from the combination of KJ and fallibilism. The same, though, is not true for (7) and (8) above, which concern temporal and modal shifts.

Intra-subjective purism, then, is predicted by the Global Warrant Principle and KJ—the very same KJ that figures so crucially (in conjunction with fallibilism) in the argument that purism generally is false. Why not go all the way, then? As long as we're accepting intra-subjective purism, why not accept purism generally? Answer: because one of the principles that show us that intra-subjective purism is true is the very same principle (in conjunction with fallibilism) that shows us that purism is false. Perhaps this gives us a reason to reject fallibilism. But here all we need to show is that the putative madness of pragmatic encroachment does not include the madness of intra-subjective pragmatic encroachment. Whatever madness there is will have to derive from the madness of varying stakes resulting in gains or losses of knowledge across (actual or possible) subjects or times. We turn to these difficulties in Section 2.4.

First, though, we want to consider a worry about whether we have perhaps overreacted to the Neta problem. It is one thing to think that Kate can know *I am on State* if and only if she can know *I am on Main*. It is quite another to think that Kate can know some proposition completely irrelevant to her current practical situation only if it is more probable than *I am on State*. Can't she remain justified in believing and know highly probable propositions about where she was born, where she will be next week, and the like? Or think of the recurring ice example. You might fail to know the ice is thick enough to hold you, because so much is at stake in your decision depending on whether it is thick enough, but surely you know all sorts of equally probable propositions—for example, that you had Cheerios for breakfast yesterday—that are completely irrelevant to the decision you face. Far from it being a virtue of KJ that it rules out such violations of intra-subjective purism, it seems a decided vice!

The result might seem even more worrisome when it comes to being justified in believing. When, because the stakes go up, you lose justification for believing that the ice is thick enough to hold you, are you likewise no longer justified in believing that you had Cheerios for breakfast yesterday? Plausibly, you do continue to believe it (as pointed out in Chapter 5). Are you no longer justified in doing so? If you are still justified, perhaps that means that the Global Warrant Principle is too powerful medicine for the ills of State and Main. But it is open to reject the Global Warrant Principle in favor of some weaker principle.[13] What should that principle be? It will depend on what the problematic features of the relationship are between Kate's belief that she is on State and her belief that she is on Main—problematic features that are not shared by the relationship between Kate's belief that she is on Main and her belief that, say, she had Cheerios for breakfast yesterday. Here are a number of possibilities:

- the kind or *source* of evidence for *I am on State* is the same as the kind or source for *I am on Main*, but different from the kind or source for *I had Cheerios for breakfast yesterday*.
- the content of *I am on State* is relevantly similar to the content of *I am on Main*, but the content of *I had Cheerios* is not relevantly similar to *I am on Main*.
- whether Kate's evidence is good enough to believe she is on State is immediately brought to mind—or should be—when Kate wonders whether her evidence is good enough to believe she is on Main. But this is not the case with the question of whether her evidence is good enough for her to believe that she had Cheerios for breakfast yesterday.
- Kate is considering (in the right way) whether that she is on State is warranted enough to justify her in believing that she in on Main, but she is not considering (in the right way) whether that she had Cheerios for breakfast yesterday justifies her in believing that she is on Main.

We take no stand on what the precise problematic features of State and Main are that are not present when discussing Kate's belief that she had Cheerios for breakfast yesterday. Let us abbreviate such problematic features by saying that Kate's belief that she is on State is *close enough* to her belief that she is on Main for problems with the latter to carry over to the former. On this loose vocabulary, some might be tempted to replace the Global Warrant Principle with the following:

> (The Local Warrant Principle) If your epistemic position with respect to p is no stronger than your epistemic position with respect to q, and p is close enough to q, then, for all ϕ, if q is not warranted enough to justify you in ϕ-ing, then neither is p.

[13] It is for this reason that we remained half-hearted in our commitment to the implications of the Global Warrant Principle in Chapter 3. See n. 11 of that chapter.

This principle, in conjunction with KJ, the proposition that, for Kate, *I am on State* is close enough to *I am on Main*, and the proposition that, for Kate, *I had Cheerios for breakfast yesterday* is not close enough to *I am on Main*, entails that if Kate's lack of warrant for *I am on Main* prevents her from knowing that she is on Main, then she doesn't know that she is on State, either. But it does not entail that she doesn't know that she had Cheerios for breakfast yesterday.[14] So, if you have worries about intra-subjective purism, this principle allows you to save Neta's intuitions about State and Main but avoid the more counterintuitive consequences of intra-subjective purism.

For our part, we remain neutral on which of the Local or Global principles is true. We don't find the consequences of intra-subjective purism particularly troubling, but neither do we find intra-subjective purism clearly true. Our goal here has been to show that there is at least one plausible and principled

[14] But *does* Kate know that she had Cheerios for breakfast yesterday? That is, is it warranted enough to justify her in, say, believing that she is on Main? It sounds odd to say it is. After all, (suppose) it has no greater warrant than the proposition that she is on Main. And that degree of warrant isn't sufficient for her to know (or be justified in believing) that she is on Main. So how is that she had Cheerios warranted enough to justify her in so believing? That this is a worry reflects the intuition behind the Global Warrant Principle. Intuitively, we want to say that it is not the case that that she had Cheerios for breakfast yesterday is warranted enough to justify her in believing that she is on Main.

But if she knows that she had Cheerios for breakfast yesterday there is something similarly odd about saying *I had Cheerios for breakfast yesterday* is not warranted enough to justify her in believing that she is on Main. Is there a way to have it both ways? Perhaps, if we allow that it can be indeterminate whether a proposition, p, is warranted enough to justify you in believing a further proposition, q. And, in cases where p isn't close enough to q, there is some plausibility in saying that it is so indeterminate. If it is indeterminate, then it may be the case that p neither determinately is warranted enough to justify believing q, nor does p determinately fail to be warranted enough to justify believing q.

Now, KJ entails that, if you know p, then p (determinately) is warranted enough to justify you in believing q. So, if p fails to determinately be warranted enough to justify you in believing q, you won't know q. But, KJ can be modified slightly to accommodate the possibility of indeterminacy:

> (KJ-modified) If you know that p, then p does not determinately fail to be warranted enough to justify you in ϕ-ing, for any ϕ.

Similar modifications can apply to the biconditional of J^KJ:

> (Biconditional J^KJ-modified) p is knowledge-level justified for you iff, p does not determinately fail to be warranted enough to justify you in ϕ-ing, for any ϕ.

If that Kate had Cheerios for breakfast yesterday determinately fails to justify her in ϕ-ing, for all ϕ that is close enough to the proposition that she had Cheerios for breakfast yesterday and only fails to be determinately warranted enough to justify her in ϕ-ing when ϕ isn't close enough, then Kate may well satisfy the right side of the modified biconditional. In that case, Kate may well have knowledge-level justification that she had Cheerios for breakfast yesterday and, thus, may well know that she did.

way for pragmatic encroachers to stave off the Neta problem. We can do this with or without committing to intra-subjective purism.

2.4 Shifts across worlds, subjects, and times

Some might think that the statement of pragmatic encroachment is not only false but *obviously* false *on its face*. But consider the slogan that if the consequences of error are devastating, you need more evidence in order to know. This slogan is very close to the statement of pragmatic encroachment, and it doesn't strike us—and we doubt it strikes you—as just obviously wrong on its face. In fact, this slogan and the statement of pragmatic encroachment do not seem particularly implausible, at least on their faces. And anecdotally, we can report that in introducing this subject conversationally to others—laypeople and philosophers alike—when we first present the view in this form, the immediate reaction is that it is too obvious to mention.

Reactions change when we spell out the implications of pragmatic encroachment for specific cases. Here, intuitions rebel. For example, if there is pragmatic encroachment on knowledge, then we should expect there to be cases in which you can truly attribute knowledge to yourself even while truly denying it to (either possible or actual) others (or yourself in another time) in seemingly the same epistemic situation:

(9) I know that *p*, but a minute ago, when the stakes were higher, I didn't know that *p*, even though I had the same evidence. (Temporal Shift)

(10) I know that *p* but, had the stakes been higher and my evidence the same, I wouldn't have known that *p*. (Modal Shift)

(11) I know that *p*, but Mary and John don't even though I have the same evidence as they do. (Cross-subject Shift)

(12) I know that *p*, but I cannot impart my knowledge that *p* to Bob by telling him that *p*, even though he has no special reason to doubt my sincerity or my reliability. (Testimonial Shift)

Likewise, we might expect you to be able to truly deny knowledge to yourself, but truly attribute it to others or your later or possible selves. These knowledge-denials, however, are problematic in a way that even (9)–(12) are not. Think of replacing (9) with 'I don't know now but when less was at stake a moment ago I did know'. In uttering this you commit yourself to '*p*' and to 'I don't know that *p*'. This takes us in the territory of Moore's paradox, which is a problem for all epistemologists, not only pragmatic encroachers.

Moorean worries can be averted by turning from the factive 'knows' to the non-factive 'has knowledge-level justification'. (13)–(16) too sound very odd:

(13) I have/don't have justification good enough to know that *p* but a minute ago, when the stakes were higher, I didn't/did, even though I had the same evidence. (Temporal Shift)

(14) I have/don't have justification good enough to know that *p* but, had the stakes been higher/lower and my evidence the same, I wouldn't/would have had justification good enough to know that *p*. (Modal Shift)

(15) I have/don't have justification good enough to know that *p*, but Mary and John don't/do, even though I have the same evidence as they do. (Cross-subject Shift)

(16) I have/don't have justification good enough to know that *p*, but I cannot/can impart justification good enough to know to Bob by telling him that *p*, even though he has no special evidence about my sincerity or my reliability. (Testimonial Shift)

(9)–(16), unlike the bare statement of pragmatic encroachment, sound odd indeed.

The question is: if there were pragmatic encroachment on knowledge, of the sort engendered by the acceptance of KJ and fallibilism, wouldn't it follow that statements like (9)–(16) would sometimes be true? If it would, this seems devastating to pragmatic encroachment.

However, notice that there will be true but odd-sounding cross-subject shifts like (11) and (14) if the speaker isn't in barn façade country but Mary and John are: 'I know I see a barn but Mary and John don't know this, even though they have the same evidence I do.' Odd-sounding testimonial shifts like (12) and (16) would also be true if Bob is in 'disingenuous testifier country' and happens to be speaking with you, the only truthful testifier around. The same goes for modal shifts: 'I know that I see a barn but, but had I been in barn façade country looking at the same barn with the same evidence I actually have, I wouldn't have known that I see a barn.' This sounds just as bad as (10) or (14). Perhaps something similar could be said for temporal shifts—some examples from Gendler and Hawthorne (2005) seem to give us Gettier-like temporal oddities like (9) and (13), at least on plausible principles about what makes for Gettier-like luck.

The point is not just that other views have similar problems. There *is* a Gettier condition on knowledge, and so the Gettier-related oddities do not undermine the claim that knowledge requires being unGettiered. Similarly, the pragmatic encroacher might say, there *is* a pragmatic condition on knowledge, and so (9)–(16) do not undermine that claim, and nor do they undermine fallibilism. So, (9)–(16) leave pragmatic encroachment intact. Just as good arguments can be marshaled in defense of the Gettier condition, so they can in defense of pragmatic conditions on knowledge (e.g. KJ) and in defense of fallibilism. These arguments are strong enough that we can learn to live with the oddities. And it is not as if no good story can be told about why the oddities can be true: they can be true because of the specified conditions on knowledge. What is harder to do than explain why the oddities are true is to explain why they're odd. But that's precisely where the Gettier parallels come in: we likewise lack wholly satisfying explanations for why the Gettier-oddities sound odd. But we are not tempted, in response, to abandon the Gettier conditions. (And it's plausible that, once we have an explanation for them, we'll have an explanation for the oddity of (9)–(16) as well.)

Of course, one might respond in this way: 'The reason that we don't abandon Gettier conditions in reaction to the particular oddities is that we don't find it theoretically particularly odd that whether you know is sensitive to external facts that affect reliability. But we do find it theoretically very odd that you need more evidence to know something if more is at stake for you in whether you're right. So, we should reject the conditions that give rise to pragmatic encroachment even if we don't reject the Gettier conditions.' This response, though, as we noted, is not compelling precisely because, when put on a theoretical level, we *don't* find it theoretically odd at all that how much evidence you need to know something is sensitive to what's at stake for you in whether you're right.

The intuitive oddity of (9)–(16) is not the only issue. Ordinary speakers do not go around asserting such statements, nor do they go around denying them. What might seem to be the more serious problem is that ordinary speakers assert simpler, less 'loaded' statements that would seem to be false if pragmatic encroachment is true. In Cohen's airport case, Mary and John assert 'Smith doesn't know', which given pragmatic encroachment is false (at least assuming that Mary and John's practical situation is appropriately high, which we can assume it is). Assuming stakes can be lowered over time without affecting evidence, then if pragmatic encroachment is true, there will be cases in which a subject knows and later does not know. The subject, however, when asked about his earlier self with the same evidence, will assert 'I don't know now and I didn't then, either'. A subject in a high-stakes situation who concedes he doesn't know that *p* is also willing to assert, if asked, 'And nor would I if the stakes were lower'. Finally, a person who, because his evidence is not good enough to act, concedes that he doesn't know, will presumably say, if asked, 'You can't know whether *p* by relying on me'. All of these statements would seem to be false if pragmatic encroachment is true. Why is it that people assert them, then?

The pragmatic encroacher has a number of approaches available as we noted in Chapter 2, but which it is worth repeating here. For one thing, she can appeal to a WAM, as Stanley (2005*b*: 102 ff.) does. In asserting the relevant knowledge-denials of others, or of yourself at other times or in other worlds, you are conveying the important truth that their strength of epistemic position—of justification, really—isn't good enough for knowledge in your own situation. As we noted in Chapter 2, however, although speakers convey such a truth, it is hard to avoid attributing error to speakers. But we argued there that the postulation of such an error is not ad hoc, because it can be explained as an over-extension of a genuine feature of knowledge—that one can rely on it.

Alternatively, the pragmatic encroacher can appeal to contextualism or relativism (we consider only contextualism). On the contextualist approach, the salience of a practical situation tends to drive up the standards for knowing so that no one can be truly said to know unless their strength of epistemic position is good enough for knowledge in the salient practical situation. (Recall here that, under pragmatic encroachment, it is part of the invariant truth-conditions on knowledge that if you know something, that thing is warranted enough to be a justifying reason for action and belief.)

Similar accounts could be deployed to explain the tendency of ordinary people to deny knowledge to themselves when they think about people in high-stakes situations who do not know. If Smith learns of Mary and John's predicament, and they press him ('So do you really know?'), he will likely concede he doesn't. If Smith merely thinks about Mary and John and concludes that they need to check further and so don't really know, he will likely say that he, too, doesn't really know. If the pragmatic encroacher appeals to a WAM, she could claim that by saying you don't know you impart an important truth, viz. that your epistemic position isn't strong enough for knowledge in the salient practical situation.[15] Appealing instead to contextualism, she could say that the salience of the high-stakes situation drives up the standards for knowing, so that it becomes true for you to say, 'and I don't know either'.

3 CONCLUSION

If we are right, then KJ is true, and so fallibilist purism is false. Which should go, fallibilism or purism? In previous work, we have argued that fallibilism is the obvious keeper, on pain of skepticism. Here, we are less sure that skepticism—at least, skepticism of a degree that is unacceptable—is the inevitable result of infallibilism, and so less sure that fallibilism is the obvious keeper. But we are also less sure that the consequences of pragmatic encroachment are as counterintuitive as we have hitherto conceded. The consequences are similar to those other epistemologists are committed to (see Section 2.1), and they also don't seem *all* that bad. Certainly they aren't so bad when phrased as cold, general principles. Moreover, some of the worst putative consequences—brought out very well by Neta's State and Main example—are not actually consequences of pragmatic encroachment at all. What's left? Intuitions about specific cases—intuitions that share key characteristics with intuitions about some common Gettier and Gettier-like cases.

Are these intuitions enough, when conjoined with fallibilism, to run a modus tollens on KJ, even though they are not enough to run a modus tollens on the corresponding Gettier conditions? What should we do when these kinds of intuitions come up against KJ and the arguments for it—arguments that embody a way of thinking about reasons and ways of reasoning that are central to the way we conduct our intellectual and practical lives? In such a situation, it is the intuitions, not the picture, that should go.

[15] Here, again, we would concede that the WAM does not avoid attributing errors to ordinary folk, but, again, we think the errors are understandable over-extensions of genuine features of knowledge.

APPENDIX 1

Conflicts with Bayesian Decision Theory?

In Chapter 3, we argue for

(KJ) If you know that *p*, then *p* is warranted enough to justify you in ϕ-ing, for any ϕ,

where to say that *p* justifies you in ϕ-ing is to say that *p* is a justifying reason you have to ϕ. KJ links knowledge to justified or rational action insofar as ϕ-ing may be practical. But Bayesians do decision theory without making any essential appeal to knowledge, or even justified (outright) belief. Our principles place these concepts front and center. This seems to set up a potential conflict between our approach and the Bayesian approach.

In this appendix, we address these worries.

1 SKETCH OF THE BAYESIAN VIEW

Our concern is with normative as opposed to descriptive decision theory, with decision theory as a theory of *rational* decision and action. What unites Bayesians in decision theory, as we see it, is a pair of positions: (1) that an adequate understanding of rational action must take into account not only the utilities of possible outcomes of various alternative actions but also their *probabilities* of occurring; (2) that utilities and probabilities must be taken into account in such a way as to satisfy the Bayesian motto, *maximize expected utility!*[1]

These two tenets leave a lot of room for debate among Bayesian decision theorists. Depending on the interpretation of probability and of utility, a form of Bayesian

[1] Thus, Jeffrey (1983): 'The Bayesian principle, then, is to choose an act of maximum estimated desirability.' Bayesians typically assume, further, that the probabilities in question, whatever they are, obey the probability axioms, that is, that they are representable by functions (or sets of functions) obeying the three Kolmogorov axioms: for all propositions X, $0 \leq \Pr(X) \leq 1$; if X is a logical truth, $\Pr(X) = 1$, and for any natural number n, if $X1, \ldots, Xn$ are pairwise incompatible, then $\Pr(X1 \text{ or} \ldots \text{or } Xn) = \Pr(X1) + \ldots \Pr(Xn)$.

We do not include satisfaction of these axioms among the essential tenets of Bayesian decision theory, mainly because, depending on one's conception of probability, they might be implausible. Some will think we shouldn't use the term 'Bayesian' to describe any decision theory under which probabilities don't satisfy the axioms. We hope such readers will indulge us in our non-standard use of the term.

decision theory might be more or less subjective. So, e.g. the radically subjective Bayesian adds to (1) and (2) the thesis that probabilities are subjective credences and that utilities are 'tastes'. A more objective Bayesian about *probabilities* might take them to be *rational* credences, or perhaps inductive or logical probabilities on the subject's evidence. A more objective Bayesian about *utilities* might take utilities to be objective values. Our account also leaves room for dispute among Bayesians over how to understand the normative relevance of the Bayesian motto. Is it relevant as a rule the agent is to use in decision-making, or as a principle which gives the necessary and sufficient conditions for an act to be rational? The difference matters when we think of agents working under misconceptions of the relevant probabilities and utilities. You might properly apply a decision-making rule but arrive at a false conclusion about what has the highest expected utility. If you act on this decision, you will have properly applied the decision-making rule but performed an action that didn't have the highest expected utility. We'll return to this issue below.

Why should we accept the basic tenets (1) and (2)? Let us start with some familiar thinking one can find in the opening pages of numerous introductions to decision theory.[2]

> Would you like to play the following game (Game 1)? A card is to be drawn at random from a normal deck of playing cards. If it is red, you win $10. If it is black, you pay $15. There's no backing out once you've agreed to play.

Though you might lose $15, you don't know you will. And, you might very well win $10. $10 would be nice, and you don't know you won't win it. So why not play? If we merely go by what we know about the outcomes of playing versus not playing, we might throw up our hands about whether to play or not. But it seems clear that playing is a bad idea. There's a 50/50 chance of winning. If you win you get $10, and if you lose you lose $15. The chances of a gain are the same as that of a loss, but the loss is a greater loss than the gain is a gain, and so you shouldn't play.

Now vary Game 1 a bit to reach Game 2. This game is just like Game 1 except it pays you $10 if the card drawn is not a black jack, though if it is a black jack, you pay $15. It does make sense to play Game 2. There's a 25/26 chance of winning $10 and only a 1/26 chance of losing $15. A very high probability of winning $10 beats a very small probability of losing $15. One can see this without doing any arithmetic.

What we seem to be doing here, in a rough-and-ready way, is evaluating the options—play or don't play—by comparing their 'expected returns', i.e. by comparing the probability-weighted averages of their payoffs. If all we went by were

[2] See, for example, the opening pages of Jeffrey's *Logic of Decision* or the chapter on rational choice in Skyrms' *Choice and Chance.*

our knowledge of what outcomes of the various alternatives would be, we would not be able to get anywhere. Probability takes up some of the slack when knowledge of outcomes fails us.

We can make an even stronger point here. There are clear cases in which you *know* that you won't do best by doing an act but in which the act is still rational to do. Consider Parfit's (2011) 'Mine Shafts' case:

> *Mine Shafts*: A hundred miners are trapped underground, with flood waters rising. We know that all these miners are in one of two shafts, but we don't know which. There are three floodgates which we could close. The results would be these:

		The miners are in	
		Shaft A	Shaft B
We close	Gate 1	We save 100 lives	We save no lives
	Gate 2	We save no lives	We save 100 lives
	Gate 3	We save 90 lives	We save 90 lives

Suppose that on the evidence available, and as we justifiably believe, it is equally likely that the miners are all in shaft A or all in shaft B. If we closed either Gate 1 or Gate 2, we would have a one in two chance of doing what would be right in the knowledge-supposing sense, because our act would save all of the hundred miners. If we closed Gate 3, we would have *no* chance of doing what would be in this sense right. But, given our beliefs and the evidence available, it would be clearly wrong for us to try to act rightly in the objective sense. We ought to close Gate 3.

In this case, you know closing Gate 3 is not the best option—that it wouldn't have the best results of the available options, because you know that closing either of Gates 1 or 2 would have better results. But you don't know which. In the absence of this knowledge, you must make do with probabilities. The expected returns of closing Gate 3 are higher than that of closing either Gate 1 or Gate 2. This seems to make closing Gate 3 the right thing to do, even though you know that closing Gate 3 is not the best available act.

One might worry that this reaction to the case undermines our principle, *Best Results*, which says that if you do know that A is best, you are justified in doing it (and also similar principles in our earlier work, for instance 'KB' in Fantl and McGrath (2007)). And if it undermines *Best Results* then it likely undermines KJ, too, which entails *Best Results*. This worry seems to us unfounded. In the example, you do *not* know that closing Gate 1 is best *nor* do you know that closing Gate 2 is best, so it doesn't follow from *Best Results* that you should do either. But the objector might persist: what about the disjunctive act, Close-Gate1-or-Close-Gate2? Don't you know that *this* is best? If so, then since you should close Gate 3, you shouldn't perform the disjunctive act, and so we would still have a counterexample to *Best Results*.

It is worth exploring this idea a bit further, to see how implausible it is. We will grant, for argument's sake, that there can be such disjunctive acts. Let's ask what it is for such an act to be best. We can think of two proposals. The first just applies the standard treatment: A-or-B is best iff it would have better results than any of the other available options. But then A-or-B *won't ever* be best, because it would never have better results than both of A and B. (If you perform A-or-B, then you perform A or you perform B (and not both, since we are assuming A and B, as in the miners' case, are *alternatives*).) We could exclude both A and B from the set of options, but that would be absurd, they clearly are options. In the miners' case, clearly one option is to close Gate 1 and another to close Gate 2! And even if we did exclude these as options, you still wouldn't know in the example that the disjunctive act Close-Gate-1-or-Close-Gate-2 is best, because you won't know that it would have better results than closing Gate 3. You don't know that if you performed Close-Gate-1-or-Close-Gate-2 the results would be better than if you performed Close-Gate 3. It might be; it might not be, with equal chances.

The second proposal treats the bestness of A-or-B as derivative from the bestness of the disjuncts: A-or-B is best iff either A is best (i.e. better than all other available acts) or B is best. (This proposal has all the plausibility of the claim that the inference from 'Post the letter' to 'Post the letter or burn the letter' is a good one. (See Kenny (1966: 67).)) Once again, we would have to insist on excluding some actions from the range of alternatives, and this time it is A-or-B which must be excluded. For, if it is included, one would have to say, when A was best, that it was better than A-or-B which is also best! Suppose we make the exclusion. There are further problems. What is it for A-or-B to be *worst*? Presumably, it is this: A-or-B is worst iff either A is worst or B is worst (where the comparison class doesn't include A-or-B). But in the example, you do know that one of {closing Gate 1, closing Gate 2} is worst, just as you know that one of them is best! So you know that the disjunctive act is both best and worst! Apparently you know—and so it's true—that this disjunctive act is better than closing Gate 3 and also that closing Gate 3 is better than it! That is to abandon the asymmetry of *better than*. Things have gone very wrong. Better to go with the first understanding of bestness for A-or-B. But as we saw under the first understanding, *Best Results* is in the clear as far as the example is concerned.[3]

[3] Notice that similar problems arise for understanding the expected utility of disjunctive acts. An analogue of the second proposal would be this: A-or-B has the highest expected utility iff either A does or B does. And similarly: A-or-B has the lowest expected utility iff either A does or B does. So A-or-B will in some cases have the highest and the lowest expected utility of the options.

2 TROUBLE BREWING

In the first game we described, the rational thing to do is refuse to play, and refusing to play has a higher expected utility than playing. In the second, the rational thing is to play, and it has the higher expected utility. In Parfit's miners' case, again, closing Gate 3, which has the highest expected utility, is the rational thing to do. And, in fact, the examples seem to provide reason to think that an act is rational iff it has the highest expected utility of the options (or at least that no other option has a higher expected utility). There are, of course, risks to generalizing from a few cases, but let us consider what the theory of rational action in these cases suggest:

(EU) What you are rational in doing is (are) the act(s) that has (have) the highest expected utility.

This is not a simple rewriting of the tenets (1) and (2) of Bayesian decision theory. Accepting it amounts to interpreting the Bayesian motto as giving the conditions for rational action, and not or not merely being a rule for decision-making. Nonetheless, EU is widely accepted. Sometimes it is hedged as a principle about ideal rationality, though many philosophers apply it to ordinary humans as well.

EU might seem to spell trouble for us in a way that tenets (1) and (2) by themselves do not. We can after all allow that sometimes you know facts about probabilities and utilities and that these can provide reasons for action. But with EU facts about such matters are directly determinative of what it is rational to do; they don't have their effect only by being reasons you have. In other words, we do fine by (1) and (2) if we merely note that you can have reasons that involve probabilities and utilities and not merely facts about how things are in the world outside us. But EU seems to leave reasons out of the picture altogether, and since knowledge is connected to rational action only through reasons, it appears the defender of EU needs to say nothing about knowledge either.

We can now formulate the challenge to us. Our principles seem to treat knowledge as central to rational action, while EU doesn't. Are the two approaches in conflict? Admittedly, it is hard to see how one could derive a contradiction from any of our principles together with EU. But the issue is not whether KJ and the like are compatible with EU in this narrow logical sense. What the Bayesian will want from us is good reason for thinking, given plausible assumptions about the scope of knowledge and justification and about the sort of practical environments human beings inhabit, that the actions our principles would lead one to count as rational would also be counted as rational by EU. If we can provide such reason, we will assuage worries about whether we are setting up our view as a rival to the Bayesian view.

Even if we could answer this challenge, a misgiving might remain. Yes, fine, KJ and the like do not conflict with EU. But what do they add to EU? In particular, why do we need to bring knowledge in the picture at all when we do decision theory?

3 SAVING EU

The quickest way to dispatch Bayesian skeptics who lay this challenge upon us is of course to deny EU. One could do so while retaining the basic Bayesian tenets (1) and (2), for it is EU that creates the potential trouble, not (1) and (2).

There are plenty of ways to call EU into question. First, one might doubt that there is such a thing as *measurable* utility. A standard way of justifying this claim is to appeal to preference or *better-than* relations which are assumed to obey certain ordering axioms, like transitivity. But transitivity has been called into question. The acceptance of EU, at least in its orthodox versions, also seems to require the controversial axiom of independence or separation, which in effect requires that the utility of any alternative in a state of nature be independent of the utility of that alternative or any other one in other states of nature.[4] Our concern here, though, is with epistemology. Are there *epistemic* problems with EU? If there are, we think the problems involve the interpretation of the Bayesian motto as specifying necessary and sufficient conditions for rational action rather than a rule for decision-making.

Let's focus for the moment on the simple examples we considered in Section 1. Putting aside worries about whether there are such things as measurable utilities, do the examples support EU? Well, the examples do support the claim that if you *know* that an act has the highest expected utility of the available acts then you have a good reason to do that act. In each example, when we imagine ourselves playing the game we imagine ourselves knowing what the gamble is, i.e. what propositions we're betting on and what the payoffs will be depending on whether it is true or false. This knowledge is either just given to us in the example (as in the miners' case) or is derived from our general background knowledge (as in the card-drawing examples). We do a little thinking about the case, and infer that one of the alternatives promises the greatest expected gain. Bearing in mind all the relevant considerations—the other things we'd know in the situation—we conclude that the thing we've determined has the highest expected utility is the thing the subject should do.

Notice that if the examples are understood in the ways just described, they support the view that facts of the form *A has the highest expected utility of the available acts*, when known, constitute reasons you have to do A. But do they support EU, which isn't about reasons at all?

[4] Cf. Broome (1991).

One might think not. Suppose that option C has the highest expected utility of the available acts, but you don't know this. Indeed, suppose you have no idea that C is available at all. (Vary the miners' case by imagining that you have the option of closing Gate 3 but aren't aware of this option.) Or suppose that in the first card-playing example you have been wrongly informed that the set of cards being used is really only a half-deck of all red cards. You would then have a justified false belief about the probability of drawing a red card, which would lead to a justified false belief that playing the game has the highest expected return. Again, you might have a justified false belief about the outcomes, having misread the description of the game as guaranteeing $100 rather than $10 if the card drawn is red. If you are under any of these justified illusions about the situation then it is not true that the rational thing for you to do is the thing which in fact has the highest expected utility.

One might respond to this by suggesting that in this case you should have done the act with the highest expected utility but have an excuse for doing another act. The excuse will be that you didn't know some relevant fact, e.g. that a certain act was available, that the probability was this rather than that, that the outcome would be this rather than that. (It's interesting, nevertheless, that we feel the need to excuse the absence of such knowledge.)

This is a poor reply. Consider the miners' case, and suppose you have a justified false belief that closing Gate 3 is unavailable. Agreed, you certainly do have an excuse for not closing Gate 3. But are you *rational* to close Gate 3? Well, you have a good reason not even to attempt to close Gate 3, namely: *I can't close Gate 3 even if I try.* To say that you should close Gate 3 and shouldn't close Gate 2 in this sort of case is like saying that when you have no idea, and no reason to believe, that the president is in Boston—reasonably thinking that he's either in Washington or New York—you are justified in believing he is in Boston because he is. It's not just that you have an excuse for failing to believe he's in Boston: it's that it is positively irrational to believe that he's in Boston. Likewise, if you take the option with the highest expected utility, despite justifiably believing that some other option, and not it, has the highest expected utility, then you don't just have an excuse for failing to take the option with the highest expected utility; you would be positively irrational if you did take that option.

One might hope to fix this problem by claiming that EU is about attempts, rather than acts, and then claiming that the rational attempt is the one with the highest expected utility. The idea would be that you can attempt just about anything. You could attempt to do C even if your evidence made the claim that C is available highly improbable. The hope would be that when we consider attempts attempting C would not be the attempt with the highest expected utility, because its expected value would be discounted so heavily by the improbability of actually doing C given that you attempt it. There are worries one could raise about this fix. Some philosophers will decry the retreat from actions to attempts. Do we really have probability 1 for all claims about attempts? If not, where does the probability weighting end? At attempts of attempts, or attempts of attempts of attempts?

But the more serious worry is about the normative significance of justified but false beliefs about expected utility considerations, not just about action-availability. Even if availability is folded into the expectation, we might have justified false beliefs about the expectation. If we do, wouldn't it be rational to act on those justified beliefs, and so to do something which does not in fact have the highest expected utility? These worries suggest that the best way to understand the motto 'Maximize expected utility!' isn't as specifying a necessary and sufficient condition for rational action—as EU does—but rather as a rule of decision-making, specifying a decisive reason for action.

There is a further response available to defenders of EU as we are currently construing it. Perhaps, when A has the highest expected utility for you, it is impossible for it to be justified for you that some other act, B, has a higher expected utility. This might be because facts about expected utility are luminous in Williamson's (2000) sense, i.e. that if they obtain in your case you are in a position to know they obtain in your case, or because of the weaker claim that you simply can't be justified in believing some proposition about expected utility without that proposition being true.

But why think facts about expected utility are epistemically privileged in either of these ways? Why can't you, without losing justification, make mistakes in calculating expected utilities or rely on reasonable estimates of probabilities and utilities that are incorrect? You could surely be justified in thinking that a deck of cards is a normal one when in fact it contained no spades at all and two sets of diamonds. Then you might justifiably believe that the probability of drawing a black card is 50%, when in fact it is 75%. Why is that impossible? There are questions about how the relevant probabilities to be used in the decision-theoretic calculation are to be calculated, of course. Perhaps the relevant probabilities to be used are the ones you are justified in believing—or know—obtain. But notice that this route makes knowledge (and justified belief) essential to the discussion of rational action in just the way that was supposed to pose a problem for us. And in any case, surely you should be able to have testimonial evidence of your expected utilities (say from a savvier friend to whom you've given all relevant information), and in general testimonial evidence can give rise to justified false belief. A normally reliable friend might tell us, falsely, that the deck is normal. Why the special pleading in the case of expected utilities?

We think the special pleading comes from a subtle shift in thinking about probabilities. When we think of the examples involving card games, dice, etc., we are thinking of the probabilities involved as objective, as roughly matters of relative frequency or propensity. We certainly *can* have justified false beliefs about such matters. Appeals to luminosity and the like are only plausible when we move from objective probabilities to epistemic probabilities (we put aside purely subjective probabilities as irrelevant to rational action). Even if we make this shift, though, luminosity is still implausible. One can always say that an ideal agent would know, and indeed assign probability 1, to all truths about his expected utilities, but we are not ideal agents. It would be *irrational* for us, being the non-ideal creatures that we are, to do so.

We think, then, that the appeal to some special sort of epistemic privilege to facts of expected utility fails. Nevertheless, the shift from objective to epistemic probabilities points to a possible way to save EU, to which we alluded above. Suppose we understand the probabilities relevant to expected utility as epistemic probabilities, measuring how justified various propositions are for you. It is then more plausible to think of expected utility as measuring the rational preferability of your available options (or their degree of justification). One might be skeptical. Can't one have justified false beliefs about expected utility, even when the probabilities are epistemic? And if so, won't this lead to counterexamples to EU? A justified false belief that an act B has the highest objective expected utility gives you a good reason to do B, a reason which makes it the case that you are rational to do B, despite the fact that B does not have the highest objective expected utility. Why would this be different when the probabilities are epistemic?

Justified but false beliefs about *objective* probabilities of outcomes make a difference to how strong your justification is for propositions about those outcomes obtaining. And, because of this fact about objective probabilities, justified false beliefs about objective expected utility can make a difference to how strongly you should prefer certain options. Since they make this difference, we can see how they can be reasons *even if they are false.* But suppose the probabilities are epistemic. Does a justified false belief about epistemic probabilities of outcomes make a difference to how strong your justification is for propositions about those outcomes obtaining? This is not obvious. The justified belief must make a difference without making itself true, in order to derive counterexamples to EU. But it is not clear that such justified beliefs wouldn't make themselves true, because it is not clear how something could make a difference to *strength of justification* without making a difference to *epistemic probabilities.*

But there is a more direct argument to consider. Suppose you have a justified false belief that A has the highest expected utility and a justified belief that EU is true. If so, you will be also be justified in believing that A is the rational thing for you to do; but if you're justified in believing *that,* then A is the rational thing for you to do. So, A is the rational thing for you to do even though A isn't the act with the highest expected utility—EU is false.

This argument assumes, in its last step, that if you are justified in thinking A is the rational thing to do, then A is the rational thing for you to do. Such an assumption rules out justified false beliefs about rationality *whatever rationality might be.* Why think *A is the rational thing to do,* when justifiably believed, must be true? Perhaps the thought is that it is a decisive reason to do A. But this, too, can be disputed. It might neither be a reason, nor decisive. It might not be a reason because that something is the rational thing to do doesn't seem like an extra reason over and above any lower level reasons that make it the rational thing to do. (A better thing to say is this: when it is true, *A is the rational thing to do* 'programs' for certain A-favoring reasons, without itself being one; when it is false, it doesn't even do this.) And it might not be decisive because, even if it were an extra reason to do A, it might be defeated by lower level reasons that make it the case that A really isn't the rational thing to do.

Our answers to worries about justified false beliefs are not decisive, but we think they give the defender of EU—who insists on epistemic probabilities—sufficient wiggle-room. But notice how they are doing this. They are doing it by ensuring that whatever your reasons determine is the rational thing to do is also sanctioned by EU. But once that happens, there is no longer any threat of conflict between EU and our principles. The challenge, recall, was to give some plausible account of why the advice given by our principles would line up with the advice given by EU. And the answer, it turns out, is that EU is false unless its advice lines up with what you have most reason to do.

4 EXPLANATORY ORDER

Recall that even if we could stave off worries about a conflict between our principles and EU, there remained misgivings about the point of bringing knowledge into the picture. Can we justify our appeal to knowledge? We can. But how precisely we justify it depends on some delicate explanatory issues.

We have claimed that what you know is warranted enough to be a reason, but we have *not* taken a stand on whether this sufficiency claim is grounded in certain explanatory relations between knowledge and reasons. One could maintain that what is known is warranted enough to be a reason because knowledge *explains* or *grounds* being warranted enough to be a reason. Alternatively, one could maintain that what is known is warranted enough to be a reason because the latter is part of what it is for p to count as knowledge. Under the first view, knowledge is deeply explanatory of reasons: things get to be reasons in part because they're known. Under the second view, knowledge lacks this explanatory depth.

We are neutral between the two views. The second concedes to the Bayesian that the theory of rational action need not take account of the notion of knowledge at all. So we would have no need to bring the concept of knowledge in on that score. But even if we cannot illuminate rational action by its connections to knowledge, we might be able to illuminate knowledge by its connections to rational action. The illumination of knowledge is a perfectly satisfactory answer to the question of why we bring knowledge into the decision-theoretic picture. And, as we explained in Chapter 6, this connection to reasons and rational action helps to explain the importance of the concept of knowledge.

If we took the first view, our answer to the Bayesian would be more daring: knowledge is at the heart of rational action because, (i), reasons are, and (ii), because reasons are explained in terms of knowledge. Clearly, reasons make a difference to rational action, and one way to account for this is to endorse (i), i.e. to think of the rational preferability of actions as grounded in reasons you have, and perhaps even that rational preferability amounts to *strength of support from reasons*.[5] Concerning (ii), we argue in Chapter 4 that it is too strong to hold that something can be a reason only if known, but that it is quite plausible to think that all and only knowledge-level justified propositions are epistemically qualified to be reasons. If one then added the claim that they are so qualified *because* your justification is knowledge-level, the having of reasons would be explained in terms of knowledge. As we said, we do not incline to this view. But we have no decisive argument against it and it would certainly provide the foundational explanatory position for knowledge that some have wished for.[6] Either of these responses provides the materials for an adequate answer to the challenge we have posed. There is no conflict between our principles and EU when understood aright. And, depending on how we think of the relevant explanatory questions, our principles might illuminate knowledge and they might instead illuminate rational action.[7] Of course, in a looser sense of 'illuminate', which isn't associated with asymmetric explanatory relations, our principles illuminate knowledge and rational action, as well as reasons. We can understand all three better by appreciating these general connections between them, connections which are not articulated by EU.

5 One worry about this claim is that factors beyond reasons can make a difference to what one is justified in doing. Perhaps a perceptual experience of a certain sort, by itself, helps to make it the case that one is justified in doing something, but a perceptual experience isn't a reason (we discuss these issues in Chapter 4).

6 Hawthorne and Stanley (2008) criticize our earlier work (2002) for getting the explanatory relations between knowledge and rational action wrong. In our earlier work, we sometimes argue from the fact that someone isn't rational to act in a certain way to the conclusion that the person does not know. However, this shows nothing about explanatory direction. If it is true, as we argue in that paper, that if you know *p*, then you're rational to act as if *p*, then if a person *isn't* rational to act as if *p*, then they don't know. So one can argue from a premise about rational action to a conclusion about the lack of knowledge. Nothing about explanatory, as opposed to logical, direction is needed to make that point.

7 There is room for debate, however, about whether reasons are explanatory of rational preferability or not. Reasons of course feed into rational preferability: adding reasons in many cases at least makes a difference to the rational preferability of options. But is this because rational preferability is partly grounded in reasons?

APPENDIX 2

Does KJ Entail Infallibilism?

Is there a direct argument from KJ to infallibilism? We discuss three attempts to provide one.

THE ARGUMENT FROM BEING CERTAIN

According to KJ, when you know that *p*, then *p* is warranted enough to justify you in any attitude or activity. One such attitude is the attitude of certainty in the truth of *p*, of having credence 1 in *p*. Therefore, according to KJ, when you know that *p*, then *p* is warranted enough to justify you in being certain that *p*. But, if *p* is warranted enough to justify you in being certain that *p* then it seems it does justify you in being certain that *p*. After all, if *p* were epistemically certain for you, if it had probability 1, then it would justify you in being certain that *p*. And if *p* is warranted enough to justify you in being certain that *p*, then *p*'s being short of epistemic certainty for you can't make a difference to whether you are justified in being certain that *p*. Therefore, if you know that *p*, you should be certain that *p*. Surely, though, you should only be certain that *p* if there is no chance that not-*p*. Therefore, if you know that *p*, there is no chance that not-*p*.

First, notice that this argument, even if sound, doesn't have anything particularly to do with the pragmatist aspects of KJ. The argument applies just as much to a version of KJ (and indeed KR) with 'ϕ' restricted to doxastic states. But the argument is unconvincing in any case. The problematic step is the claim that if *p* were epistemically certain for you then it justifies you in being certain that *p*. The fallibilist can quite reasonably make the following response. *p*, regardless of its degree of certainty, never justifies you in being certain of it. Even if we bump up your epistemic position with respect to *p* so that there is a zero-chance for you that not-*p*, *p* would not be a reason you have for believing there is a zero-chance that not-*p*. What would the reasoning look like: *p*, so there is no chance that not-*p*? This is clearly fallacious. To have a reason which justifies certainty, you need a reason to think there is no epistemic chance that not-*p*, and *p* is not such a reason. If *p* is bumped up to certainty, you may well be justified in being certain that *p*. But it won't be *p* that's justifying you, but rather some set of facts about the strength of your evidence for *p*. In general, *p* does not justify assigning to *p* a credence of 1.

Of course, infallibilists might just equate believing that *p* with having credence 1 in *p*. Therefore, if *p* is warranted enough to justify believing that *p*, then *p* is warranted enough to justify being certain that *p*. This argument, though, requires an infallibilist assumption—that believing *p* is equivalent to having credence 1. KJ, therefore, does not entail infallibilism simply because ϕ-ing ranges over *being certain*.

THE ARGUMENT FROM ACQUISITION OF REASONS

Suppose whether you are justified in believing *q* hinges on whether *p* is a reason you have to believe *q*. If *p* is a reason you have, you are justified in believing *q*, but if not, not. Whether *p* is a reason you have, then, makes a difference to whether *p* justifies you in believing *q*. But, if KJ and fallibilism are true, you can gain *p* as a reason for believing *q* if what's at stake for you changes, even if your strength of epistemic position with respect to *p* remains constant. But, if your strength of epistemic position for *p* remains constant, your strength of epistemic position with respect to *q* remains constant as well, even when you gain *p* as a reason to believe *q*. If KJ is true, then, fallibilism allows that you can gain a reason for believing *q* even though your strength of epistemic position with respect to *q* doesn't increase. In short, the following Gain of Reasons principle is false:

(GOR) Gaining a new reason for believing *q* increases your strength of epistemic position for *q*.

GOR seems clearly right, however. So KJ + fallibilism has an absurd consequence. In other words, KJ entails that fallibilism is false.

In fact, GOR is implausible, regardless of what epistemic threshold a proposition must surpass to be a reason you have. Consider the relation between *p* and the disjunction *p*-or-*q*. And call the epistemic threshold a proposition must surpass to be a reason you have, 'T'. When your warrant for *p* surpasses T, then *p* is a reason you have to believe *p*-or-*q*. Now imagine that your epistemic position with respect to *p* gradually strengthens, though not yet to T. As *p* gets more warranted for you, so does *p*-or-*q*. The relation seems to be linear, assuming that *p* and *q* are suitably independent.

What happens when your warrant for *p* reaches T? If GOR is right, then as your warrant for *p* linearly passes T, your justification for *p*-or-*q* jumps non-linearly because, not only does *p*-or-*q* get the added support conferred by an increase in the degree to which *p* is warranted, it gets a little extra support conferred by the fact that *p* is now a reason you have to believe *p*-or-*q*. This is implausible on its face, and its implausibility is not lessened when thinking about specific ways that your warrant for *p* might increase. Suppose *p*'s warrant is increased by your getting more evidence for *p*. Then, as *p* gets the crucial evidence that makes *p* a reason you have for believing *q*, your degree of justification for *q* benefits not only from the added evidence for *p*, but from an addition of p itself. Why would q benefit in these ways from p when p itself is not so benefited?

Propositions get no extra boost when the propositions they are supported by become your *reasons*—no boost that they do not get from the ordinary increase in your strength of epistemic position with respect to those reasons.

THE ARGUMENT FROM HYPOTHETICAL GAMBLES

KJ tells us that if you know something it is warranted enough to justify you in ϕ-ing, for any ϕ. There is no particular trouble for fallibilism as long as ϕ-ing is taken to be some currently available action. But it might seem that once ϕ-ing includes any and all preferences everything changes. Suppose you know that your grandfather ('Grandpa') smoked a pipe. You've been told about his pipe-smoking and seen many photographs of him smoking a pipe, though you never met him. Is *Grandpa smoked a pipe* warranted enough to be a reason you have to prefer accepting to rejecting a gamble on whether he smoked a pipe which pays a very small payoff if he did and ends your life if he didn't? If *Grandpa smoked a pipe* is warranted enough to be a reason to have this preference, it seems it *is* a reason to have it, and if it is a reason, it seems it is a justifying reason. And if you have a justifying reason to have this preference, then if later in your life you are offered the gamble, you should accept it. But this is wrong: you shouldn't accept the gamble if offered it.

Generally, it seems that if KJ is right, then if you fallibly know p, you have a justifying reason to prefer accepting to rejecting high-stakes gambles on p no matter how small the payoff if p and how big the loss if not-p. So you are justified in having such a preference. But if you are justified in having the preference, then if you are later offered the gamble you should take it. But you *shouldn't take such a gamble if offered.* It seems that the only way out of this difficulty, without abandoning KJ, is to abandon fallibilism. If and only if your probability for p is 1 will you be justified accepting such bets on p if offered. KJ seems to require infallibilism.

These worries may sound somewhat familiar. They constitute a practical analogue to a well-known paradox attributed to Saul Kripke. Suppose you know that your grandfather smoked a pipe. If you know this, you also know that any evidence against it is misleading. But isn't that a reason—a justifying one—to be prepared to ignore any counterevidence that comes your way? If so, then when you get counterevidence, say in the form of an elaborate explanation from your mother, confirmed independently by your aunts and uncles, of how it was a family joke, etc., won't you be right to insist dogmatically that this evidence is misleading? But surely you *wouldn't* be right to do this.

Kripke's paradox is called the *dogmatism* paradox. The paradox is this: knowledge doesn't seem to justify dogmatism and yet there is a simple and powerful argument that it does. An infallibilist may be able to tolerate the conclusion that knowledge justifies dogmatism, but a fallibilist won't. Its practical analogue might be called the *recklessness* paradox.[1] Knowledge doesn't seem to justify recklessness about possible gambles and yet there is a simple and powerful argument that it does. Here, too, the infallibilist can tolerate the conclusion that knowledge does justify recklessness, but no fallibilist can.

We think these paradoxes can be solved together. The key to the solution, in our view, is the concept of *junk knowledge*.[2] Take the dogmatism paradox first. Before getting the counterevidence, you do know that any evidence against *p* will be misleading, but after you get the counterevidence C, you cannot come to know that the counterevidence C is misleading, for you cease to know *p* and so cease to know that any evidence against *p* is misleading. Your knowledge that any evidence against *p* is misleading is junk knowledge: you lose it when you actually get evidence against *p*. You lose it because you lose your basis—namely, *p*—for inferring that all evidence against *p* is misleading. In the recklessness paradox, junk knowledge enters in the same way. You know *p*, and so you know that accepting any high-stakes gamble on whether *p* that pays some small amount if *p* would have better results than refusing it, regardless of the penalty if not-*p*. When the gamble is offered and made credible, however, you lose your knowledge that *p*, and with it you lose your knowledge that taking any high-stakes gamble on *p* would have better results than refusing it. And so you are not in a position to rely on that proposition to gain knowledge that taking the gamble offered you would have better results than refusing it. And so that proposition is not a reason you have to accept the gamble. (If it was, you would have a justifying reason to accept it, but you don't.) Before the gamble is offered, you have only junk knowledge about the comparative results of taking versus refusing the high-stakes bet on *p*, before the bet is offered. If the conditions arise wherein you could use it to derive knowledge using instantiation and modus ponens, you lose knowledge of it.

So, here is what the appeal to junk knowledge buys the fallibilist. Yes, were you put in a position to *use* the apparent dogmatism-justifying or recklessness-justifying knowledge, you would lose that knowledge, and so it would not be a reason you have for dismissing the counterevidence or taking the gamble. If you know that *p*, then if you later get counterevidence, you won't be justified in dismissing it; and if

[1] One way of answering these paradoxes is to attack the relevant instance of the closure of knowledge. So, in the dogmatism case, the idea would be that although you know the relevant proposition *p*, you do not know that any evidence against *p* is misleading, and that is why you have no reason to be dogmatic. In the practical case, similarly, the idea would be that although you know *p*, you do not know that it would be better to take rather than refuse the high-stakes bet if offered, and so you have no reason to have the reckless preference. However, as Conee effectively argues, denying closure doesn't seem to help with a crucial datum to be explained. While it does explain why you shouldn't dogmatically insist, after presented with counterevidence against *p*, that it is misleading, it doesn't explain why you lose knowledge that *p* (2001: 112).

[2] See Sorensen (1988) and also Conee (2001).

you know that p, then if you later are offered an appropriate high-stakes gamble, you won't be justified in accepting it.

Is this solution adequate? Yes, the knowledge involved is junk, but doesn't it—before it is 'put to the test'—justify a dogmatic attitude in the theoretical case and justify a reckless attitude in the practical analogue? Isn't this bad enough?

Let us consider the theoretical case first. Before getting the counterevidence, you have junk knowledge of:

(1) If all my relatives independently deny that Grandpa smoked a pipe, they are all wrong.

Does this junk knowledge justify a dogmatic attitude? To answer the question we have to be clear about what dogmatic attitude we have in mind. A dogmatic attitude is one which disposes you to dogmatic beliefs/rejections. If you believe (1), this need not be dogmatic, since if you retain your belief only so long as it is justified, you will not use modus ponens to conclude that your relatives are all wrong if you learn that they deny that Grandpa smoked a pipe. What would be a dogmatic attitude is this: the conditional belief that your relatives are wrong given that they independently deny that Grandpa smoked a pipe. At least this would be dogmatic if conditional beliefs obey conditionalization: that is, if when you have a conditional belief that q given p, then if you merely add p to your stock of beliefs you believe q.

So, you are justified in believing the conditional (1) but not justified in having the corresponding conditional belief? How could that be? You are justified in believing the conditional in part because you lack any reason to believe its antecedent. In the absence of any such reason, the conditional is just as probable for you as *Grandpa smoked a pipe* is, and that means it is very probable. However, you are justified in the corresponding conditional belief only if the conditional probability of the consequent of (1) is high given its antecedent, which of course it isn't.

We can put all of this in terms of theoretical KJ. The dogmatism paradox is not a threat to theoretical KJ, because although you know the conditional (1), and it fails to justify you in having the dogmatic conditional belief, it is still warranted enough to do so. When your knowledge of a conditional is junk, its being junky stands in the way of its justifying the corresponding conditional belief. The conditional nevertheless is *warranted enough* to justify you in the conditional belief.

Next, the practical case. Suppose, again, that you know that Grandpa smoked a pipe. You therefore know the truth of the conditional:

(2) If I am offered the appropriate gamble, I would do best to take it.

Can we find a reckless attitude that this justifies? You would be reckless to form a preference which, upon learning that you are offered the gamble, would lead you to accept it. This would be a *conditional preference*: preferring to accept rather than reject the appropriate gamble given that it is offered to you.

Does your junk knowledge of (2) justify you in having this conditional preference? No, at least on the plausible assumption that the justification of a conditional preference for A over B given *p* goes by the conditional expected values of A and B given *p*. The conditional expected value of your taking the high-stakes bet given that it's offered is lower than that of your rejecting the bet given that it is offered. The full KJ is not threatened here any more than the theoretical restriction of KJ is threatened in the dogmatism case. The conditional—(2)—which you know to be true—is warranted enough to justify you in the conditional preference. What stands in the way is its being junk knowledge.

Glossary

Action: the principle that if you know that *p*, then you are proper to act on *p* when the question of whether *p* is relevant to the question of what to do.

Belief—kinds of:

graded: the doxastic state wherein one has a certain degree of confidence or credence in a proposition.

outright or binary: the doxastic state of believing *simpliciter.*

Belief—outright, views of:

Kaplan's assertion view of: you believe that *p* iff you are disposed to assert that *p* were your sole aim to assert the truth as it pertains to *p*.

Lockean view of: you believe that *p* iff your credence for *p*, whether thin or thick, is greater than some fixed threshold below 1 on the confidence scale.

Strong Pragmatic view of: you believe that *p* iff your credence for *p* is high enough for *p* to be your motivating reason for ϕ-ing, for any ϕ.

Weak Pragmatic view of: you believe that p iff your credence for *p* is high enough for *p* to be your motivating reason for ϕ-ing, for some connected ϕ.

Best Results: the principle that if you know that act A will have the best results of all available acts, then you are rational to do A.

Certainty:

credal or doxastic: a psychological status a proposition, *p*, has for you when you give *p* credence 1.

epistemic: an epistemic status a proposition, *p*, has for you when there is no chance for you that not-*p*.

Conclusive Reasons Link: the principle that if you know that *p* is a conclusive reason there is for you to ϕ, then you have a conclusive reason to ϕ.

Contextualism:

content-based: the view that the semantic content of knowledge-attributing sentences vary with the context of use.

speech act: the view that what is asserted by the use of a knowledge-attributing sentence varies with the context of use.

Decision theory, cognitive: the theory that you are justified in believing something just in case believing it maximizes expected cognitive value.

Encroachment:

general formula for: there is X-encroachment on an epistemic property F iff subjects can differ in whether they (are in a position to) have F with respect to a proposition *p* due to differences in X-factors holding fixed all truth-relevant factors with respect to *p*.

pragmatic: there is pragmatic encroachment on an epistemic property F iff subjects can differ in whether they (are in a position to) have F with respect to a proposition *p* due to differences in pragmatic factors holding fixed all truth-relevant factors with respect to *p*. (For example, there is pragmatic encroachment on being in a position to know iff subjects can differ in whether they are in a position to know that *p* due to differences in pragmatic factors holding fixed all truth-relevant factors with respect to *p*.)

Equivalence thesis, the: a principle about justification according to which *p* is knowledge-level justified for you iff you are justified in believing that *p*.

Error theory: any theory that entails that a suitably wide range of ordinary beliefs that are normally thought to be true are false.

Externalism:

moderate: the view that, (i) knowing that *p* requires being justified in believing that *p*, and (ii) the conditions on being justified in believing that *p* are entirely externalistic.

radical: the view that knowledge requires satisfying certain externalistic conditions but does not require any justification, however weak.

Fallibly instantiating epistemic property F: see fallibly knowing—conceptions of, with 'know' replaced by 'F'.

Fallibly knowing—conceptions of:

epistemic conception of, strong: the conception of fallible knowledge under which to know fallibly that *p* is to know that *p* despite there being a non-zero epistemic chance, for you, that not-*p*.

epistemic conception of, weak: the conception of fallible knowledge under which to know fallibly that *p* is to know that *p* despite having a non-maximal justification for *p*.

logical conception of: the conception of fallible knowledge under which to fallibly know is to know on the basis of non-entailing evidence.

Fallibilism—about knowledge: the doctrine that fallible knowledge is possible.

Fallibilism—about knowledge, doctrines of:

epistemic, strong (Strong EF): the doctrine that fallible knowledge under the strong epistemic conception is possible.

epistemic, weak (Weak EF): the doctrine that fallible knowledge under the weak epistemic conception is possible.

logical (LF): the doctrine that fallible knowledge under the logical conception is possible.

Fallibilism—about epistemic feature F: see fallibilism—about knowledge, doctrines of, with replacements of 'know' with 'F'.

Foxboro: a town of just over 16,000 people located approximately 22 miles southwest of Boston, MA, and the home of the New England Patriots.

The Gain of Reasons principle (GOR): a principle about gaining reasons according to which gaining a new reason for believing *q* increases your justification for *q*

Impurism: the denial of purism.

Infallibilism: the denial of fallibilism.

Invariantism (standard use):

moderate: the conjunction of invariantism (strict use), the denial of relativism, the denial of impurism, and the denial of skepticism.

skeptical: the conjunction of invariantism (strict use), the denial of relativism, the denial of impurism, and skepticism.

Invariantism (strict use): the denial of contextualism.

JJ*: the principle that if you are justified in believing that *p*, then *p* is justified enough to justify you in ϕ-ing, for any ϕ.

JJ: the principle that 'what is justified can justify', i.e., if you are justified in believing that p, then p is warranted enough to justify you in ϕ-ing, for any ϕ.

JJ, credal variant of the biconditional version of: the principle that you are justified in believing p iff you are justified in being such that your credence for p is high enough for p to be your motivating reason for ϕ-ing, for all ϕ.

$J^K J$: the principle that 'what is knowledge-level justified can justify', i.e., if p is knowledge-level justified for you, then p is warranted enough to be a reason you have to ϕ, for any ϕ.

$J^K R$: the principle that 'what is knowledge-level justified can be a reason you have', i.e., if p is knowledge-level justified for you, then p is warranted enough to be a reason you have to ϕ, for any ϕ.

Justification, knowledge-level: the status a proposition has iff it is justified enough for you for you to know it. More formally: p is knowledge-level justified for you iff no weakness in p's justification stands in the way of you knowing that p.

KJ: the principle that 'what you know can justify', i.e., if you know that p, then p is warranted enough to justify you in ϕ-ing, for any ϕ.

KP: the principle that 'what you know can permit', i.e., if you know that p, then p is warranted enough to permit you to ϕ, for any ϕ.

The Knowledge-Reasons Principle (KR): the principle that 'what you know can be a reason you have', i.e., what you know is warranted enough to be a reason you have for ϕ-ing, for any ϕ.

Position to Know: the epistemic status of having epistemic position strong enough for knowledge. More carefully: you are positioned to know that p iff p is warranted enough, for you, to be known by you.

Purism:
- about epistemic feature E: the view that any two subjects with the same strength of epistemic position with respect to p are such that both or neither (are in a position to) exemplify E with respect to p.
- about knowledge: an epistemological view according to which any two subjects with the same strength of epistemic position with respect to p are such that both or neither are in a position to know that p.

Purism, intrasubjective

about epistemic feature F: the view that for any two propositions *p* and *q* and subject S, if S has the same strength of epistemic position with respect to *p* as with respect to *q*, then S either exemplifies E with respect to both *p* and *q* or neither.

Reasons Link: the principle that if you know that the fact that *p* is a reason there is for you to ϕ, then you have a reason to ϕ, namely *p*.

Relativism—epistemic, assessment: an epistemological view according to which how strong your epistemic position must be—which epistemic standards you must meet—in order for a knowledge attribution, with a fixed content, to be true of you can vary with the context of assessment.

Resolution: a desideratum for theories of outright belief according to which if you believe that *p*, then your mind is made up that *p*.

Safe Reasons: a principle about having reasons according to which if *p* is a reason you have for ϕ-ing, then *p* is warranted enough to justify you in ϕ-ing, for any ϕ.

Salience: a mechanism by which the content or truth-value of knowledge-attributions is sometimes purported to vary; it usually operates by either the attributor or the subject considering or taking seriously counterpossibilities that hadn't been previously considered or taken seriously.

Skepticism: the view that a suitably wide range of ordinary knowledge-claims are false.

Subject Sensitive Invariantism (SSI): the conjunction of impurism and the denial of contextualism.

Transparency: a desideratum for theories of outright belief according to which strength of justification for *p* is directly proportional to the strength of justification one has for believing *p*.

The *truth standard*: a desideratum on theories of outright belief according to which if you believe *p* and *p* is false, then you are mistaken about whether *p*, and if you believe *p* and *p* is true, then you are right about whether *p*.

The Unity thesis: a principle about reasons according to which, if *p* is warranted enough to be a reason you have for believing that *q*, for any *q*, then *p* is warranted enough to be a reason you have for ϕ-ing, for any ϕ.

Valuable as such: a status a relation, R, has iff, necessarily, for any R-ing state of affairs, the fact that it is an R-ing state of affairs *prima facie* makes it valuable.

WAMmy—double: the combined strategy of employing a WAM both on a proposition and on its negation. See also WAM.

Warrant:

for *p*: a measure of your strength of epistemic position for *p*.

enough to justify you in ϕ-ing: the status *p* has for you when no weaknesses in your epistemic position with respect to *p* stand in the way of *p* justifying you in ϕ-ing.

enough to know: the status *p* must have for you such that no weaknesses in your epistemic position with respect to *p* stand in the way of you knowing that *p*; amounts to being in a position to know.

Warranted assertibility maneuver (WAM): a strategy for defusing counter-intuitive consequences of one's theory by attempting to show that a proposition which appears false is nonetheless true but infelicitous to assert or that a proposition which appears true is nonetheless false but felicitous to assert.

References

Alston, William P. (2005). *Beyond 'Justification': Dimensions of Epistemic Evaluation.* Ithaca, NY: Cornell University Press.

Armstrong, D. M. (1973). *Belief, Truth, and Knowledge.* Cambridge: Cambridge University Press.

Audi, Robert (2002). 'Sources of Knowledge'. In P. Moser (ed.) *Oxford Handbook of Epistemology.* Oxford: Oxford University Press: 71–94.

Bach, Kent (2005). 'The Emperor's New "Knows"'. In G. Preyer and G. Peter (eds.) *Contextualism in Philosophy: Knowledge, Meaning, and Truth.* Oxford: Oxford University Press: 51–90.

—— (forthcoming). 'Applying Pragmatics to Epistemology'. *Philosophical Issues* 18.

Baron, Marcia (2005). 'Justification and Excuses'. *Ohio State Journal of Criminal Law* 2: 387–413.

Birch, Susan A. J. and Bloom, Paul (2004). 'Understanding Children's and Adults' Limitations in Mental State Reasoning'. *Trends in Cognitive Sciences* 8: 255–60.

Blackson, Thomas A. (2004). 'An Invalid Argument for Contextualism'. *Philosophy and Phenomenological Research* 68: 344–5.

Blaizot, J. P., Iliopoulos, J., Madsen, J., Ross, G. G., Sonderegger, P., and Specht, H. J. (2003). 'Study of Potentially Dangerous Events During Heavy-Ion Collisions at the LHC: Report of the LHC Safety Study Group'. Geneva: CERN.

BonJour, Laurence. (1985). *The Structure of Empirical Knowledge.* Cambridge, MA: Harvard University Press.

—— (1986). 'Can Empirical Knowledge Have a Foundation?' In P. Moser (ed.) *Empirical Knowledge.* 2nd edn. Totowa, NJ: Rowman & Littlefield: 97–120.

—— (2001). 'Toward a Defense of Empirical Foundationalism'. In M. R. DePaul (ed.) *Resurrecting Old-Fashioned Foundationalism.* Lanham, MD: Rowman & Littlefield: 21–40.

—— (2002). *Epistemology: Classic Problems and Contemporary Responses.* Lanham, MD: Rowman & Littlefield.

Braithwaite, R. B. (1932–3). 'The Nature of Believing'. *Proceedings of the Aristotelian Society* 33: 129–46.

Bratman, Michael (1992). 'Practical Reasoning and Acceptance in a Context'. *Mind* 101: 1–15.

Broome, John (1991). *Weighing Goods.* Oxford: Oxford University Press.

Brown, Jessica (2005). 'Comparing Contextualism and Invariantism on the Correctness of Contextualist Intuitions'. *Grazer Philosophische Studien* 69: 71–99.

—— (2006). 'Contextualism and Warranted Assertability Manoeuvers'. *Philosophical Studies* 130: 407–35.

—— (2008). 'Subject-Sensitive Invariantism and the Knowledge Norm for Practical Reasoning'. *Noûs* 42: 167–89.

Buckwalter, Wesley (manuscript). 'Knowledge isn't Closed on Saturdays'.

Cappelen, Herman and LePore, Ernest. (2005). *Insensitive Semantics: A Defense of Semantic Minimalism and Speech Act Pluralism.* Oxford: Blackwell Publishing.

Carroll, Lewis (1895). 'What the Tortoise Said to Achilles'. *Mind* 4: 278–80.

CERN (2008). 'Safety at the LHC'. May 8, 2008. <http://press.web.cern.ch/public/en/LHC/Safety-en.html>.

Chisholm, Roderick (1966). *Theory of Knowledge.* 1st edn. Englewood Cliffs, NJ: Prentice-Hall.

—— (1977). *Theory of Knowledge.* 2nd edn. Englewood Cliffs, NJ: Prentice-Hall.

—— (1989). *Theory of Knowledge.* 3rd edn. Englewood Cliffs, NJ: Prentice-Hall.

Christensen, David (2004). *Putting Logic in its Place: Formal Constraints on Rational Belief.* Oxford: Oxford University Press.

Clifford, William (1999). *The Ethics of Belief and Other Essays.* Amherst, NY: Prometheus Books.

Cohen, L. J. (1989). 'Belief and Acceptance'. *Mind* 98: 367–89.

Cohen, Stewart (1986). 'Knowledge and Context'. *The Journal of Philosophy* 83: 574–85.

—— (1988). 'How to Be a Fallibilist'. *Philosophical Perspectives* 2 (Epistemology): 91–123.

—— (1999). 'Contextualism, Skepticism, and the Structure of Reasons'. In J. Tomberlin (ed.) *Philosophical Perspectives.* Cambridge: Blackwell: 57–89.

Conee, Earl (2001). 'Heeding Misleading Evidence'. *Philosophical Studies* 103: 99–120.

Conee, Earl and Feldman, Richard (2004*a*). *Evidentialism: Essays in Epistemology.* Oxford: Oxford University Press.

—— (2004*b*). 'Making Sense of Skepticism'. In E. Conee and R. Feldman (eds.) *Evidentialism: Essays in Epistemology.* Oxford: Oxford University Press: 277–306.

Dancy, Jonathan (2000). *Practical Reality.* Oxford: Oxford University Press.

—— (2003). 'What do Reasons Do?' *Southern Journal of Philosophy* 41 (supplement): 95–113.

DePaul, Michael (2004). 'Truth Consequentialism, Withholding and Proportioning Belief to the Evidence'. *Philosophical Issues* 14 (Epistemology): 92–112.

—— (2009). 'Ugly Analyses and Value'. In A. Haddock, A. Millar, and D. H. Pritchard (eds.) *Epistemic Value.* Oxford: Oxford University Press: 112–38.

DePaul, Michael and Grimm, Stephen (2007). 'Review Essay on Jonathan Kvanvig's *The Value of Knowledge and the Pursuit of Understanding*'. *Philosophy and Phenomenological Research* 74: 498–514.

DeRose, Keith (1991). 'Epistemic Possibilities'. *The Philosophical Review* 100: 581–605.

——(1992). 'Contextualism and Knowledge Attributions'. *Philosophy and Phenomenological Research* 52: 913–29.

——(2002). 'Assertion, Knowledge, and Context'. *The Philosophical Review* 111: 167–203.

——(2004). 'The Problem with Subject-Sensitive Invariantism'. *Philosophy and Phenomenological Research* 68: 346–50.

——(2005). 'The Ordinary Language Basis for Contextualism, and the New Invariantism'. *Philosophical Quarterly* 55: 172–98.

Dougherty, Trent and Rysiew, Patrick (2009). 'Fallibilism, Epistemic Possibility, and Concessive Knowledge Attributions'. *Philosophy and Phenomenological Research* 78: 128–32.

Dretske, Fred (1981). *Knowledge and the Flow of Information*. Cambridge, MA: MIT Press.

Edwards, Gareth (2005). 'End Day'. Television Broadcast. BBC.

Fantl, Jeremy and McGrath, Matthew (2002). 'Evidence, Pragmatics, and Justification'. *The Philosophical Review* 111: 67–94.

——(2007). 'On Pragmatic Encroachment in Epistemology'. *Philosophy and Phenomenological Research* 75: 558–89.

Feldman, Richard (1981). 'Fallibilism and Knowing that One Knows'. *The Philosophical Review* 90: 77–93.

——(2003). *Epistemology*. Upper Saddle River, NJ: Prentice Hall.

——(2007). 'Knowledge and Lotteries'. *Philosophy and Phenomenological Research* 75: 211–26.

Feltz, Adam and Zarpentine, Chris (manuscript). 'Do You Know More When It Matters Less?'

Foley, Richard (1993). *Working Without a Net*. Oxford: Oxford University Press.

Frances, Bryan (2005). *Scepticism Comes Alive*. Oxford: Oxford University Press.

Fumerton, Richard (1995). *Metaepistemology and Skepticism*. Lanham, MD: Rowman & Littlefield.

——(2001). 'Classical Foundationalism'. In M. R. DePaul (ed.) *Resurrecting Old-Fashioned Foundationalism*. Lanham, MD: Rowman & Littlefield: 3–20.

Ganson, Dorit (2008). 'Evidentialism and Pragmatic Constraints on Outright Belief'. *Philosophical Studies* 139: 441–58.

Gendler, Tamar Szabó and Hawthorne, John (2005). 'The Real Guide to Fake Barns: A Catalogue of Gifts or Your Epistemic Enemies'. *Philosophical Studies* 124: 331–52.

Goldman, Alvin (1979). 'What Is Justified Belief?' In G. S. Pappas (ed.) *Justification and Knowledge*. Dordrecht: Reidel: 1–23.

—— (1999). *Knowledge in a Social World.* Oxford: Oxford University Press.

—— (forthcoming). 'Williamson on Knowledge and Evidence'. In D. Pritchard (ed.) *Williamson on Knowledge.* Oxford: Oxford University Press.

Gordon, Robert M. (1987). *The Structure of Emotions.* Cambridge: Cambridge University Press.

Greco, John (2009). 'What's Wrong with Contextualism?' *The Philosophical Quarterly* 58: 416–36.

Harman, Gilbert (2007). 'Epistemic Contextualism as a Theory of Primary Speaker Meaning'. *Philosophy and Phenomenological Research* 75: 173–9.

Harman, Gilbert and Sherman, Brett (2004). 'Knowledge, Assumptions, Lotteries'. *Philosophical Issues* 14 (Epistemology): 492–500.

Hawthorne, John (2004). *Knowledge and Lotteries.* Oxford: Oxford University Press.

Hawthorne, John and Stanley, Jason (2008). 'Knowledge and Action'. *Journal of Philosophy* 105: 571–90.

Hazlett, Allan (2006). 'How to Defeat Belief in the External World'. *Pacific Philosophical Quarterly* 87: 198–212.

Henderson, David (2009). 'Motivated Contextualism'. *Philosophical Studies* 142: 119–31.

Hetherington, Stephen (2005). 'Knowing (How It is) that P: Degrees and Qualities of Knowledge'. *Veritas* 50: 99–107.

Hinton, J. M. (1969). 'Review of *Theory of Knowledge*'. *The Philosophical Review* 78: 383–86.

Huemer, Michael (2001). *Skepticism and the Veil of Perception.* New York: Rowman and Littlefield.

—— (2007). 'Moore's Paradox and the Norm of Belief'. In S. Nuccetelli and G. Seau (eds.) *Themes from G. E. Moore.* Oxford: Oxford University Press: 142–57.

Hyman, John (1999). 'How Knowledge Works'. *The Philosophical Quarterly* 49: 433–51.

James, William (1962). 'The Will to Believe'. In W. Barrett and H. D. Aiken (eds.) *Philosophy in the Twentieth Century.* New York: Random House: 241–58.

Jeffrey, Richard C. (1983). *The Logic of Decision.* Chicago: University of Chicago Press.

—— (1992). *Probability and the Art of Judgment.* Cambridge: Cambridge University Press.

Kahneman, Daniel and Tversky, Amos (1979). 'Prospect Theory: An Analysis of Decision and Risk'. *Econometrica* 47: 263–92.

Kaplan, Mark (1996). *Decision Theory as Philosophy.* Cambridge: Cambridge University Press.

Kenny, A. J. (1966). 'Practical Inference'. *Analysis* 26: 65–75.

King, Jeffrey (2002). 'Designating Propositions'. *The Philosophical Review* 111: 341–71.

Klein, Peter (1980*a*). *Certainty*. Minneapolis: University of Minnesota Press.

—— (1980*b*). 'Misleading Evidence and the Restoration of Justification'. *Philosophical Studies* 37: 81–99.

—— (1981). *Certainty: A Refutation of Scepticism*. Minneapolis: University of Minnesota Press.

Koch, Benjamin, Bleicher, Marcus, and Stöcker, Horst (2009). 'Exclusion of black hole disaster scenarios at the LHC'. *Physics Letters B* 672: 71–76.

Kvanvig, Jonathan (2003). *The Value of Knowledge and the Pursuit of Understanding*. Cambridge: Cambridge University Press.

—— (2004). 'Pragmatic aspects of knowledge?' Blog. March 18, 2008. <http://fleetwood.baylor.edu/certain_doubts/?p=13>.

—— (2009). *Epistemic Optionality*. Oxford: Oxford University Press:

Kyburg, Henry (1970). *Probability and Inductive Logic*. New York: Macmillan.

Lackey, Jennifer (2006). 'Pritchard's *Epistemic Luck*'. *The Philosophical Quarterly* 56: 284–9.

Lehrer, Keith (2000). *Theory of Knowledge*. Boulder, CO: Westview Press.

Levi, Isaac (1980). *The Enterprise of Knowledge*. Cambridge, MA: MIT Press.

Lewis, David (1979). 'Scorekeeping in a Language Game'. *Journal of Philosophical Logic* 8: 339–59.

—— (1996). 'Elusive Knowledge'. *Australasian Journal of Philosophy* 74: 549–67.

Lyons, Jack (2008). 'Evidence, Experience, and Externalism'. *Australasian Journal of Philosophy* 86: 461–79.

McDowell, John (1993). 'Wittgenstein on Following a Rule'. In A. W. Moore (ed.) *Meaning and Reference*. Oxford: Oxford University Press:

—— (1994). 'The Content of Perceptual Experience'. *The Philosophical Quarterly* 44: 190–205.

MacFarlane, John (2005*a*). 'The Assessment Sensitivity of Knowledge Attributions'. In T. S. Gendler and J. Hawthorne (eds.) *Oxford Studies in Epistemology*. Oxford: Oxford University Press: 197–233.

—— (2005*b*). 'Knowledge Laundering: Testimony and Sensitive Invariantism'. *Analysis* 65: 132–8.

—— (2009). 'Nonindexical Contextualism'. *Synthese* 166 (2): 231–50.

McGrath, Matthew (2005). 'Propositions'. *Stanford Encyclopedia of Philosophy*. May 9, 2008. <http://plato.stanford.edu/entries/propositions/>.

Maher, Patrick (1986). 'The Irrelevance of Belief to Rational Action'. *Erkenntnis* 24: 363–84.

—— (1993). *Betting on Theories*. Cambridge: Cambridge University Press.

May, Joshua, Sinnott-Armstrong, Walter, Hull, Jay G., and Zimmerman, Aaron (forthcoming). 'Practical Interests, Relevant Alternatives, and Knowledge Attributions: An Empirical Study'. *European Review of Philosophy* 9.

Mellor, D. H. (1980). 'Consciousness and Degrees of Belief'. In D. H. Mellor, (ed.) *Prospects for Pragmatism: Essays in Memory of F. P. Ramsey*. Cambridge: Cambridge University Press: 139–73.

Millar, Alan (1991). *Reasons and Experience*. Oxford: Clarendon Press.

Moltmann, Friederike (2003). 'Propositional Attitudes without Propositions'. *Synthese* 135: 77–118.

Moore, G. E. (1993). *Principia Ethica*. Cambridge: Cambridge University Press.

Moran, Richard (2001). *Authority and Estrangement: An Essay on Self-Knowledge*. Princeton, NJ: Princeton University Press.

Moyal-Sharrock, Danièle (2003). 'Logic in Action: Wittgenstein's *Logical Pragmatism* and the Impotence of Scepticism'. *Philosophical Investigations* 26: 125–48.

Muir, Hazel (2008). 'Particle smasher "not a threat to the Earth"'. May 8, 2008. <http://www.newscientist.com/article.ns?id=dn13555>.

Nagel, Jennifer (2008). 'Knowledge Ascriptions and the Psychological Consequences of Changing Stakes'. *Australasian Journal of Philosophy* 86: 279–94.

—— (2010). 'Knowledge Ascriptions and the Psychological Consequences of Thinking about Error'. *Philosophical Quarterly* 60: 286–306.

Neta, Ram (2007*a*). 'Anti-intellectualism and the Knowledge-Action Principle'. *Philosophy and Phenomenological Research* 75: 180–7.

—— (2007*b*). 'Propositional Justification, Evidence, and the Cost of Error'. *Philosophical Issues* 17: 197–216.

Neta, Ram and Phelan, Mark (manuscript). 'Evidence that Stakes Don't Matter for Evidence'.

Nozick, Robert (1981). *Philosophical Explanations*. Cambridge, MA: Harvard University Press.

Overbye, Dennis (2008). 'Asking a Judge to Save the World, and Maybe a Whole Lot More'. *New York Times*. New York.

Owens, David (2008). 'Freedom and Practical Judgement'. March 17, 2008. <http://ssrn.com/abstract=1094368>.

Parfit, Derek (2011). *On What Matters*. Oxford: Oxford University Press.

Peirce, C. S. (1931). *Collected Papers*, ed. C. Hartshorne, and P. Weiss. Cambridge, MA: Harvard University Press.

Peirce, Charles Sanders (1897). 'Fallibilism, Continuity, and Evolution'. In *Collected Papers*, ed. C. Hartshorne and P. Weiss. Cambridge, MA: Harvard University Press: 141–75.

Plantinga, Alvin (1993). *Warrant: the Current Debate*. Oxford: Oxford University Press.

Pollock, John (1986). *Contemporary Theories of Knowledge*. Totowa, NJ: Rowman & Littlefield.

Pritchard, Duncan (2001). 'Radical Scepticism, Epistemological Externalism, and "Hinge" Propositions'. In D. Salehi (ed.) *Wittgenstein-Jahrbuch 2001/2002*. Berlin: Peter Lang: 97–122.

Pritchard, Duncan (2005). *Epistemic Luck.* Oxford: Oxford University Press.

Reed, Baron (2002). 'How to Think About Fallibilism'. *Philosophical Studies* 107: 143–57.

—— (forthcoming). 'A Defense of Stable Invariantism'. *Noûs.*

Riggs, Wayne (2003). 'Balancing Our Epistemic Goals'. *Noûs* 37: 342–52.

Ross, W. D. (2002). *The Right and the Good.* Oxford: Oxford University Press.

Royzman, Edward B., Cassidy, Kimberly Wright, and Baron, Jonathan (2003). ' "I Know, You Know": Epistemic Egocentrism in Children and Adults'. *Review of General Psychology* 7: 38–65.

Rudner, Richard (1953). 'The Scientist *qua* Scientist Makes Value Judgments'. *Philosophy of Science* 20: 1–6.

Rysiew, Patrick (2001). 'The Context-Sensitivity of Knowledge Attributions'. *Noûs* 35: 477–514.

—— (2007). 'Speaking of Knowing'. *Noûs* 41: 627–62.

Santas, Gerasimos (2001). *Goodness and Justice: Plato, Aristotle, and the Moderns.* Malden, MA: Blackwell Publishers.

Sartre, Jean-Paul (1993). *Being and Nothingness.* New York: Washington Square Press.

Schaffer, Jonathan (2006). 'The Irrelevance of the Subject: Against Subject-Sensitive Invariantism'. *Philosophical Studies* 127: 87–107.

Schroeder, Mark (2007). 'The Humean Theory of Reasons'. *Oxford Studies in Metaethics* 2: 195–219.

—— (2008). 'Having Reasons'. *Philosophical Studies* 139: 57–71.

Sellars, Wilfrid (1970). 'On Knowing the Better and Doing the Worst'. *International Philosophical Quarterly* 10: 5–20.

Sidgwick, Henry (1884). *The Methods of Ethics.* London: Macmillan.

Skyrms, Brian (1999). *Choice and Chance,* 4th edn. Belmar, MA: Wordsworth.

Snowdon, Paul (1980/1). 'Perception, Vision, and Causation'. *Proceedings of the Aristotelian Society* 81: 175–92.

Sorensen, Roy (1988). 'Dogmatism, Junk Knowledge, and Conditionals'. *The Philosophical Quarterly* 38: 433–54.

Sosa, Ernest (1991). *Knowledge in Perspective.* Cambridge: Cambridge University Press.

—— (2007). *A Virtue Epistemology: Apt Belief and Reflective Knowledge,* vol. 1. Oxford: Oxford University Press.

Stainton, Robert (forthcoming). 'Contextualism in Epistemology and the Context Sensitivity of "Knows" '. In J. C. Campbell, M. O'Rourke, and H. Silverstein (eds.) *Knowledge and Skepticism.* Cambridge, MA: MIT Press.

Stalnaker, Robert (1984). *Inquiry.* Cambridge, MA: Bradford Books, MIT Press.

Stanley, Jason (2005*a*). 'Fallibilism and Concessive Knowledge Attributions'. *Analysis* 65: 126–31.

—— (2005*b*). 'Knowledge and Practical Interests'. Oxford: Oxford University Press.

Stine, Gail (1976). 'Skepticism, Relevant Alternatives, and Deductive Closure'. *Philosophical Studies* 29: 249–61.

Stroll, Avrum (1994). *Moore and Wittgenstein on Certainty*. Oxford: Oxford University Press.

Sturgeon, Scott (2008). 'Reason and the Grain of Belief'. *Noûs* 42: 139–65.

Sutton, Jonathan (2007). *Without Justification*. Cambridge, MA: MIT Press.

Unger, Peter (1974). 'Two Types of Skepticism'. *Philosophical Studies* 25: 77–96.

—— (1975). *Ignorance*. Oxford: Oxford University Press.

—— (1984). *Philosophical Relativity*. Minneapolis: University of Minnesota Press.

Wagenseil, Paul (2008). 'Lawsuit: Huge Atom Smasher Could Destroy World'. April 8, 2008. <http://www.foxnews.com/story/0,2933,342854,00.html>.

Wasserman, Wayne (1980). 'Chisholm's Definition of the Evident'. *Analysis* 40: 42–4.

Weatherson, Brian (2005). 'Can We Do Without Pragmatic Encroachment?' *Philosophical Perspectives* 19 (Epistemology): 417–43.

Williams, Michael (1996). *Unnatural Doubts: Epistemological Realism and the Basis of Scepticism*. Princeton, NJ: Princeton University Press.

Williamson, Timothy (2000). *Knowledge and its Limits*. Oxford: Oxford University Press.

Wittgenstein, Ludwig (2001). *On Certainty*. Oxford: Basil Blackwell.

Index

Made in the USA
Middletown, DE
02 December 2015